Your Options Under the New Law

Answer these questions to figure out whether you should consider bankruptcy under the new bankruptcy law:

1. **Can you pay off your debts (except mortgages) within three years while maintaining an objectively tolerable standard of living?**

   YES: Congratulations! You're probably on fairly solid financial footing.

   NO: Consider bankruptcy. Depending on your circumstances, your options may be

   - Chapter 7, in which many of your debts are forgiven immediately and you surrender nonexempt property (96 percent of filers don't lose any of their assets).

   - Chapter 13, where you pay a portion of your debts over three to five years.

2. **Is your median income greater than the median income for your state? See Appendix B.**

   YES: Your repayment plan must run for five years if you go the Chapter 13 route. Your Chapter 7 may be dismissed if your debts are primarily consumer debts *and* you flunk the Means Test. See Chapter 5.

   NO: You automatically pass the Means Test. If you choose Chapter 13, your repayment plan can span only three years. The five-year repayment plan is not required (meaning that you're not stuck committing all of your disposable income to a repayment plan for five years).

3. **Do you have nonexempt property that you want to keep? Do you need time to catch up on your mortgage? Do you owe taxes or support obligations that you want to pay off over time without being hassled?**

   It varies by state, but generally homesteads, pensions, cars, and household goods are exempt.

   YES: Consider Chapter 13 bankruptcy. If your income is greater than the median, you have to pay for five years. Otherwise, a three-year plan is an option.

   NO: Consider Chapter 7 bankruptcy.

4. **Are your debts primarily consumer debts and your income greater than the median?**

   YES: Take the Means Test, outlined in the next step.

   NO: Choose either Chapter 7 or Chapter 13 — whichever is more beneficial to you. See Chapter 4.

5. **Do you pass the Means Test?**

   Deduct the following monthly expenses from your gross monthly income:

   - IRS living, housing, and transportation expenses (excluding mortgage and car payments). See Chapter 5.

   - Mandatory payroll deductions (taxes, FICA, and repayments on pension loan) and future support obligations

   - Health insurance premiums

   - Debt payments, such as regular mortgage and car payments, 1/60 of past due mortgage and car payments, and 1/60 of past due support obligations

6. **Is the difference between your monthly expenses and gross monthly income less than $100? (If the difference is more, proceed to Step 7.)**

   YES: You pass the Means Test and may choose between Chapter 7 and Chapter 13.

   NO: You *may* be restricted to Chapter 13. See Chapter 5.

7. **Is the difference between your monthly expenses and gross monthly income between $100 and $166.66 per month and less than 25 percent of your unsecured nonpriority debts (regular obligations such as credit cards and medical bills divided by 60)?**

   YES: You pass the Means Test.

   NO: You're limited to Chapter 13.

8. **Is the difference between your monthly expenses and gross monthly income more than $166.67 per month?**

   YES: You're limited to Chapter 13.

   NO: Choose between Chapter 7 or Chapter 13 — whichever is more beneficial to you.

Personal Bankruptcy Laws For Dummies, 2nd Edition

Cheat Sheet

What the New Bankruptcy Law Means to You

- Mandatory credit counseling within 180 days before filing bankruptcy
- A slim chance (less than 3 percent) that you may not be eligible for bankruptcy
- Pay stubs received within 60 days prior to bankruptcy must be filed with the court.
- Creditors are entitled to a copy of most recent tax return
- Mandatory attendance at a financial management class after filing bankruptcy
- Increased attorney fees and court filing fees

What Bills You Should Pay First When You Can't Pay Everyone

- Rent (unless you plan to move)
- Utilities
- Car (if you want to keep it)
- Mortgage (if you want to keep your home)
- Fines
- Child support and spousal support
- Income taxes

What Debt Collectors Can't Do

- Call you early in the morning, late at night, or at any other unreasonable time or place.
- Harass you.
- Contact you at work if your employer prohibits personal calls.
- Threaten you.
- Tell anyone (other than your spouse, lawyer, or cosigner) that you're in debt.
- Bug you once you've told them to bug off.

What to Do When Debt Collectors Break the Rules

First, tell them you know what the Fair Debt Collection Practices Act is and how to use it. Then, use it by filing a complaint to the Federal Trade Commission, Correspondence Branch, 600 Pennsylvania NW, Washington, D.C. 20580.

For Dummies: Bestselling Book Series for Beginners

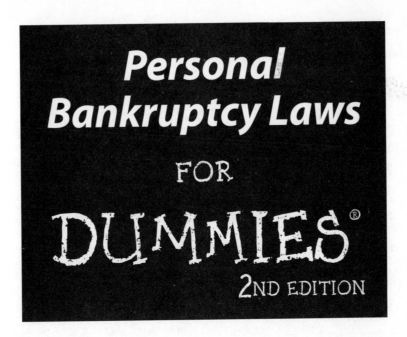

Personal Bankruptcy Laws

FOR

DUMMIES®

2ND EDITION

by James P. Caher and John M. Caher

WILEY

Wiley Publishing, Inc.

Personal Bankruptcy Laws For Dummies,® 2nd Edition

Published by
Wiley Publishing, Inc.
111 River St.
Hoboken, NJ 07030-5774
www.wiley.com

WILEY

About the Authors

James P. Caher, a practicing attorney with 30 years of experience, is a nationally recognized expert on consumer bankruptcies and authority on the Bankruptcy Abuse Prevention and Consumer Protection Act of 2005.

Jim coauthored, with his brother John, *Debt Free! Your Guide to Personal Bankruptcy Without Shame* (Henry Holt, 1996) and two highly regarded books for lawyers: *Discharging Marital Obligations in Bankruptcy* (LRP, 1997) and *Discharging Credit Card Debts in Bankruptcy* (LRP, 1998).

In addition, Jim has published scores of articles for bankruptcy professionals and is frequently called upon to analyze and interpret the complicated provisions of the 2005 bankruptcy law. He was labeled the "online guru" by a national legal weekly because of his regular appearances on the Internet as an expert analyst on bankruptcy law. Jim also serves on the editorial board of the American Bankruptcy Institute.

Jim graduated from Niagara University and then earned his law degree from Memphis State University Law School, where he was a member of the Law Review and recipient of the American Jurisprudence Award for Excellence in the field of debtor-creditor relations. He filed his first consumer bankruptcy case shortly after graduating in 1975. Jim lives and practices in Eugene, Oregon.

John M. Caher is a legal journalist who has written about law and the courts for most of his 25-year career.

Currently the Albany bureau chief for the *New York Law Journal*, John previously was state editor and legal affairs reporter for the *Times Union* of Albany, New York. His legal reportage has won more than two dozen awards, including prestigious honors from the American Bar Association, the New York State Bar Association, the Erie County Bar Association, and the Associated Press.

John coauthored, with his brother Jim, *Debt Free! Your Guide to Personal Bankruptcy Without Shame* (Henry Holt, 1996). He is the author of *King of the Mountain: The Rise, Fall and Redemption of Chief Judge Sol Wachtler* (Prometheus Books, 1998). In addition, John was the principal writer assisting former U.S. Treasury Secretary William E. Simon in preparation of his memoirs. Mr. Simon's autobiography, *A Time for Reflection,* was published in 2003 by Regnery.

John is a 1980 graduate of Utica College of Syracuse University, where he received his bachelor's degree in journalism, and a 1993 graduate of Rensselaer Polytechnic Institute, where he earned a master's degree in technical communications/graphics. John lives in Clifton Park, New York.

Dedication

This book is dedicated to the memory of our parents, James C. and Dolores Caher (a.k.a. "Big Jim and Fitz"), who died way before their time but left us with their own life examples of personal responsibility, fairness, justice, affinity for the underdog, basic decency, and common sense. It is also dedicated to the five grandchildren they should have known and would have adored and enjoyed beyond measure: Sean and Brendan Caputi of East Aurora, New York, and Erin, Kerry, and Norah Caher of Clifton Park, New York.

Authors' Acknowledgments

For the second edition of this book, just like the first, our respective spouses Kate Donnelly and Kathleen Caher were there every step of the way with their love, support, and encouragement.

Also for the second edition of our book, just like the first, Michael J. O'Connor took time from his busy law practice to offer expert analysis of our effort. Mike, an outstanding bankruptcy attorney in his own right and prominent partner in O'Connor O'Connor Mayberger & First PC in Albany, New York, has always been there when we needed him, and we would like to publicly acknowledge our humble appreciation for his efforts.

We also acknowledge the continuing dedication of our long-time agent, Sheree Bykofsky of Sheree Bykofsky Associates in Manhattan, and the insights of the talented folks at Wiley Publishing who made this come together, especially our project editor, Kelly Ewing, and acquisitions editor, Stacy Kennedy.

Publisher's Acknowledgments

We're proud of this book; please send us your comments through our Dummies online registration form located at www.dummies.com/register/.

Some of the people who helped bring this book to market include the following:

Acquisitions, Editorial, and Media Development

Project Editor: Kelly Ewing

(Previous Edition: Marcia L. Johnson)

Acquisitions Editor: Stacy Kennedy

General Reviewer: Michael J. O'Connor

Editorial Manager: Michelle Hacker

Editorial Supervisor and Reprint Editor: Carmen Krikorian

Editorial Assistants: Hanna Scott, Nadine Bell

Cartoons: Rich Tennant (www.the5thwave.com)

Composition Services

Project Coordinator: Jennifer Theriot

Layout and Graphics: Andrea Dahl, Stephanie D. Jumper, Barry Offringa

Proofreaders: Leeann Harney, TECHBOOKS Production Services

Indexer: TECHBOOKS Production Services

Publishing and Editorial for Consumer Dummies

Diane Graves Steele, Vice President and Publisher, Consumer Dummies

Joyce Pepple, Acquisitions Director, Consumer Dummies

Kristin A. Cocks, Product Development Director, Consumer Dummies

Michael Spring, Vice President and Publisher, Travel

Kelly Regan, Editorial Director, Travel

Publishing for Technology Dummies

Andy Cummings, Vice President and Publisher, Dummies Technology/General User

Composition Services

Gerry Fahey, Vice President of Production Services

Debbie Stailey, Director of Composition Services

Contents at a Glance

Table of Contents

Introduction

. . . .

*W*elcome to the second edition of *Personal Bankruptcy Law For Dummies* — your antidote to BARF (Bankruptcy Abuse Reform Fiasco).

You're probably in financial trouble, or you wouldn't have picked up this book. Unfortunately, your troubles got a lot more complicated in October 2005, when a law new drastically altered the time-honored and court-tested rules of bankruptcy and changed much of what we told you in the first edition.

It's officially called the Bankruptcy Abuse Prevention and Consumer Protection Act of 2005 — a euphemism if ever there was one. Many judges and other bankruptcy judges know it by a more colorful and, we think, more accurate name: BARF. And that's how we generally refer to it in this book.

BARF was bought and paid for by creditors, and there's almost nothing in this 501-page "amendment" to the Bankruptcy Code that spells anything but "indigestion" for the average consumer. That said, there are ways to keep BARF at bay. If you know some tricks, you'll make out just fine. You just have to know where to step and not step. In this book, we show you the way.

About This Book

If you ever go to Ireland, an Irish phrase that you just have to know is "It's clearly signposted all the way." It usually comes up in a tavern, or anywhere else you may stop to ask for directions. Invariably, you'll be sent on your merry way with these promising words.

Now, the ignorant may assume that phrase means that the way to your destination is obvious, and prominent signs appear anywhere you can make a wrong turn. But, what a foolish assumption! What it really means is that no such signs are anywhere to be found, and you're going to get hopelessly lost. That's how our ancestors got here. One wrong turn in Dublin, and, the next thing they knew, they were in Buffalo.

What's that have to do with bankruptcy? Nothing, except that most of the bankruptcy books we've encountered are "clearly signposted all the way" and about half as understandable as an Irish roundabout. Do you go around the traffic circle to the left or right when you drive on the left, and how come there's a cow in the passing lane? You just can't get there from here without wading through a mountain of manure.

So we, The Brothers Caher, decided to make the world of bankruptcy a little more intelligible and a little more navigable. Yeah, we thought about fixing Ireland first, but getting lost adds to the fun and charm of our ancestral homeland. Nothing's fun or charming about getting lost in the dragon-plagued dungeons of bankruptcy law, especially when it's raining BARF.

Conventions Used in This Book

We're pretty conventional guys, and here are some of the conventions used in the book:

Debtor is you, the person who owes someone else money. Also, a person filing bankruptcy is called a *debtor* instead of a "bankruptcy." *Court,* unless otherwise stated, means U.S. Bankruptcy Court. *Trustee* is the Chapter 7 Bankruptcy trustee. *Credit-card company* refers to banks and other lending institutions that issue loans processed by companies like Visa and MasterCard.

BARF (Bankruptcy Abuse Reform Fiasco) is the monument to Murphy's Law that made such a mess of consumer bankruptcies.

And *Congress* refers to the knuckleheads in Washington who replaced a law they didn't understand with one they haven't read to fix a problem that doesn't exist, requiring you to wallow in BARF and us to rewrite our book.

What You're Not to Read

Feel free to cherry pick. If you're looking for just-the-facts-ma'am, gloss over the aptly designated Technical Stuff (you can always go back if you need more than a bird's eye view). You can skate by the anecdotes (all tagged with an icon) and the sidebars (the stuff printed on gray background) as well.

Foolish Assumptions

We assume that you understand the English language and never went to law school. To that end, unless we tell you otherwise, a word means what it means in plain-old English, not legalese. If we're about to get all lawyerly on you, we warn you.

How This Book Is Organized

So you're thinking that perhaps, just perhaps, bankruptcy is your way out? You may be right. We guide you through all the thickets of bankruptcy law so that you can figure that one out for yourself. This book covers everything you need to know, and we've tried real hard to organize a ton of material so that you can immediately put it to practical use. Here's a brief rundown of what you find in each section of the book.

Part 1: Bankruptcy: The Big Picture

Torn over the question of whether bankruptcy is for you? The aim of this first part is simply to put your mind at ease and get you to evaluate the bankruptcy option on a simple, objective, intelligent standard: Do the benefits outweigh the drawbacks? We explain the process and the pitfalls and, as an added bonus, we describe some quick and effective ways to immediately stop the financial bloodletting. We also include a brand new chapter just on the "Means Test," the lynchpin of BARF.

Part 11: Avoiding Bankruptcy

Most folks will do almost anything to avoid bankruptcy, and all too many only make matters worse by putting off that day of reckoning. We understand your reluctance to file bankruptcy (although in our experience, people are usually better off filing bankruptcy sooner rather than later). In this section, we explain a variety of debt-busting techniques to keep the bill collectors off your back until you get on your feet again.

Part 111: Keeping Your Stuff

The credit industry would have you believe that when you file bankruptcy, an army of predators and scavengers descends on the tranquility of your homestead and yanks the bowl of porridge right out from under your kids' spoons. Well, the fact of the matter is that although you may — *may* — lose some of your possessions in bankruptcy, the really important stuff is strictly off-limits to your creditors. This section spells out what's yours, what's potentially at stake, and what you can do to make sure that your most important possessions remain in your own good hands.

Part IV: Getting Rid of (Most of) Your Debt

Bankruptcy eliminates most of your debts, but some problems (like taxes, child support, and school loans) may stick around even if you file. In this section, we explore those lingering obligations and explain what you can do to get the biggest bang for your bankruptcy buck.

Part V: Strategies for a Successful Bankruptcy

With apologies to Yogi Berra, "It ain't over 'til it's over" — and in some cases, it ain't even over when it's over. You have to put in a little effort to get the most relief from your bankruptcy filing. This section offers oodles of suggestions about how you can make the process run smoothly and effectively, and how you can avoid some troublesome traps.

Part VI: Enjoying Your Fresh Start

Phew! You made it. You survived bankruptcy, and you're determined to never return to the bad old days of debts, delinquencies, and diabolical collection agents. Thanks to the American tradition of justice, fair play, and sympathy for the underdog, you have a new lease on your financial life. Here, we work on restoring your credit and, once and for all, putting all your bad financial experiences behind you.

Part VII: The Part of Tens

Hey, this wouldn't be a *For Dummies* book without the tens — and we include such nuggets as the ten most common questions that we get about bankruptcy and the ten things you can do right now to ease your mind. In fact, you may want to scan the common questions right now.

Icons Used in This Book

Your road to financial salvation has many twists and turns, and you have to know when to zig and when to zag. So we include a bunch of eye-catching, head-bopping iconic reminders to draw attention to particular points or hazards and to warn you in advance of the boring technical stuff.

These little bull's-eyes point out helpful tidbits and strategic moves you or your lawyer may want to consider.

This icon points out the legal and logistical bombs that may blow up in your face if you're not minding your p's and q's.

These icons are reminders of points made previously. An awful lot of information is included in this book, and we don't expect you to keep it all in your head. This is a gentle reminder.

Yikes, some complicated, convoluted information is coming your way! We've made it as easy to understand as possible, but some stuff is just plain mind-boggling. Dive in at your own peril. We won't be offended, however, if you skip ahead. Well, Jim (the lawyer) may be offended. Forget about him.

The rules for what's called a *Chapter 7 bankruptcy* — one where you wipe out all your debts and surrender certain assets — are different from the other most common consumer bankruptcy, a Chapter 13. When you see this icon, you know we're talking only about Chapter 7.

The rules for what's called a *Chapter 13 bankruptcy* — one where you pay off a portion of your debts over time — are different from the other most common consumer bankruptcy, a Chapter 7. When you see this icon, you know we're talking only about Chapter 13.

Legal principles are much easier to understand when you can see how they apply in the real world. We include plenty of examples and identify them with this icon.

Where to Go from Here

Relax. As daunting as all this information seems, it's really not that bad. We suggest reading the first two chapters from start to finish now, before flipping to the stuff that's really worrying you (taming bill collectors, dealing with the IRS, and so on). In short order, you'll have a pretty good idea of whether bankruptcy is right for you.

Part I
Bankruptcy:
The Big Picture

The 5th Wave   By Rich Tennant

"Einstein over there miscalculated our startup costs, and we ran out of money before we could afford to open a 24-hour store."

In this part . . .

Is bankruptcy the best option for you, or even an option for you? What happens if you file? What happens if you don't? And what's this new bankruptcy law mean? Do you need a lawyer? How can you stop the hemorrhaging? Where do you even start? If you don't already know the answers to these questions — and maybe even if you think you do — start your journey here. Many people begin with the assumption that even considering bankruptcy is an admission of failure. Actually, it can be a first step toward taking responsible control of your financial future. Read this part to see how bankruptcy is a legitimate tool and to understand the implications of exercising — and not exercising — your right to a fresh start.

Chapter 1

Considering Bankruptcy

Maybe you were socked with an unexpected and uninsured medical expense, and you didn't have the savings to cover the bills. Perhaps you lost your job, and you can no longer juggle your car and mortgage payments. Maybe you dipped into personal assets in a desperate (and futile) bid to salvage your business. Perchance your husband split and left you holding a big bag of joint debts. You likely bought into the easy-credit, instant-gratification, shop-till-you-drop mentality encouraged by lenders and retailers and found yourself mired in financial quicksand. In any case, things got out of hand and now you're up to your ears in debt.

Finance companies are warning that if you don't pay up, and soon, they're going to take your home and car. Credit-card firms are threatening to haul your butt into court. Debt collectors are pursuing you relentlessly. Your finances are a disaster. Your personal and professional relationships are strained. You're losing sleep, and you're becoming a perfect candidate for ulcers. Welcome to the club. Millions of Americans are in the same leaky boat.

Thankfully, you have a way — a perfectly legitimate way — to stop foreclosures and repossessions, put an end to lawsuits, protect your paycheck from garnishments, get those menacing debt collectors off your back, and regain control of your life: bankruptcy.

But bankruptcy is shrouded in myth and prejudice. You may have even felt a twinge of embarrassment buying this book.

If you're like many folks, the first step on the road to financial recovery is overcoming your feelings of inadequacy, shame, guilt, and fear of the unknown.

In this chapter, we encourage you to put myth and prejudice aside and look calmly at the advantages and disadvantages of bankruptcy. Then, and only then, can you make a rational decision about whether bankruptcy is the best choice for you and your loved ones. You have things to gain, and things to lose, in bankruptcy. This chapter gives you a glimpse of what's at stake with bankruptcy in kind of a broad way and serves as a gateway to the rest of the book.

Viewing Bankruptcy in a Historical Context

In the United States, the concept of bankruptcy is unique. Here, bankruptcy is viewed — legally and perceptually — as a means to an end, and not as "the end" of a debtor's financial life. America's Founding Fathers provided for bankruptcy right in the Constitution. A series of laws passed (and sometimes repealed) by Congress during the 1800s shaped the American view of bankruptcy as not only a remedy for creditors, but also as a way to give honest yet unfortunate debtors financial rebirth. The Bankruptcy Act of 1898 established that debtors had a basic right to financial relief without creditor consent or court permission. American bankruptcy laws have come to be recognized as far more compassionate and much less punitive to debtors than the laws of other countries.

Like much of American law, the country's bankruptcy statutes reflect the constant tension between the competing interests of debtors and creditors. Think of it as a perpetual tug of war, with each side striving mightily but never pulling their opponent all the way over the line. To this day, the balance of influence between creditors and debtors is in an ever-present state of flux. Sometimes debtors have the upper hand. Other times, creditors get the edge. At the moment, thanks to a new law that took effect in October 2005, creditors are holding the trump card.

The constant, however, is that Americans have always been (and remain) entitled to a fresh start. The obstacles that you must clear to obtain this fresh start are not constant; they're always changing.

Bankruptcy's roots

The word *bankruptcy* evolved from an Italian phrase *banca ratta* that means "broken bench or table." In medieval times, when a merchant failed to pay his debts, creditors would ceremoniously break the bench or table from which he conducted his business. The forgiveness of debts, on the other hand, has biblical roots.

Consider the Old Testament: "At the end of every seven years, you are to cancel the debts of those who owe you money. This is how it is done. Everyone who has lent money to his neighbor is to cancel the debt: he must not try to collect the money: the Lord himself has declared the debt canceled." (Deuteronomy 15: 1–2).

Debt forgiveness also is a prominent New Testament theme. In Matthew 18:21–27, Jesus relates the story of a servant who was indebted to his master. The master ordered the servant and his entire family into slavery but, upon reconsideration, he forgave the debt. Jesus used the parable to explain the virtue of debt forgiveness. (On the other hand, the apostle Paul admonishes debt in Romans 13:8, "Render therefore to all their dues . . . owe no man any thing." So maybe we can't afford to get too pious here.)

In any case, throughout history, creditors have not exactly displayed an attitude of Judeo-Christian charity toward debtors. Neither have governments.

The early Romans hacked up and divided the bodies of people who didn't pay their debts. In early England, people who were in over their heads financially were tossed in dungeons. The initial bankruptcy law, passed in 1542 during the reign of Henry VIII (the guy who kept beheading his wives), viewed debtors as quasi criminals but, for the first time, provided remedies other than imprisonment or mutilation.

Apparently, creditors finally realized that killing, maiming, or imprisoning debtors only ensured that they'd never get their money and that even if the debtor survived, he'd never be able to support himself and his family or become a productive member of society.

During the more enlightened reign of Queen Elizabeth I, a comprehensive bankruptcy law was passed (one that remained in effect for more than a century). The aim of the 1570 bankruptcy law was most certainly *not* to grant relief to debtors. Rather, it was designed to help creditors. It applied only to merchants (ordinary debtors still were imprisoned) and essentially laid out procedures by which a bankruptcy commissioner could seize the debtor's assets, sell them, and divide the proceeds among creditors. Debtors who did not cooperate had one of their ears lopped off.

The very idea of a bankruptcy law aiding debtors or forgiving debts remained a somewhat unimaginable concept until 1705, when Parliament enacted the first law that enabled a person to wipe out unpaid financial obligations. However, the terms were rather harsh: Consent of the creditor was required, and anyone who fraudulently sought bankruptcy relief faced the death penalty.

Before the United States won its independence, the various colonies handled bankruptcy their own respective ways, and little uniformity existed from colony to colony — except for the fact that settlers generally maintained the British tradition of jailing debtors (which extended to one of the British Empire's greatest literary stars, Charles Dickens.). In fact, Robert Morris, known as the "financier of the American revolution" and a signer of the Declaration of Independence, spent three years in debtors' prison (and six years in the United States Senate). Supreme Court Justice James Wilson fled Pennsylvania to avoid a similar fate.

Modern-day bankruptcy is rooted in the Bankruptcy Code of 1978, a federal law that was produced after more than ten years of careful study by judges and scholars. More recently, creditors and their lobbyists essentially rewrote what was a pretty well reasoned and fair law in their own image. The result was the "Bankruptcy Abuse Prevention and Consumer Protection Act of 2005" — often known as the Bankruptcy Abuse Reform Fiasco, or BARF. It's not good for consumers. It's not good for the economy. It flies in the face of the risk-reward principles at the core of capitalism. And, in the long run, it's probably not all that good for the credit industry, which wrote it.

So how did a one-sided, ill-considered bucket of BARF happen to pass both houses of Congress as well as presidential scrutiny?

Some cynics think the eight-year lobbying campaign by the credit-card industry and the $100 million spent on campaign contributions may have had something to do with it. Some speculate that lawmakers, blinded by campaign contributions and sound-bite moralizing about personal responsibility (we are, by the way, all for personal responsibility — both for borrowers and *lenders*), simply didn't pay a whole lot of attention to the fine print in an incredibly complex amendment that's about the size of a metropolitan telephone book.

How these provisions will be implemented, applied and interpreted remains a mystery, and it will take years and years of cases and judicial opinions to sort it out. The simple fact of the matter is that neither we, your lawyer, nor even your local bankruptcy judge know for sure how or when the higher courts will decipher all this stuff and figure out how to apply it to circumstances never imagined by the people who wrote and voted for this bill.

Debunking Bankruptcy Myths

Bankruptcy is an economic decision, not a morality play, and you needn't be deceived into viewing it as anything else. The following sections look at some of the usual red herrings that are cast about by the credit industry.

People who go bankrupt are sleazy deadbeats

People file for bankruptcy because they're in debt. The more debt there is, the more bankruptcies there are. Well, duh! It really is that simple.

American bankruptcy

Our forefathers had radical ideas when it came to bankruptcy.

The founders of this country foresaw the possibility that honest people might suffer severe economic misfortune or make poor choices (Thomas Jefferson, certainly one of the most productive and accomplished individuals in the history of the world, was perpetually on the brink of bankruptcy during his later years), and had the wisdom to provide for bankruptcy in the U.S. Constitution.

After the Constitutional Convention of 1787, the framers of the Constitution added a bankruptcy clause empowering Congress to pass uniform bankruptcy laws to prevent some states from establishing debtors' havens. In 1800 — 11 years after the ratification of the Constitution — Congress passed (by a single vote) a national bankruptcy law that enabled debtors to wipe out unpaid debts. But the provision was repealed three years later because of creditor complaints. Consequently, states began passing their own bankruptcy laws, a practice that was struck down by the U.S. Supreme Court.

By 1833, the federal government abolished debtors' prisons. Honest debtors would no longer be incarcerated. But bankruptcy was still viewed as a remedy for creditors, not debtors.

The tide began to shift when Congress, spurred by the powerful oratory of Daniel Webster, passed the Bankruptcy Act of 1841, a seminal event that established clearly that bankruptcy law was for debtors *and* for creditors. For the first time in history, the advocates for debtors had prevailed over the interests of creditors.

The victory, however, was short-lived. Only three years later, creditors succeeded in having the law withdrawn. A similar choreography occurred just after the Civil War: Congress passed the Bankruptcy Act of 1867, which again enabled debtors to wipe out their debts. Eleven years later, creditors got it repealed. The threshold problem was this: Debt elimination was viewed as a privilege, dependent on creditor consent or court permission, not a fundamental right.

In the late 1890s, a revolutionary and uniquely American idea emerged — namely, that bankruptcy relief needed to be available to an honest person without consent or permission from others. This concept, which has come to be known as the *unconditional discharge,* was carved into the Bankruptcy Act of 1898.

Regardless of the long history and legal tradition underlying the unconditional discharge, creditors never cease trying to turn the clock back to the days when your bankruptcy relief required their permission.

Whenever the political climate appears favorable, creditors predictably scamper to Congress, whine about their losses, and claim that the "crisis" of "out-of-control" bankruptcies threatens to undermine the whole of Western civilization.

And therein lies the roots of BARF!

(See Charles Jordan Tabb, *The History of the Bankruptcy Laws in the United States,* American Bankruptcy Institute Law Review, Vol. 3:5, 1995.)

The credit industry stereotypes folks who file bankruptcy as worthless dead-beats taking advantage of a loophole-ridden legal system to dump their moral obligations on the backs of the rest of us. This stereotype is false, discrimina-tory, and manifestly unfair. Sure, bankruptcies have increased dramatically along with consumer debt, although the number of bankruptcies per $100 million on consumer debt has remained remarkably constant. From the 1970s to the 1980s, filings virtually doubled. The pace continued to increase in the 1990s, with bankruptcy filings setting new records year after year, even with a seemingly robust economy and near full employment. In fact, by the mid-1990s, bankruptcy filings, on a per capita basis, were running some eight times ahead of those of the Great Depression. About 1 out of every 75 house-holds in America have a member who has filed bankruptcy.

And who are these people filing for bankruptcy? Chances are they're your neighbors, regardless of what neighborhood you live in. Bankruptcy is an equal opportunity phenomenon that strikes every socioeconomic bracket.

The fastest growing group of bankruptcy filers are older Americans. More than half of those 65 and older are forced into bankruptcy by medical debts. Also, more families with children, single mothers, and single fathers are being driven into bankruptcy — the presence of children in a household triples the odds that the head of the household will end up in bankruptcy.

In any case, the image of the sleazy, deadbeat bankruptcy filer is a phantom and a scapegoat for irresponsible lending. The bankruptcy filer can be more accurately described as an ordinary, honest, hardworking, middle-class con-sumer who fell for aggressive and sophisticated credit marketing techniques, lost control, and unwittingly surrendered his financial soul to the devil that is debt.

Bankruptcy is the easy way out for folks who can pay their bills

Creditors have been making this claim since the 1800s, and it's as demonstra-bly wrong today as it was back then.

In recent years, the credit industry funded several *studies* — a handy euphemism for propaganda, the more accurate description — that suppos-edly support their argument that people are skipping to bankruptcy court to skip out of their obligations. Every one of these self-serving reports has been debunked by independent sources — every single one. Several of these stud-ies were even discredited by two financial arms of Congress, the General Accounting Office and the Congressional Budget Office.

Bankruptcy isn't the cause of debt, but rather is the result. And it isn't the disease, but rather is the cure. Restricting access to bankruptcy court won't solve the problem of debt any more than closing the hospitals will cure a plague.

Bankruptcy threatens the ethical foundations of our society

Gee, you'd think that bankruptcy was the greatest threat to apple pie and motherhood since Elvis Presley and bell-bottom jeans!

Credit-card companies furiously push plastic on virtually anyone willing to take it. At present, more than one billion credit cards are in circulation — that's about a dozen for every household in America. Lenders mail out billions of credit-card solicitations every year. Low- and moderate-income households, high school students, and the mentally disabled — or, in their vernacular, "emerging markets" — are popular targets of lenders.

According to the Administrative Office of the United States Courts, consumers between the ages of 18 and 25 are one of the largest growing segments (next to senior citizens) of bankruptcy filers — students and other young people who lack the maturity and resources to handle debt.

Anyone with a brain can figure out that extending credit to folks with no income, no assets, and no track record is kind of dumb (not to mention morally questionable). But creditors are more than willing to ignore the dangers of tomorrow so that they can reap exorbitant interest rates today. They're counting on — literally banking on — your ignorance of the situation. They encourage robbing Peter to pay Paul by using credit-card advances to pay off credit-card bills. They convince many middle-class consumers to bleed all the equity out of their homes through aggressively marketed home-equity loans — with much of it going to finance consumable products (mall junk) rather than the homestead of the American Dream. That hundreds of solid, middle-class folks find themselves in bankruptcy court isn't surprising.

But why, in the face of increasing credit-card losses, does the credit industry continue dispensing credit with utterly reckless abandon? The answer is simple: Because it's profitable . . . extremely profitable. Since 1997, bankruptcy filings have increased 17 percent, while credit-card profits have soared 163 percent!

It's enough to make you BARF

A five-year study published in the medical policy journal *Health Affairs* in February 2005 found that between 1981 and 2001, medical-related bankruptcies increased by 2,200 percent — six times the increase in the number of all bankruptcies during the same period. And most of the medical filers were not the uninsured poor, but middle-class folks with health insurance. According to the study, it's not lack of insurance that wipes people out; it's copayments, deductibles, and uncovered services.

Honest folks pay a "tax" to support those who are bankrupt

That honest taxpayers are supporting people who are bankrupt is nothing short of an outright, bald-faced lie. The theory, trumpeted in press releases, is that hundreds of thousands of Americans routinely ignore their obligations, intentionally or recklessly drive up their debts, and then declare themselves insolvent, stiffing creditors, and ultimately, every God-fearing, bill-paying, hard-working, patriotic American.

Creditors note that they write off about $40 billion in debts annually, which works out to about $400 to $500 for every American household. Thus, the reasoning goes, if access to bankruptcy were restricted, the credit industry wouldn't suffer losses that it must pass along to consumers. So, they say, BARF is good for consumers.

They're not saying, take note, that they'll pass along any savings to their customers, and historically that has not been their practice. Besides, do you really believe that the credit industry paid politicians tens of millions of dollars to enact BARF in order to save you money? Not likely.

Understanding What You Can Gain Through Bankruptcy

If you have no way of paying your bills, you certainly need to consider bankruptcy. If you have an income but cannot repay your debts in full within three years while maintaining a reasonable standard of living, bankruptcy may be a wise option. (Chapter 2 can help you calculate your potential to pay your debts based on current income and expenses.)

Bankruptcy isn't the solution when your motive is anything other than reasonable relief from your debts. The U.S. Bankruptcy Code was established to assist *honest debtors*, not to provide a haven for chiselers and charlatans. If your aim is to jerk some creditor around, weasel out of debts you can easily pay, evade child support, or generally just stiff someone, bankruptcy is the wrong route. Bankruptcy should not be used for vengeance or as a stopgap measure. It should not be used as a ploy or a bargaining chip. You should not file bankruptcy unless you're serious about following through.

Bankruptcy can

✔ Halt almost every kind of lawsuit.

✔ Prevent garnishment of any wages you earn after filing.

✔ Stop most evictions if bankruptcy is filed before a state court enters a judgment for possession.

✔ Avert repossessions.

✔ Stop foreclosures.

✔ Prevent your driver's license from being yanked for unpaid fines or judgments. (The stay doesn't prevent revocation or suspension of your driver's license for failing to pay court-ordered support.)

✔ Bring IRS seizures to a skidding stop.

Bankruptcy generally *won't* prevent

✔ Criminal prosecutions

✔ Proceedings against someone who cosigned your loan, unless you file a "Chapter 13" repayment plan and propose paying the loan in full (see Chapter 4)

✔ Contempt of court hearings

✔ Actions to collect back child support or alimony, unless you file Chapter 13 and propose to pay that obligation off during the life of your plan (see Chapter 17)

✔ Governmental regulatory proceedings

In recent years, some self-proclaimed "mortgage consultants" and "foreclosure service" outfits have made a business out of essentially tricking their clients into filing bankruptcy. These con artists exploit the bankruptcy laws to delay foreclosure, collect rents from the property during the delay, and then head for the hills. In the end, unsuspecting clients usually lose their homes and wind up with a bankruptcy on their records without realizing they'd even filed for bankruptcy. Bottom line: Discuss your options with an experienced bankruptcy attorney, not some fly-by-night flimflam operation. See Chapter 3 for tips on finding a good lawyer.

Stopping creditors in their tracks

The moment that you file a bankruptcy petition, a legal shield called the *automatic stay* kicks in, prohibiting creditors from contacting you, suing you, repossessing your property, or garnishing your wages.

After you file, a creditor can ask for permission to proceed with a repossession or foreclosure. But the creditor must obtain permission in advance, and the bankruptcy court judge may very well turn them down, if you propose a reasonable plan for paying that particular debt. (The following sections cover filing bankruptcy to eliminate some bills and pay others.)

Whenever a creditor is foolish enough to ignore the automatic stay, he'll have a federal judge on his back and may well get zapped with a fine and an order to pay your attorney fees.

Wiping out most of your debts

Bankruptcy wipes out or *discharges* most debts. Credit cards, medical bills, phone charges, loans, and judgments all are usually *dischargeable*. However, some obligations generally are not eliminated in bankruptcy, and these *nondischargeable* debts include

- ✔ Student loans (see Chapter 18)
- ✔ Alimony and child support (see Chapter 17)
- ✔ Damages for a personal injury you caused while driving illegally under the influence of drugs or alcohol (see Chapter 16)
- ✔ Debts from fraud (see Chapters 11 and 16)
- ✔ Financial obligations imposed as part of a criminal conviction (see Chapter 16)
- ✔ Taxes arising during the past three years (see Chapter 15)

Catching up on back mortgage and car payments

Sometimes, even dischargeable debts may continue to haunt you when they are tied to one of your essential possessions. For example, you can wipe out loans secured by your home or car, but the creditor can still foreclose on your house or repossess your vehicle if you don't pay.

In a Chapter 13 bankruptcy (one where you pay what you can toward your debts and the remainder is forgiven), you can propose a partial repayment plan to avoid foreclosure and make up back mortgage payments over a five-year span. You can prevent repossession of your car by catching up on back payments of the life of the plan. In some situations, you have to pay only what the vehicle is worth — rather than the whole loan balance (see Chapters 11 and 12).

Filing bankruptcy to pay some debts over time

Although some debts are not dischargeable, filing a Chapter 13 reorganization enables you to pay debts such as support obligations or back taxes over a five-year period and protects you from being hassled while you're paying down the balances. You can also gradually catch up on missed mortgage payments. In the meantime, most of your other debts are eliminated while you just pay for current expenses and keep current on future house and car payments.

Using bankruptcy to pay all your debts

Sometimes filing bankruptcy actually provides a way of paying all your debts rather than escaping them.

If the value of your property is sufficient to pay all your debts if only you had enough time to sell your assets, bankruptcy can be used to hold aggressive lenders at bay until your property is sold for the benefit of all your creditors — and possibly producing a surplus for you.

Here's how it works. Say, for example, that you own investment property worth $150,000, on which you have a mortgage of $100,000, and that you have other debts totaling $25,000.

If you can sell the property, you can pay off the mortgage and other debts and still have something left over for yourself. But if the mortgageholder forecloses, neither you nor your creditors are likely to receive a cent. Although the property *is* put up for public auction in a foreclosure, bidders rarely show up, and the only bidder typically is the mortgageholder, which merely bids the amount that's owed on the mortgage. In other words, the mortgage company ends up owning the property without paying any cash. Filing bankruptcy interrupts the foreclosure so that the property can be sold for everyone's benefit. See Chapter 12 for more on how foreclosures work and how you can actually use the bankruptcy process to save your home.

Noncitizens of the U.S. of A.

You don't even have to be an American citizen to qualify for a fresh start. Neither citizenship nor even formal resident-alien status is required. As long as you have property or a business in the U.S., you're eligible for bankruptcy relief. But courts disagree on just what "property in the United States" constitutes, and some have rejected attempts by foreigners to create eligibility by simply obtaining a U. S. mailbox or establishing a nominal bank account. Others take a more liberal view.

For example, Ernestine didn't live, work, or do any business in the United States, but she had a few hundred bucks in a bank account. The court said Ernestine was eligible to file bankruptcy in the United States — expressing bewilderment as to why American credit-card companies would offer massive amounts of credit to a foreigner with no job and $522 to her name.

Knowing What You Can Lose in Bankruptcy

Although bankruptcy may be that miracle cure you sought for your financial woes, you may encounter some unpleasant side effects. The disadvantages of filing bankruptcy are

- ✔ **You can lose assets.** Depending on how much your home is worth and where you live, it is possible, but unlikely, that you'll lose it by filing bankruptcy. (If you're really worried about what will happen to your stuff, check out Part III, especially Chapter 10.) In most bankruptcies, debtors don't have to give up any of their belongings, but . . .

- ✔ **Bankruptcy is a matter of public record.** As more and more records are stored on computers and accessible on the Internet, searching that data becomes easier and easier for anyone who's interested. In other words, if your nosey neighbor wants to know whether you filed bankruptcy, how much you owe, and who you owe it to, the information may be just a few mouse clicks away,

- ✔ **Bankruptcy affects your credit rating.** Bankruptcy may have a negative effect on your credit rating, but that fact may well fall into the "So what?" category for you. Even with a bankruptcy on your record, your odds of obtaining credit are very good. With a little work and perseverance, you can reestablish credit almost immediately. Some credit-card companies actually target folks right after bankruptcy because they know that these people are free of all their existing debts and probably won't be eligible to file another bankruptcy any time soon. For a few years after bankruptcy, you may have to pay higher interest rates on new credit, but this result will ease over time, even if your credit report still shows a bankruptcy. So, don't pay too much attention to the horror stories bill collectors tell you about the disastrous effect bankruptcy has your credit. (In Chapter 21, we walk you through rebuilding your credit after bankruptcy.)

✔ **Friends and relatives can be forced to give back money or property.** If you repaid loans to friends or relatives or gave them anything within the past year, they can be forced to repay a trustee the money they received, if you don't know what to watch out for. (We tell you what to watch out for in Chapter 19.) You can usually avoid these kinds of problems by carefully timing your bankruptcy filing.

✔ **Bankruptcy can strain relations with loved ones, especially parents who were raised in a different era.** (In Chapter 2, we give you some pointers on easing the strain.)

✔ **A stigma may still be attached to filing bankruptcy.** This drawback is especially true in small communities, but is much less likely to be a problem in cities, where newspapers rarely bother printing the names of nonbusiness bankruptcies.

✔ **Bankruptcy may cause more problems than it solves when you've transferred assets to keep them away from creditors.** (You can find out more about this problem in Chapter 19.)

✔ **You can suffer some discrimination.** Although governmental agencies and employers aren't supposed to discriminate against you for filing bankruptcy, they may still do so in a roundabout way. Prospective employers may also refuse to hire you (see Chapter 25 for more on employment discrimination).

Considering Alternatives to Bankruptcy

Bankruptcy isn't for everyone, and sometimes better solutions are available. We explain them in Chapter 7. If it appears that the negatives outweigh the positives, another route may be your best choice. Depending on your situation, the best alternative may be

✔ Selling assets to pay debts in full

✔ Negotiating with creditors to reduce your debts to a manageable level

✔ Restructuring your home mortgage

✔ Taking out a home-equity loan

✔ Doing nothing at all if you have nothing, expect to acquire nothing, and don't care about your present or future credit rating

In any event, you need to weigh your decision on a simple, rational scale. Ask yourself whether the benefits outweigh the drawbacks. Many people, ravaged by guilt and shame, think they need to fully exhaust every alternative before considering bankruptcy, including

- Making payments that never reduce the principal balance owed
- Taking out second mortgages to pay credit-card debts
- Borrowing against pensions
- Withdrawing funds from retirement accounts
- Obtaining loans from friends and relatives
- Taking second jobs

You must think seriously about the strain your financial distress places on your health, marriage, and family. Granted, bankruptcy is a very serious step that you shouldn't take lightly, but that doesn't mean you have to wait until you've lost everything. Think of it in these terms: If you have some blocked arteries, it just may be smarter to have bypass surgery *before* you have a heart attack. The same is true of bankruptcy. Think of bankruptcy as preventative medicine.

Introducing the Different Types of Personal Bankruptcy

Consumer bankruptcies are covered mainly under two parts of the U.S. Bankruptcy Code:

- *Chapter 7 liquidation,* which enables you to eliminate most of your debts but may require you to forfeit some of your assets for distribution to creditors.

- *Chapter 13 reorganization,* which enables you to pay off all or a portion of your debts during a three- to five-year time span but doesn't require you to forfeit any of your belongings or assets to pay *unsecured debts* (those that are not secured by property, such as your car or another valuable asset). See Chapter 11 for more on the difference between secured and unsecured debts.

Likewise, other special kinds of bankruptcy exist. *Chapter 11 bankruptcy* is available to individuals but primarily is used for large business reorganizations. *Chapter 12 bankruptcy,* which is similar to Chapter 13 bankruptcy, addresses the unique problems faced by family farmers and family fishermen. As a practical matter, almost all consumer cases are covered under Chapter 7 or Chapter 13 of the code.

Liquidations (Chapter 7)

Chapter 7, commonly referred to as *straight bankruptcy,* is often what people mean or think of when they use or hear the term generically.

In its simplest form, Chapter 7 wipes out most of your debts and, in return, you may have to surrender some of your property. Chapter 7 doesn't include a repayment plan. Your debts are simply eliminated forever. If you buy a lottery ticket the day after filing and hit the jackpot, yippee! for you and tough beans for your creditors. You obviously can voluntarily pay back your creditors if you suddenly strike it rich, but, legally, you don't owe a dime after your debt is discharged. Most property you receive after filing Chapter 7 doesn't become part of your bankruptcy, but there are a few exceptions. Income tax refunds for prebankruptcy tax years go to pay your debts as well as divorce property awards, inheritances, and life insurance that you become entitled to receive within 180 days of bankruptcy. See Chapter 10 on what assets are at risk.

Theoretically, a debtor's assets can be seized and sold for the benefit of creditors. All nonexempt assets owned on the petition date are fair game. They can be sold, with the proceeds distributed to your creditors. But in practice, 96 percent of consumer bankruptcies are *no-asset cases,* meaning that no property is taken away from the debtor because it's all exempt or worth so little that it's not worth the trouble.

In order to qualify for Chapter 7, if you earn more than the median income for your state, you'll have to pass a new *Means Test* (see Chapter 5) where you show that you don't have enough income to pay a significant portion of your debts. Although the test is ungodly complicated, when all is said and done, just about everyone can pass. The toughest part is just assembling the information you have to provide. You can find helpful worksheets in Chapter 2.

Consumer reorganizations (Chapter 13)

Chapter 13 involves a repayment plan in which you pay all or part of your debts during a three- to five-year period. In a Chapter 13, you propose a debt repayment plan that requires court approval and thereafter keeps creditors at bay as long as you keep making payments. This plan can be a great relief, when you're able to establish and live within the confines of a budget.

A budget plan that demands frugality to the point of misery is doomed to fail ("Frugality is misery in disguise," observed Pubilius Syrus some 2,000 years ago). One that is reasonable has a good chance of succeeding. The operative word, however, is *reasonable.* See Chapters 2 and 22 for more on creating and living within a budget.

Every Chapter 13 plan must pass two tests:

- ✔ The *best-interest test,* which mandates that unsecured creditors be paid at least as much as they would receive if you filed a Chapter 7 instead of a Chapter 13.

- ✔ The *best-efforts test,* which requires that you pay all your disposable income (the amount left over after paying reasonable living expenses) to the trustee for at least the first 36 months of your plan. If your monthly income is more than the median for your state, allowable expenses will be based on *Internal Revenue Collection Financial Standards,* and the plan must run for five years. Otherwise, the amount of your payment will be based on your actual expenses, so long as they are reasonable.

When you're done, you're done. Most creditors have gotten all they're going to get. Life goes on. See Chapter 4 to see what type of bankruptcy is best for you.

Weighing the Consequences of Not Filing Bankruptcy

In the same way that filing bankruptcy can have negative consequences, *not* filing can also have negative consequences. If you're eligible for bankruptcy, but opt against filing, creditors have a number of options they can pursue, depending on whether a particular debt is secured by your property.

Claims secured by your car

If your car secures a debt, the creditor can repossess the vehicle and sell it to cover the loan. The proceeds of a repossession sale usually aren't enough to pay the debt, so you'll lose the car and still have to pay the balance that you owe on it — the worst of both worlds.

Although the law requires a creditor to sell a car in a "commercially reasonable" manner, that doesn't necessarily mean that the creditor will receive nearly as much as you can by selling it yourself. Before allowing repossession, you may want to try selling the vehicle. Your chances of getting more money for the car are greater than the finance company's. See Chapter 11 for more on how bankruptcy can affect your car. If you and your lawyer agree that it's best to get rid of the car because you just can't afford it, you can voluntarily surrender it to the lender rather than wait for them to repossess it. Despite what people may tell you, your credit report will not look that much better, but at least you'll avoid the hassle of finding your car gone when you come out of the supermarket, or the embarrassment of a tow truck showing up at your house.

Claims secured by your home

Mortgage companies can't simply boot you out of your home and onto your derrière if you miss a few payments. They must first go through a foreclosure procedure to extinguish your ownership rights. Although not all foreclosures involve court proceedings, all do take time — at least three months in most cases and frequently much longer. You can continue to live on the property until the foreclosure is completed. Chapter 12 has more on the workings of foreclosures.

Student loans

Government agencies can *garnish* (siphon off) up to 10 percent of your disposable income without going to court. A garnishment is almost like a withholding tax — the money is gone from your paycheck before you ever see it. You also need to be aware that Congress canceled state statutes of limitations on student loans. In other words, you can't just wait it out. You must deal with student loans. They won't disappear on their own. See Chapter 18 for more on student loans.

Support obligations

Although debtors' prisons are officially a thing of the past, a divorce court can still send you to jail for neglecting your support obligations, and some states have programs to revoke professional licenses — such as licenses for practical nurses or accountants or cosmetologists — of people who haven't kept up with their support. Chapter 17 covers support obligations.

Fines and restitution

If you've been ordered to pay a fine or make restitution in connection with a criminal proceeding and don't pay, accommodations at the local jail may await you. Don't tempt the judge, because some of them don't need much tempting to have you hauled off in handcuffs. See Chapter 16 for more on fines.

Taxes

The IRS has truly scary powers to seize your bank account, pension, real property, or even the shirt off your back. State taxing authorities also have similar special powers. In addition, your town or city, student loan creditors, or your ex-spouse or kids may be able to grab your tax refund whenever you owe alimony or support. Chapters 9 and 15 cover taxes.

Lawsuits

Creditors with other types of claims can't do much without first suing you and obtaining a judgment. To do this, they must serve you with legal documents and give you a chance to dispute the debt in court. If you don't respond, a default judgment can be entered against you. That means the ruling goes against you even though you never presented your case.

Using the Statute of Limitations

Most debts — student loans being the most notable exception — eventually evaporate simply through the passage of time. In most cases, the *statute of limitations* (the time period within which an action must be commenced) is six years or less. But whenever a judgment has been entered against you, it can be as long as 20 years.

Sometimes the statute of limitations (usually ten years) can make federal taxes disappear. See Chapter 9.

The trick is figuring out when the statute of limitations clock begins ticking. Sometimes, just making partial payments or acknowledging a debt can start the time running all over again. And you sure don't want that to happen.

Chapter 2

Stopping the Bleeding

Demoralizing debt can seem like a perpetual storm cloud hovering over your days and putting a damper on all life's pleasures. As bleak as your outlook may seem, the forecast really isn't that dismal. A ray of sunshine is striving to break through those clouds, and we're going to help you find it. Remember, however, that maintaining a positive, can-do attitude is essential. Although considering personal bankruptcy is no time for self-pity, understanding that you're not a loser, you're not alone, and that your predicament is symptomatic of a new culture that emerged during the last half-century is definitely important.

Realizing You're Not Alone

If you're like most debtors, you probably feel as if you've been hemorrhaging green stuff for so long that your financial blood vessels are bone-dry. And you're probably down on yourself in a big way. Although you must accept responsibility for your own mistakes — and bear the cross even when your predicament is just the result of rotten luck — you're also probably riding a crazy but predictable wave that has engulfed several million other Americans.

Lenders perpetually make pitches for more spending and more borrowing, which on the credibility scale is somewhere up there with the Boston strangler promoting the Heimlich maneuver. Even political institutions have signed on to the consumerism fad. National leaders tell us in times of economic downturn that spending more and more is our patriotic duty, further extending our debt load. What's good for the credit-card companies, apparently, is good for America — at least in the eyes of consumer lenders.

Odds are you've consciously (or subconsciously) swallowed this bait hook, line, and sinker. And odds are you've already paid the piper in the currency of stress and anxiety. It doesn't take a mind reader to predict that you (and others in your situation) are probably

- Fighting with your spouse over money
- Watching in helpless horror as more and more and more of your monthly income falls down the debt drain
- Sweating even the minimum payments on your credit cards
- Neglecting routine and preventive medical and dental care because you can't pay the doctor's bill, and even the copay seems daunting
- Taking advances on one credit card to cover payments on another — the very definition of robbing Peter to pay Paul
- Dodging calls from creditors and pretending to be someone else when they call
- Using your credit card for small purchases and then buying more things you don't need because you're embarrassed to go into a drugstore and charge only a bottle of aspirin
- Saving those unsolicited cash advance checks from lenders, just in case
- Waking up in the middle of the night worrying about money

Welcome to the club — a really big club. Now that you're a member, you have only one thing to do: Clear your head and put a tourniquet on your wound this instant. True, the problem may not be entirely of your making. It is, however, entirely your responsibility to get out of trouble, so go for it! You need to make a rational determination about what you ought to do and how you ought to do it.

Preventing Further Damage Now

Imagining things being much bleaker than they seem right now is probably difficult, but if you're on the brink of bankruptcy, you need to be extremely careful; otherwise, you'll only muck up your situation.

Until you've met with a bankruptcy lawyer and know just where you stand, do not

- ✔ **Borrow any more money.** Period. No balance transfers. No bill consolidation loans. No pension loans. No home-equity loans. And certainly no loans from friends or relatives.
- ✔ **Make any payments on debts to friends, business partners, or relatives.**
- ✔ **Provide information about your income or expenses to any credit counseling or debt consolidation outfit.**
- ✔ **Call or write to any creditor who does not already know how to contact you.**
- ✔ **Get married — or divorced.**
- ✔ **Sell any valuable assets.**
- ✔ **Make any gifts (other than charitable contributions that you normally make) or transfer property in an attempt to keep those assets away from creditors.**
- ✔ **Ignore lawsuits.**
- ✔ **Give any creditor a postdated check.**
- ✔ **Reveal to a creditor who holds the title to your car that you're considering bankruptcy.**
- ✔ **Agree to pay joint debts if you're in the middle of a divorce matter.**
- ✔ **File any past-due income tax returns.** (However, have them prepared and ready to file.)
- ✔ **Make any unusual or large contributions to a pension fund.**
- ✔ **Make any withdrawals from your pension.**
- ✔ **Move out of your homestead or enter into a contract to sell it.**
- ✔ **Allow a foreclosure sale to occur or give a creditor a deed in lieu of foreclosure.**
- ✔ **Leave any money on deposit in an institution where you owe money.**
- ✔ **Allow health insurance to lapse.**
- ✔ **Voluntarily leave your job.**

Watch out for credit-card arbitration proceedings.

Some credit-card companies have partnered with an outfit called the "National Arbitration Forum." It is nothing more than a kangaroo court, established so that creditors can get stealth judgments — often on bogus claims — against consumers without the hassle of going through a real court with a real judge.

How do they get away with this? They're sneaky. Along with all the other junk they stick in the envelopes with their monthly statements is often an official and binding notice that collections issued will be resolved through arbitration, not litigation. Those sessions will probably not take place anywhere convenient to you — like your local courthouse. Rather, they'll occur in some other location, possibly far from your home.

It usually starts with a legalistic notice that arbitration proceedings have been started against you, and that if you do not respond, an award may be turned into a real court judgment against you. They're counting on you not responding, of course, and most folks don't. And then you're screwed.

So if you receive one of these notices, don't ignore it if you have any reason at all to question the amount of the claim against you. Study the instructions that come with the notice and force them to at least prove that you owe them money.

Throughout this book, we show you how these and other seemingly innocent actions can complicate your bankruptcy and your life. If you've already done some of the *don'ts*, don't despair. Just make sure to tell your lawyer, who may be able to fix things.

Comparing Your Income with Your Spending

When you know what *not* to do (see the preceding section), you can focus on what you *can* do to improve your situation. And the first thing to do is make an honest, objective, unemotional assessment of what you have, what you owe, and what you can do to balance the scales.

Figuring out where you stand or where you're going without knowing just how much you make and spend is tough. Taking the time to complete the two worksheets outlined in Tables 2-1 and 2-2 helps you

✔ Provide insight into whether you can solve your problems without bankruptcy

✔ Assemble the information your lawyer needs to file bankruptcy

✔ Establish a budget for the future so you don't get into financial trouble again

Focusing on how much income you have

Table 2-1 helps you calculate the first half of the financial equation — your monthly income.

Focusing on monthly income and expenses would be wise, so you may have to prorate some figures. *Prorating* means, for example, that when you're paid every two weeks, you double the amount of your paycheck. Whenever you receive an annual bonus, divide it by 12.

Several of the sources to which you can look for this information are

✔ Your paycheck

✔ Last year's income tax return

✔ Records of any alimony you receive (not the amount you're supposed to get, but the actual amount you received)

Table 2-1	**Your Net Income**		
	You	*Your Mate*	*Combined Amount*
Current gross wages, salary, and commissions	$	$	
Estimated overtime pay	$	$	
Subtotal gross income			$
PAYROLL DEDUCTIONS			
Payroll taxes and Social Security	$	$	
Insurance	$	$	
Union dues	$	$	
Contributions to pension	$	$	
Repayments on pension loan	$	$	

(continued)

Table 2-1 *(continued)*

	You	Your Mate	Combined Amount
Support payments deducted from pay	$	$	
Other payroll deductions	$	$	
Subtotal of payroll deductions			$
TAKE-HOME PAY	$	$	$
Gross income from business, profession, or farm (expenses of running the operation are accounted for on the expenses worksheet)	$	$	
Gross income from rental properties (expenses are accounted for on the expenses worksheet)	$	$	
Social Security and other government assistance	$	$	
Retirement income	$	$	
Other income	$	$	
TOTAL INCOME	$	$	$

Coming to grips with where your money goes

Chances are, you don't really know where all your money goes. It probably seems like you just never have enough, despite living a rather modest lifestyle.

We suggest that you carry around a little notebook so that you can record *every* expenditure that you make for a month. You say you dropped $10 in the collection basket at church? Write it down. Maybe you picked up a box of cookies at the convenience store . . . make a note. Even if it's only a cup of coffee or a soda, record it. Sure, it sounds like a hassle — and it is, but that's the point. The pain of having to write down every expenditure makes you less likely to spend the money. It just becomes more trouble than it's worth.

Keeping track of all your expenditures enables you to do the following:

- ✔ Prepare a realistic budget
- ✔ Lay the groundwork for bringing your spending under control, regardless of whether you end up filing bankruptcy
- ✔ Make a more informed decision about whether bankruptcy is the best solution
- ✔ Intelligently weigh pros and cons of a Chapter 7 liquidation versus a Chapter 13 reorganization
- ✔ Provide a ready record of some of the information necessary to complete bankruptcy papers, if you decide to go that route

Be sure to record expenses that are not monthly and tend to fall into the out-of-sight-out-of-mind category. Insurance, real property taxes, income taxes not withheld from wages, vacation expenses, tuition, and Christmas spending are a few examples. When you pay car insurance every six months, divide the amount of this payment by six. When you pay some bills weekly, multiply by 52 and then divide by 12 to arrive at the monthly payment amount.

Include payments on *past* credit-card charges, but as for future charges, record the items purchased.

Table 2-2 should help.

Table 2-2	Where Does My Money Go?	
Type of Expense	*Monthly Average*	*Total*
HOUSING		
Rent	$	
Mortgage payments	$	
Real property taxes (if not included in mortgage payments)	$	
Furniture/appliance purchases	$	
Home maintenance/repairs	$	
Total Housing Expense		$
UTILITIES		
Gas/electric/oil	$	

(continued)

Table 2-2 *(continued)*

Type of Expense	Monthly Average	Total
Water	$	
Regular phone	$	
Cable TV	$	
Total Utilities Expense		$
FOOD		
Groceries	$	
Eating out	$	
Total Food Expense		$
CLOTHING EXPENSES		
New clothes	$	
Laundry	$	
Total Clothing Expense		$
MEDICAL EXPENSES		
Doctors/dentists/other medical professionals	$	
Drugs	$	
Eyeglasses	$	
Other medical expenses	$	
Total Medical Expense		$
TRANSPORTATION EXPENSES		
Gasoline	$	
Maintenance/repairs	$	
License and other fees	$	
Parking	$	
Public transportation	$	
Other transportation expenses	$	
Total Transportation Expense		$

Type of Expense	Monthly Average	Total
DEBT PAYMENTS		
Credit cards	$	
Auto loans	$	
Student loans	$	
Other payments	$	
Total Debt Payment		$
TAXES NOT DEDUCTED FROM PAY		
Estimated tax payments	$	
Taxes paid when annual return filed (remember to divide by 12)	$	
Payments on back taxes	$	
Other tax payments	$	
Total Tax Payment		$
RECREATION EXPENSES		
Cell phone	$	
Internet	$	
Movies, sporting events, concerts	$	
Books	$	
Vacation and travel	$	
Gifts	$	
Pet expenses	$	
Other recreational expenditures	$	
Total Recreation Expense		$
INSURANCE		
Homeowners (unless included in mortgage payment)	$	
Auto insurance	$	

(continued)

Table 2-2 *(continued)*

Type of Expense	Monthly Average	Total
Health insurance (unless deducted from pay)	$	
Life insurance (unless deducted from pay)	$	
Other insurance	$	
Total Insurance Expense		$
VICES		
Tobacco	$	
Alcohol	$	
Gambling	$	
Other	$	
Total Vice Expense		$
PERSONAL ITEMS		
Haircuts, beauty products (including makeup)	$	
Health club memberships	$	
Other	$	
Total Personal Items Expense		$
SUPPORT AND ALIMONY PAYMENTS		
Back alimony and child support (not deducted from pay)	$	
Current alimony and child support payments	$	
Total Support Payments		$
OFFSPRING		
Allowance	$	
Tuition	$	
Day care	$	
Toys and presents	$	
Money given to adult children	$	
Other	$	
Total Offspring Expense		$

Type of Expense	Monthly Average	Total
PERSONAL EDUCATIONAL EXPENSES		
Tuition	$	
Books	$	
Supplies	$	
Other	$	
Total Educational Expense		$
BUSINESS EXPENSES		
Total monthly expenses of business, profession, or farm	$	
Total monthly expenses of owning and operating rental property	$	
Other business expenses	$	
Total Business Expense		$
OTHER EXPENSES		
Charitable contributions	$	
Miscellaneous expenses	$	
Total Other Expense		$
TOTAL MONTHLY EXPENSES		$

Assessing Your Spending Habits

Congratulations! You've just taken the most important step on the road to financial recovery. To varying degrees, we all live in a self-imposed fog when it comes to spending money. Spending becomes a comfortable habit — just the way you go about your daily business — and habits are always hard to break. But now you're on your way.

Now that you've committed yourself to recovery, we can take a closer look at where your money is going, consider the possibility that overspending has become a habit and, if so, examine ways to deal with it.

The devil's in the details: Scrutinizing your expenses

Okay, documenting your expenses has proven the obvious: You've wasted money, and probably made some lousy financial decisions. Who hasn't? (If you haven't assessed your spending habits, see the section "Comparing Your Income with Your Spending," earlier in this chapter.) But now that you have a handle on the problem, you're in position to take control. In Chapter 22, we offer some suggestions for a simpler lifestyle through financial "downshifting."

With the right attitude, eliminating unnecessary expenditures can be a little like a treasure hunt. There's extra money somewhere; you just have to find it.

Although we wouldn't presume to tell you how much to spend on any particular item — that's your call — here are a few things to zero in on:

- **Credit-card payments.** If a big chunk of your monthly income is going to pay credit-card bills (and for minimum payments at that), bankruptcy may be far and away the best solution. Right now, you're just spinning your wheels — paying interest without significantly reducing the principal amount of the debts. Say that you've got a fairly modest credit-card debt of about $3,000. At 17 percent interest — and a lot of times the interest rate is a whole lot higher — you'll be indebted to the credit-card company for about 35 years if you just make minimum payments.

- **Daily dribbles.** We all live our lives against a background of daily patterns that eventually become habits. Many times, these habits include unnecessary spending that provides no real benefit or enjoyment. What seems like small stuff eventually adds up. Consider the $2 latte you get on the way to work, a $1 you put in the soda pop machine, and the $2.50 you spend for an afternoon snack — all without thinking about it. Over the course of a year, you've blown $1,430. To put it in perspective: If you invested this money for 20 years at 10 percent interest, you'd end up with more than $80,000!

- **Extravagances.** Admittedly, one person's luxury is another's necessity, but you really need to think long and hard before plopping down $100 for a restaurant meal or $60 to watch a pay-for-view prize fight on television. It's sometimes helpful — albeit painful — to figure out how much work you had to do to pay for a particular treat. For example, if a night on the town costs you a day and a half of work, you may think twice about the return on your investment.

- **Impulse purchases.** A little later in this chapter, in the section "Getting a Handle on What You Own," we ask you to list all your belongings, but for now, just make a trip to your attic, basement, and garage. If you're like most people — and us — you'll see tons of stuff you've bought but rarely if ever use. Simplify.

✔ **Gifts.** Studies show that many folks spend lavishly on gifts they would never buy for themselves. Christmas, of course, is the granddaddy of budget-busters.

✔ **Overwhelming mortgage payments.** If you obtained your mortgage recently, most of your monthly payment goes toward the interest. So, you may not have much equity, and the home may not be worth keeping — especially if it's a second mortgage. For more on this topic, see Chapter 12.

✔ **Killer car payments.** New cars are awfully pricey these days, partly because they're more dependable and longer lasting. If you're struggling to maintain payments on a new car, you may want to consider selling your expensive car and buying something more affordable. Plenty of reliable, moderately priced used cars are on the market today.

Are you a spendaholic?

Similar to an addiction, compulsive spending can be a disease. If you're so afflicted, you may need professional assistance. Debtors Anonymous, a group dedicated to helping folks curb excessive spending habits, has compiled a checklist of the common signs of compulsive behavior. Ask yourself the following questions:

✔ Are your debts making your home life unhappy?

✔ Does the pressure of your debts distract you from your daily work?

✔ Are your debts affecting your reputation?

✔ Do your debts cause you to think less of yourself?

✔ Have you ever given false information to obtain credit?

✔ Have you ever made unrealistic promises to your creditors?

✔ Does the pressure of your debts make you careless of the welfare of your family?

✔ Do you ever fear that your employer, family, or friends will find out the extent of your total indebtedness?

✔ When faced with a difficult financial situation, does the prospect of borrowing give you an inordinate feeling of relief?

✔ Does the pressure of your debts cause you to have difficulty sleeping?

✔ Has the pressure of your debts ever caused you to consider getting drunk?

✔ Have you ever borrowed money without giving adequate consideration to the rate of interest you're required to pay?

✔ Do you usually expect a negative response when you're subject to a credit investigation?

✔ Have you ever developed a strict regimen for paying off your debts, only to break it under pressure?

✔ Do you justify your debts by telling yourself that you're superior to the "other" people, and when you get your "break," you'll be out of debt overnight?

If you answer yes to eight or more of the previous questions, you may be a compulsive spender. An organization called Debtors Anonymous can help. You can check out their Web site at www.DebtorsAnonymous.org, call them at (781) 453-2743, or write to them at Debtors Anonymous, General Service Office, P.O. Box 920888, Needham, MA 02492-0009.

You also may want to take a look at Chapter 22 to help reorder your spending priorities.

Getting a Handle on What You Own

After you figure out what your spending habits and your earnings are (see the sections earlier in this chapter), it's also a good time to get an equally firm grasp on what you *own*. Documenting your assets does the following:

✔ Creates a basis for figuring out what property you may lose by filing bankruptcy

✔ Lets you know if avoiding bankruptcy by selling things is a viable option

✔ Demonstrates how little you have to show for thousands of dollars of credit-card debt

Use Table 2-3 to document what you own. If you need some help figuring out how much you stuff is worth, take a look at Chapter 10.

Documenting your assets when you're close to bankruptcy is depressing.

Table 2-3	What You Own
Asset	*Value*
REAL PROPERTY	
Your home	

Asset	Value
Other real property	
Timeshares	
MOTOR VEHICLES	
BANK ACCOUNT BALANCES	
HOUSEHOLD GOODS	
Furniture	
Appliances	
Audio and video equipment	
Computers and accessories	
Other household items	
ART OBJECTS AND COLLECTIBLES	
JEWELRY	
FIREARMS	
HOBBY EQUIPMENT	
STOCKS, BONDS, AND OTHER INVESTMENTS	

(continued)

Table 2-3 *(continued)*

Asset	Value
CASH VALUE OF LIFE INSURANCE	
INTERESTS IN ANY TRUSTS	
BUSINESS INTERESTS	
MONEY THAT YOU ARE OWED	
Alimony and support	
Bonuses at work	
Accounts receivable	
Claims where you can sue someone	
Commissions	
Tax refunds	
MONEY YOU ARE ENTITLED TO BECAUSE SOMEONE DIED	
Life insurance	
Distributions from an estate	
PATENTS AND COPYRIGHTS	
TOOLS AND MACHINERY USED FOR WORK	

CASH VALUE OR PENSIONS

OFFICE EQUIPMENT NOT INCLUDED IN HOUSEHOLD GOODS

BUSINESS INVENTORY

OTHER ASSETS

Figuring Out How Much You Owe

Purveyors of consumer credit want you to think in terms of monthly payments instead of considering the total amount you'll owe. It's a lot easier to sell that new car when the customer focuses on a $400 monthly payment rather than on a $25,000 albatross. But when it comes to assessing your financial condition, knowing the total amount of your debts is critical.

Home and car loans should be considered separately from other debts for two reasons:

✔ These loans can be reduced or eliminated if you sell the house or car.

✔ Bankruptcy affects home and car loans differently than other debts.

You can find out how much you owe on these loans by phoning the creditor. If you're behind in payments, also find out how much it will take to bring the loan current (as opposed to the amount required to pay the loan in full).

Filling the blanks in Table 2-4 helps you get a grip on what you owe.

Table 2-4	How Much Do You Owe on Mortgage and Car Loans?			
	Total Balance Owed	Monthly Payment	Value of Home/Car	Arrearage (Amount You're Behind)
Residence				
Other real estate				
Cars				

Calculating how much you owe on other debts is a little tougher.

Ordering credit reports is one place to start. See Chapter 6 for tips on getting credit reports.

You can frequently determine the amounts owed on judgments, child support, alimony, fines, and restitution obligations from documents on file in the courthouse.

You can get a rough idea of how much you owe on income taxes by looking at copies of your income tax returns, but this method won't give you the amount of penalties and interest that has accrued. See Chapter 9 and Chapter 15 for more info on dealing with tax obligations.

Hopefully, you have a rough idea of how much you owe on student loans. If not, you'll probably have to find out more than you want to about how the student loan industry works just to find out whom to ask. Check out Chapter 18.

After you know what you owe, use Table 2-5 to help you keep track of it.

If creditors don't how where you live, or have given up on you, don't ring their bell by calling them.

Table 2-5	How Much Do You Owe on Other Debts?
Type of Debt	Total Amount Owed
Judgments	
Income taxes	

Type of Debt	Total Amount Owed
Child support and alimony	
Student loans	
Fines and restitution obligations	
Medical bills	
Credit-card balances	
Loans to friends and relatives	

At this point, you may want to jump to Chapter 4 to discover which types of bankruptcy are available and to Chapter 7 to check out alternatives to bankruptcy.

Chapter 3

Meeting the Players

. . . .

In This Chapter

▶ Appreciating why you need a lawyer

▶ Finding a lawyer you can trust, and figuring out how to pay her

▶ Identifying friends and foes

. . . .

*I*n your pursuit of a fresh financial start, you'll encounter a rather large cast of characters, at least indirectly. One player, and only one, is unequivocally on your side: your lawyer. Others, such as the trustee, look out for the interests of your creditors. And the judge is supposed to function as a neutral arbiter. This chapter identifies the troupe, their roles on the bankruptcy stage, and how those factors relate to you and your goals. It also includes — in the sidebar at the end — a brief vocabulary list for you to look at so that you can understand what everyone is talking about.

Finding Professional Help

One of the challenges of putting your financial house in order is getting an accurate, trustworthy, and unbiased assessment of your particular options. Obtaining objective advice is absolutely essential because you're going to be bombarded with conflicting information and opinions about bankruptcy.

Despite their best intentions, friends or relatives may mislead you. And so can the following groups of people:

✔ **Credit counselors,** who ostensibly help with budgeting and dealing with creditors, may inappropriately discourage you from filing for bankruptcy, and, instead, push for a secret agenda. Although they may appear to be independent, many of them are on creditors' payrolls, so their interests may be completely at odds with yours.

✔ **Debt consolidators,** offering to replace your many monthly bills with a single "low-interest, easy payment loan," sometimes use sophisticated marketing ploys to dazzle you into believing that you can get out of debt by borrowing more money. You can't.

✔ **Bill collectors** are willing to tell you just about anything to squeeze some money out of you.

You need to act with your head, and not your heart, when making a cold, calculated, harsh judgment of what truly is in your best interests. This section explains why you need a lawyer, how to find one, and how to deal with legal and other costs associated with filing bankruptcy.

Answering why a lawyer is a must

An old adage says that a lawyer who represents himself has a fool for a client. Nowhere is that statement more true than in the area of bankruptcy law, and never was it truer than today. Bankruptcy law is incredibly complex particularly in the wake of the Bankruptcy Abuse Reform Fiasco (or BARF, as we and many others refer to the laws enacted in 2005), and many attorneys with successful general practices have difficulty keeping up to date.

With a new and remarkably obtuse new law on the books, even attorneys and judges struggle to figure out just what Congress meant when it rewrote the bankruptcy code. The Bankruptcy Abuse Reform Fiasco — or BARF — is so poorly conceived and ill-written that it will take the courts ages to figure out just what Congress has done (not that the folks in Congress have any clue). A conscientious bankruptcy lawyer will have to monitor developments regularly just to stay in the game, and that's the person you need at your side. Filing bankruptcy is *not* the time to rely on paralegals and document preparation services. They just don't have the time, expertise, or stomach to deal with BARF. And neither do you.

Don't listen to anyone who tells you that he handled his own bankruptcy and everything went just fine. Prior to BARF, some folks did manage to successfully file bankruptcy without a lawyer, but things have changed — dramatically!

Finding a good lawyer

Certainly no shortage of "free" advice exists out there, but most of it is worth about what it costs — nothing, if that. When you're serious about considering bankruptcy, you need a lawyer — simple as that. So how do you go about finding one?

You can check with friends and relatives who have filed bankruptcy, and, if you already know a reputable attorney whose firm does *not* handle bankruptcy cases, he is likely to know a good source of advice. They won't knowingly send their clients to hacks. (For tips about meeting with your lawyer, see Chapter 6.)

Understanding what to expect from your lawyer

Some lawyers offer a "free" initial consultation, which means the only way that they make any money is if you end up filing bankruptcy. That approach can skew their judgment.

You're probably better off paying an attorney for an hour of his or her time, expecting to pay roughly $100 to $200 per hour. When you're paying a fee, you have every right to insist on a consultation with the attorney who actually would be handling your case, not some paralegal or assistant. Whenever a law firm won't make this commitment or tries to shift you to someone else, take your business and your money elsewhere.

Paying the piper

Filing a Chapter 7, the type of bankruptcy that doesn't involve any kind of repayment plan, costs you a $274 court fee. A Chapter 13 filing, where you repay a portion of your debts over time, costs $189. Legal fees vary widely, depending on where you live and how complicated your case is.

In the past, lawyers would typically charge a fixed fee for personal bankruptcy, with additional charges for an unusually complicated case. Under BARF, a "routine" bankruptcy case doesn't exist anymore. They're all complicated. Ultimately, your attorney fees depend on how much time the lawyer spends on your case. You can minimize that effort by getting all your ducks in a row before meeting with the attorney. If you've collected all your asset and debt information and read enough of this book to forego the most basic questions, you can cut down on the billable hours.

In a Chapter 7 bankruptcy, all attorney fees must be paid before filing. You can pay fees over an extended time period in a Chapter 13 filing.

Considering your current financial situation, you're probably wondering where you're going to find money to pay for your bankruptcy filing. Here are a few suggestions:

✔ After you decide to file bankruptcy, you don't need to make any more payments on debts that ultimately will be eliminated (such as most credit-card debts). That alone is likely to free up a fair amount of cash to apply toward your legal and court costs.

✔ You can sell assets to raise the money. This move is smart one whenever you'd otherwise be forced to forfeit these assets when you file bankruptcy.

✔ A friend or relative can give you the money to file, if you ask nicely. An employer may even pony up bankruptcy fees to focus the employee's attention on the job rather than on his or her financial problems and avoid the hassle of dealing with creditors trying to attach or garnish the employee's wages.

Surfing for consumer info on the Internet

Information that you glean from the Internet can be a godsend. It also can also be god-awful.

Some Web sites are sponsored by debt consolidation companies, which earn fees from debtors and creditors when they convince the former to undertake debt repayment plans; even folks with no hope of success and clients who'd be far better off in bankruptcy. For that matter, even well-intentioned sites sometimes provide erroneous information. Oops.

Still other sites that appear consumer-oriented actually sell advertising to mortgage lenders and credit-card issuers. So-called experts on these sites frequently try to convince people to borrow even more, often by advising visitors to take out second and third mortgages against their homes when they actually need to file bankruptcy and start out fresh.

That said, we've found that the following Web sites are consistently reliable and informative:

✔ **Consumer Federation of America (www. ConsumerFed.org):** The Consumer Federation of America (CFA) in Washington, D.C. is a terrific source. In our experience, the folks at the Consumer Federation are informed, diligent, and up-to-date. Many consumer-rights folks, and more than a few policymakers, rely on the CFA to honestly and thoroughly evaluate the real impact of legislation on real, live consumers.

✔ **National Consumer Law Center (www. ConsumerLaw.org):** The National Consumer Law Center (NCLC) offers ton of useful and reliable consumer information on its Web site.

✔ **Debtors Anonymous (www.Debtors Anonymous.org):** Debtors Anonymous provides a wealth of insight on compulsive spending and offers the opportunity to chat with others about money problems without anyone trying to lend you money, sell you something, or sign you up for some screwy debt repayment plans.

Borrowing money to pay attorney fees is a dicey proposition; the idea, after all, is getting out of debt, not accumulating more. In any case, one definite is "Don't borrow money from anyone without first revealing your plan to file bankruptcy." If you do, that creditor may claim that you're guilty of fraud and try to keep the debt from being wiped out. See Chapters 13 and 15.

Getting to Know the Players

Bankruptcy is an adversarial process in which individuals with competing interests struggle against one another to — hopefully — achieve a balanced and fair result. Bankruptcy court is the playing field, and the judge is the referee. The people you can encounter in the bankruptcy system all have different roles to play.

Although the players act politely and respectfully toward each other most of the time, keep in mind that the only person responsible for looking out for your best interests is your lawyer.

Bankruptcy judge

The justice system is blessed with scores of dedicated, thoughtful bankruptcy judges who conscientiously strive to fairly balance the competing interests. Some judges, of course, are better than others, but in the scheme of things, that also means that others are downright bad. Some judges are biased, and some have agendas. And even good judges sometimes make mistakes. Luckily, rulings by bankruptcy judges can be reviewed by other federal judges — and sometimes even the United States Supreme Court.

Unlike some other federal jurists, bankruptcy judges don't enjoy lifetime appointments. The federal court must reappoint them when their 14-year terms expire. Recently, several well-respected judges were denied reappointment because creditors' groups lobbied powers with political muscle, claiming the judges were too sympathetic to debtors. This development — we'll go so far as to call it a trend — can't help but weigh on judges.

Regardless, in our experience, few judges (consciously) allow outside influences to color their decision making. And the decisions of those who do tend to be reversed on appeal. In other words, be aware that the judge *may* not be as objective as you'd hope, but don't lose any sleep over it.

In all likelihood, you'll never even see the bankruptcy judge who handles your case. Other players usually can resolve issues through negotiation and settlement, and the judge is called in only when a problem is encountered. Still, you can feel reassured in knowing that if all else fails, you can always take it to the judge and make a federal case out of it.

Case trustee

The most visible player in a bankruptcy filing is the *case trustee.* Your relationship with this trustee differs depending on whether you file a Chapter 7 liquidation or a Chapter 13 reorganization.

Chapter 7: The panel trustee

The trustee in a Chapter 7 bankruptcy is appointed at random from a panel of (usually) lawyers. You encounter your case trustee when you meet a *341 meeting,* where debtors answer questions about their assets and financial affairs (see Chapter 6).

A Chapter 7 trustee's main mission is selling property and doling the proceeds out to creditors. Any *nonexempt property* — stuff that can be taken to satisfy your debts — is up for grabs, and so is money received within six months of filing bankruptcy from life insurance, inheritances, or divorce property divisions. The trustee also can recover some transfers and payments that you made before filing bankruptcy (see Chapter 19 for more details). For his troubles, the case trustee gets a commission based on how much money is collected.

After reviewing your bankruptcy documents, the case trustee asks you some questions to determine whether any assets can be sold to cover your debts. Although the Chapter 7 trustee isn't necessarily your friend, he needn't be your enemy either. Most case trustees are reasonable people just trying to fulfill their roles within the confines of the law. So, try not to take it personally.

Granted, the thought of someone scrounging through your belongings and putting them up for sale is inherently offensive. But you don't need to worry that the trustee will turn your living room into a Salvation Army store. In 96 percent of Chapter 7 cases, no assets actually are liquidated, because they're all exempt or because they're not worth enough to bother with.

Be aware, however, that a trustee is likely to pounce on anything that looks like easy pickings — like income tax refunds for past years and the current year. But remember that he can't take future tax refunds.

Bumping heads with Uncle Sam

Chrissie was, like, totally not into completing the financial questionnaire her lawyer gave her. So-oh, she pretty much made up the answers while watching MTV. Chrissie didn't really mean to deceive anyone, but digging up all that stuff is a drag, and she really had more fun things to do. So, she winged it. Who'd ever care?

Chrissie's papers were so riddled with errors that the judge had a fit, refused to wipe out her debts, fined her — and referred the matter to federal prosecutors for possible criminal action. Chrissie totally couldn't deal with that!

But the U.S. Attorney could. And did.

Bum-mer!

If the trustee doesn't pursue an asset, it's yours after your bankruptcy case is closed — provided that you accurately described it on your bankruptcy papers. For that reason, making sure that your paperwork is complete, accurate, and honest is extremely important. Besides, doing so may keep you out of jail.

The trustee also asks about payments and transfers of assets that you made prior to bankruptcy to see whether he can recover them for the benefit of creditors (see Chapter 19).

Chapter 13: The standing trustee

A Chapter 13 trustee has a different role, and you meet him or her at your 341 meeting. The trustee questions you about your assets and scrutinizes your income and expenses and generally tries to make sure that your repayment plan meets technical requirements and has a reasonable chance of succeeding.

Unlike a Chapter 7 trustee, a Chapter 13 trustee doesn't typically liquidate any property. Instead, the trustee collects monthly payments that you make under a Chapter 13 repayment plan and receives a commission based on these payments. The longer that you make required payments, the more the trustee earns. So the Chapter 13 trustee has an incentive in helping you succeed with your repayment plan.

Some Chapter 13 trustees sponsor personal financial management courses, hoping that your attending them will increase your chances for successfully completing the repayment plan. So far, the jury is out on whether debtor education leads to higher Chapter 13 success rates. But if the option is there, take it. You've nothing to lose.

U.S. Trustee

The U.S. Trustee, an employee of the U.S. Department of Justice, is an entirely different creature than the case trustee. A U.S. Trustee heads one of 21 regional offices. The head of the entire United States Trustee program, the Executive Director, is a political appointee of the U.S. Attorney General and, by extension, of the current president.

The U.S. Trustee:

- Oversees private trustees and makes sure that they properly account for all funds they receive.

- Watches out for fraud in bankruptcy cases and refers questionable matters to the U.S. Attorney for criminal prosecution.

- Conducts, in theory, 341 meetings. In practice, this chore usually is delegated to the trustee assigned to your particular case.

- Grades the *Means Test* (this part of the new bankruptcy law is designed to determine whether you're really broke enough to file Chapter 7). If you flunk and are unwilling or unable to commit to a Chapter 13 repayment plan, the U.S. Trustee may ask the court to dismiss your bankruptcy.

- Can help whenever special accommodations must be made for the 341 meeting. For example, if you're disabled or need an interpreter, the U.S. Trustee tries to provide appropriate assistance.

Talking the legal lingo

Legal eagles and legal beagles talk their own language, and, oftentimes, the legalistic meaning of a word or concept is different than the generic definition. So having a basic familiarity with legalese is a good idea so that you can communicate effectively with the lawyerly sorts you'll likely encounter whenever you decide to take this journey.

Automatic stay: The instant your bankruptcy petition is filed, an automatic court order keeps the creditors at bay. They can't garnish your wages, repossess your car, start or continue foreclosure proceedings, sue you, or even contact you about your debts. And, if they do, they'll have a federal judge — and probably an angry one at that — to answer to.

Bankruptcy Abuse Prevention And Consumer Protection Act of 2005 (also known as the Bankruptcy Abuse Reform Fiasco or "BARF": The most extensive revision of the bankruptcy code since 1978. The law, written and paid for by the consumer credit industry, applies to all bankruptcies filed on or after October 17, 2005. Despite the official name, nothing in the law really protects consumers. A more accurate name would be the "irresponsible lender protection act," but we'll settle for BARF.

Collateral: An asset that backs up a specific debt.

Confirmation: A court order making a Chapter 13 plan binding on the debtor and all creditors.

Discharge: When your case is over, a court order wipes out or "discharges" your debts.

Exempt property: Some property is yours to keep, regardless of the bankruptcy. Those possessions are said to be *exempt* — or off limits to creditors.

Foreclosure: The way a creditor turns collateral into cash. When the collateral is *real property* (essentially land and buildings), an actual lawsuit sometimes (but not always) is required. Many states provide a method of nonjudicial foreclosure in which real property is sold at public auction at a specified time — typically about four months — after notice of the sale has been published. When the collateral is *personal property,* a nonjudicial sale can be held with as little as ten days' notice. Foreclosure should be distinguished from repossession, which, by itself, doesn't terminate your interest in the collateral.

Joint bankruptcy: Your spouse doesn't have to file bankruptcy just because you're filing, but if both of you go that route, the petition is called a *joint bankruptcy.*

Lien: Some debts are backed up by specific assets (collateral), which the creditor can seize if you don't pay. For example, when you buy a house, the bank holds a mortgage that places a *lien* on your home as collateral for the mortgage. Similarly, your car oftentimes is used as collateral for a loan. Again, that is a *lien.*

Means Test: The keystone of BARF and the main hurdle to those searching for financial salvation. A complicated set of calculations that is supposed to identify those consumers who can pay a significant portion of their debt and therefore should be required to do so instead of immediately shedding their obligations in Chapter 7. When all is said and done, the test applies only to debtors earning more than the median income for their state. Even when it does apply, just about everyone who jumps through all the hoops will pass it and qualify for Chapter 7.

No-asset case: A Chapter 7 case in which the value of a debtor's assets isn't high enough to bother liquidating any of them.

Personal property: Anything you own that's not attached to land — and that includes your car, household goods, bank accounts, pensions, and so on — is considered *personal property,* as opposed to *real property,* and is subject to special rules in bankruptcy. In some states, even mobile homes are considered personal property, as long as they're not permanently tied to the ground.

Petition date: The date that your bankruptcy petition is filed.

Property of the estate: Everything that you own as of the petition date is deemed *property of the estate* and therefore is potentially at risk in bankruptcy.

Reaffirmation: Even if bankruptcy would wipe out a debt, you can promise to repay what you owe. And why would you want to do that? Good question! See Chapter 13 for situations where *reaffirmation* may make sense.

Redemption: Say you bought a refrigerator and stove for $1,500, and those appliances now are worth only $500, but you still owe $1,000. *Redemption* enables you to keep the refrigerator and stove by making a lump sum payment of $500. The remainder of the debt is wiped out.

Repossession: Where a creditor obtains possession of collateral if you don't pay.

341 meeting: About 40 days after filing your bankruptcy petition, a meeting is scheduled at which a trustee (the person who represents the interests of creditors in bankruptcy matters) and creditors can quiz you about your assets and debts. It's named a 341 meeting after a particular section of the U.S. Bankruptcy Code.

Creditors

Although creditors certainly are players in the process, you shouldn't have much to do with them after your case is filed. They may attend the 341 meeting and ask a few questions, but most won't bother.

Any contact that you have with creditors will probably be only in the context of surrendering collateral or making arrangements to keep it after you file (see Chapter 10).

Chapter 4

Deciding Which Type of Bankruptcy Is Best for You

*P*ersonal bankruptcy comes in a variety of flavors. You can find advantages and disadvantages to using any bankruptcy option, and we explore those pluses and minuses in this chapter.

The vast majority of consumers opt for *Chapter 7,* where you immediately eliminate most of your debts, surrender any *nonexempt assets* — those that can be sold off for the benefit of creditors — and go merrily on your way. Another common choice is *Chapter 13,* where you keep your stuff but have to make payments to a trustee for several years. After that, any remaining balances on most debts are wiped out.

In addition, if you can qualify as a family farmer or family fisherman, another option, *Chapter 12,* is probably the way to go. And finally, there's *Chapter 11,* a form of bankruptcy commonly used for business reorganizations, that may just provide a remedy for you.

Deciding Whether to Fly Solo or As a Married Couple

Many married people assume that they're automatically responsible for each other's debts. Wrong.

You are, of course, liable for your own debts and any monetary obligations that you accept by cosigning for a loan or a credit card obtained by your spouse or significant other. When you cosign, you tell the creditor that if your mate doesn't pay up, you will.

An ancient *doctrine of necessaries,* concocted in an era when only husbands were the breadwinners, states that if a husband wasn't bringing home the bacon, his wife could go out and buy essential items by charging them to his credit.

In our enlightened era , however, the doctrine of necessaries pops up when, for example, a hospital argues that a wife is responsible for her husband's medical services. Hospitals frequently claim that under the doctrine of necessaries, both spouses are liable for services provided to one spouse or to one of their dependents. Although that argument is a mile wide and an inch deep (and often unsuccessful), when medical expenses overwhelm you, filing a joint bankruptcy usually is easier than battling with hospitals.

If you live in one of nine community-property states (Arizona, California, Idaho, Louisiana, Nevada, New Mexico, Texas, Washington, and Wisconsin), the rules are different. Husbands or wives frequently find themselves on the hook for their spouses' debts because so-called community property of both is subject to debts incurred by either. *Community property* includes the earnings of either spouse and all property acquired by either the husband or the wife during the marriage, except for gifts and inheritances.

Even if you and your spouse must file bankruptcy, you don't have to file jointly. In fact, you may find advantages to filing separately (see Chapters 5, 10, and 12).

And, just in case you're wondering, you must actually be married to file a joint bankruptcy. If you aren't, you and your significant other — even if you're in a long-term, committed relationship that closely resembles marriage — must file separate bankruptcies even if most of the debts are joint. And under the federal Defense of Marriage Act, 1 U.S.C. 7, a same-sex partner cannot qualify as a spouse under the Bankruptcy Code, even in states recognizing same-sex marriages.

Looking at Your Probable Bankruptcy Choices

Your basic choice is between a bankruptcy that doesn't involve any type of repayment plan (Chapter 7 bankruptcy), and one that does (Chapters 11,12, and 13). You need to base your decision on what's best for you and your family, not on what you think will make your creditors happy.

Chapter 7: Straight bankruptcy

Chapter 7, which occasionally is referred to as *straight bankruptcy,* is essentially the belly-up version that most people envision when they hear the word *bankruptcy*. If you file under Chapter 7, most of your debts are eliminated, and some of your property may go to your creditors. You don't have any repayment plan; your debts simply disappear.

Assets that are *nonexempt* (or ripe for picking by creditors) may be seized and sold by the trustee, with the proceeds distributed to your creditors. In the real world, however, most consumer bankruptcies fall in the category of *no-asset* cases. In other words, you have nothing for creditors to take, except the shirt on your back and various other items that are off-limits. That's a pretty nifty deal and, if things work out, you've little to lose except your debt.

The law is not about to let you bounce from one spending spree to another with bankruptcy functioning as your escape hatch, so for the most part, if you go bankrupt today, you can't file again for another eight years. As a technical matter, you can still file under Chapter 7, even if you got a bankruptcy discharge within the past eight years — but there's no sense in doing so. If you had your debts wiped out in bankruptcy less than eight years ago, your latest financial obligations would not be discharged with a new Chapter 7, so filing would be pointless.

Two caveats, though. The eight-year restriction

✔ Applies only if you actually received a discharge in the earlier case. If your case was dismissed prior to completion, the eight-year rule doesn't apply, and you're free to file anew.

✔ Does not apply if your prior bankruptcy was a Chapter 13 reorganization, and creditors received at least 70 percent of their claims.

Note that the eight-year restriction applies only when the second case is filed under Chapter 7. If the second case is filed under Chapter 13, different rules apply. See the section "Chapter 13: Debt repayment plans," later in this chapter.

Confronting the Means Test

The main obstacle to Chapter 7 is the *Means Test,* a creation of the BARF law that Congress passed in 2005. The Means Test (we'll resist the urge to call it the "mean test" — on second thought, no, we won't) requires a complicated set of calculations that are supposed to identify those consumers who can pay a significant portion of their bills and should be required to do so instead of shedding all their obligations in Chapter 7. The Means Test doesn't apply to debtors earning less than the median income for their state, and most of those earning more than the median are still able to pass.

We've devoted all of Chapter 5 to passing the Means Test. For now, the thing to remember is that if you're broke and have little left over at the end of month for debt payments, one way or the other (assuming that you receive good advice), you'll be able to pass the Means Test, although it will surely be a pain in the butt for both you and your lawyer.

Good faith

In addition to looking at your ability to pay, some judges also consider whether you're acting in *good faith.* They may ask whether

- ✔ Your bankruptcy was necessitated by sudden illness, calamity, or unemployment.
- ✔ You made unnecessary eve-of-bankruptcy purchases far exceeding your ability to pay.
- ✔ Your bankruptcy paperwork is complete and accurate.

Although you eventually must check with a bankruptcy specialist who's familiar with local judges to get a reading on what to expect, you can do one thing immediately to avert a possible good-faith problem: Make darned sure that your bankruptcy papers are accurate and that you list each and every income and each and every expense. Guesstimating just doesn't cut it. When you don't know the answer, look it up . . . don't make it up.

Chapter 13: Debt repayment plans

In filing a Chapter 13 bankruptcy, you propose a debt repayment schedule, and, for the next 36 to 60 months, you pay what you can afford. The two types of payments that you may have to make are

- ✔ To a trustee, who doles out money to creditors.
- ✔ So-called *payments outside the plan,* which are payments that are coming due after you file and are paid directly to the creditor.

Creditors usually end up receiving only a small percentage of what they're owed and typically must settle for pennies on the dollar. After that, you're home-free.

You can't eliminate debts in Chapter 13 if you have received a discharge in a prior case filed under Chapter 7, 11, or 12 within the past four years, or a discharge in a case filed under Chapter 13 within the past two years.

ANECDOTE

A committed mate saves the day

Moira and Scott lived together for 12 years. Instead of working, Moira ran the household, helped raise Scott's boys, and attended to Scott's infirm mother.

During their relationship, Scott took care of all household expenses and agreed to do so during the life of Moira's Chapter 13 bankruptcy case. The judge was so impressed by Moira's and Scott's commitment to each other that he held that Scott's voluntary contributions to Moira qualified as income for Chapter 13 purposes and approved her Chapter 13 plan.

Even if you can't *eliminate* debts, if the above restrictions apply, you can still use Chapter 13 to keep creditors off your back while you pay them in full over three to five years. Only individuals with regular income (no corporations, no partnerships) can file under Chapter 13. The source of your income isn't important (assuming, of course, that you didn't rob the local convenience store or get it in some other illegal fashion), provided that it is regular and stable. Your income can be wages, self-employment profits, unemployment benefits, or even assistance from friends and family.

REMEMBER

To qualify for Chapter 13, your debts must fall within specific limits. Your *unsecured debts* — those where nothing, like a car, can be repossessed if you don't pay — can't be more than $307,675. *Secured debts* can't exceed $922,975. You can find out more about secured and unsecured debts in Chapter 11.

WARNING!

Certain debts, known as *priority claims,* must be paid in full over the life of any Chapter 13 plan. The most common priority claims are support obligations and recent taxes. Really big child-support obligations that you can't possibly pay off over 60 months or tax arrearages, as a practical matter, make you ineligible for Chapter 13 because those debts must be paid in full over a maximum of 60 months. If you can't repay those bills within five years, you're better off not filing under Chapter 13.

The length of your repayment plan depends on how much you earn and whether you have any *nonexempt assets* — stuff that could be taken to satisfy the claims of creditors. Every plan must satisfy two tests: the best-interest test and the best-efforts test.

- ✔ **Best-interest test:** Unsecured creditors must receive at least as much as they'd get when you file a Chapter 7 bankruptcy rather than a Chapter 13. If all your property is exempt and unsecured creditors would receive nothing in a Chapter 7, the best-interest test isn't a factor. On the other hand, when you have nonexempt property, your plan must propose to pay at least that much.

Mike makes the grade

Mike chooses Chapter 13 because he's got a home he wants to keep, as well as a family heirloom — an antique piano worth $5,000, and not exempt from creditors if he goes Chapter 7. Mike earns less than the median income for his state and, after paying routine monthly living expenses, had just $500 left at the end of the month to cover his $35,000 in credit card debts and $4,000 in mortgage arrearages. To satisfy the best-interests test under a 36-month plan, Mike needs to pay $250 per month to cover the mortgage payments and the cost of the piano. He essentially has to buy the piano back from creditors even though it never changes hands. So, he's looking at $4,000 for the mortgage + $5,000 for the piano, which equals $9,000. And $9,000 divided by 36 (the number of months the repayment plan will run) is $250. But that's only half the story, because Mike also has to worry about the best-efforts test. When that's factored in, he's got to pay all of his disposable income — $500 — for 36 months. Then, finally, his mortgage is current, his credit card bills are a distant memory — and the baby grand keeps humming away in the family home.

Look at it this way: If you own investment property worth $10,000 and file a Chapter 7 bankruptcy, the trustee probably will sell the property and distribute the proceeds among creditors. On the other hand, if you file under Chapter 13, you keep the property, but you still have to pay at least as much as creditors would otherwise receive had you gone the Chapter 7 route — their share of the $10,000.

✔ **Best-efforts test:** Chances are you can't possibly pay unsecured creditors in full, and the court and your creditors know that. So, although the law doesn't expect you to make good on everything, it nevertheless requires you to do the best you can. If your monthly income is more than the median for your state, allowable expenses are based on Internal Revenue Collection Financial Standards, and the plan must run for five years. Otherwise, the amount of your payment is based on your actual expenses, so long as they're reasonable. See Chapter 5 for the lowdown on which expenses are allowed under the Internal Revenue Collections Financial Standards.

In Chapter 13, you won't have any extra cash burning a hole in your pocket, but you will have what you need to get by. You'll even have a modest entertainment allowance.

Deciding Between Chapter 7 and Chapter 13

Your lawyer must take the time to fully discuss the relative advantages and disadvantages of your choice between Chapter 7 and Chapter 13, but in some situations, making the right choice can be devilishly difficult. This section provides some general guidelines for you.

Recognizing when Chapter 7 is best

Chapter 7 probably is your best choice when all the following statements are true:

- ✔ You don't have any assets that you'd have to surrender to a trustee.

- ✔ You're current on home and car payments, or willing to give them up.

- ✔ You don't have much money left over each month after paying expenses.

- ✔ You haven't received a bankruptcy discharge in an earlier case filed within the past eight years.

Considering Chapter 13 as your number-one option

Chapter 13 is probably the way to go in any of these situations:

- ✔ You want to catch up on mortgage payments.

- ✔ You need time to pay off past-due support obligations.

- ✔ You owe tax debts that you want to pay off without interest or penalties.

- ✔ You received a discharge in a bankruptcy case filed within the past eight years.

- ✔ You earn enough money to pay monthly expenses with ease and want to do your best to repay creditors at least some amount.

Discovering the advantages of Chapter 13

We discuss the upshot of Chapter 13 in detail throughout the book, but as a general proposition, the benefits are

- ✔ You can pay taxes over time, *possibly* — note we emphasize *possibly* — without interest or penalties.

- ✔ Your overdue alimony and child support can be stretched out and paid off over three to five years.

- ✔ You can get your house and car payments up to date over the life of the plan.

- ✔ You can reduce payments on some secured loans to the value of the collateral. If, for example, collateral securing a loan is worth only $2,000 but you owe $5,000, you'd have to pay only $2,000, not the full amount of the loan. This option is not available when you financed the purchase of a in motor vehicle within 910 days before bankruptcy or financed the purchase of other types of personal property acquired within one year prior to bankruptcy. In these situations, you must either pay the full amount of the debt or surrender the collateral. See Chapter 11 for more on *purchase money security interests* — where the item you buy serves as collateral for a loan for its purchase price.

- ✔ You can keep nonexempt property.

- ✔ You can get some bankruptcy relief even though you received a discharge in a prior Chapter 7, 11, or 12 bankruptcy case filed less than eight years ago.

- ✔ You can protect a cosigner from creditor harassment by proposing to pay the cosigned debt over the life of the plan.

Another advantage of Chapter 13 is that you can back out when you change your mind, or if things don't play out as expected. Conversely, after you file Chapter 7, you can't get out without the court's permission — and that can be pretty tough to get.

Having the leeway to jump out of Chapter 13 doesn't mean you can hop back when the mood strikes you. You have to wait 180 days before you can file again if your case was dismissed at your request after a creditor asked the court for relief from the *automatic stay,* which stops collection activities after a case is filed; *or* because you disobeyed an order of the court.

Exploring disadvantages of Chapter 13

One obvious disadvantage of Chapter 13 is that it usually takes at least three years to complete. During this time

- ✔ You may feel like you're on a leash . . . because you are.

- ✔ You'll probably have to give up your income tax refunds.

- ✔ You may receive an unexpected windfall and then lose it to the trustee.

- ✔ You won't be allowed to incur any more debts without the trustee's consent.

- ✔ You can lose your job and your ability to maintain payments, resulting in dismissal of your case.

- ✔ You may risk your homestead exemption (see Chapters 10, 12, and 20) if you move or sell your home.

Some people claim that a Chapter 13 filing is less detrimental to your credit rating than a Chapter 7. We're skeptical. When you file under Chapter 7, you may actually be a more attractive credit risk. Reason: Your slate is clean, your old debts are gone — and you can't file a Chapter 7 to escape new debts for eight years.

About two-thirds of Chapter 13 plans fail. Then, the bankruptcy protections disappear, and the debt collectors are b-a-a-a-ck!!! They'll resume all their collection efforts, and there's a real good chance they'll force you into Chapter 7 in hopes of getting something out of you. (Some Chapter 13 plans, those based on reality, are very successful. In Chapter 6, we guide you through a Chapter 13 filing so that your chances of success are much higher than the raw statistics would indicate.)

Advantages of Chapter 13 over nonbankruptcy repayment plans

Filing Chapter 13 usually is better than repayment agreements worked out by consumer counseling outfits because

- You pay only a small percentage of your total debts. Nonbankruptcy repayment plans usually require you to pay your debts in full (except perhaps some interest).
- You can deal with secured debts such as your home and car. Nonbankruptcy plans typically do not address those debts.
- You don't need the permission of the creditor to cut your obligation.
- You can invoke the automatic stay, which immediately stops creditors from pursuing you.
- You'll be allowed to catch up on back alimony and support obligations. (Nonbankruptcy plans don't deal with those problems.)

For a quick comparison of the eligibility requirements for Chapter 7 and Chapter 13 bankruptcies, check out Table 4-1.

Table 4-1	Comparing Eligibility Requirements for Chapter 7 and Chapter 13	
Your Situation	**Chapter 7**	**Chapter 13**
Debts not primarily consumer debts	Not subject to Means Test.	Makes no difference whether debts are consumer debts
Debts primarily consumer debts	Must compare income to state medians to determine whether Means Test applies.	Makes no difference whether debts are consumer debts

(continued)

Table 4-1 *(continued)*

Your Situation	*Chapter 7*	*Chapter 13*
Income at or below median	Eligible regardless of how much owed or amount of expenses. Means Test not a problem.	Eligible for three-year plan with payments determined by actual expenses rather than IRS guidelines.
Income above median	Subject to Means Test to see whether you can pay a significant amount of debts.	Chapter 13 plan must run for five years with expenses determined by IRS collection standards.
Amount of debt owed	Amount of unsecured debt may determine eligibility for those subject to Means Test. If your income after expenses is less than $100, you *pass* the Means Test no matter how much you owe. By the same token, if your surplus income is $167 per month or more, you *flunk* the Means Test regardless of how much you owe. But if your surplus income is between $100 and $167, you pass the Means Test if your debts are so high that your surplus income would not be enough to pay 25 percent over five years.	Maximum secured debt limit of $922,975 and unsecured debt limit of $307,675. No minimum debt requirement.
Previous Chapter 7 or Chapter 13 discharge.	Not eligible for Chapter7 discharge if Chapter 7 is filed less than eight years after filing of prior case unless the discharge was a Chapter 13 discharge and creditors in that case were paid at least 70 percent.	Not eligible for Chapter 13 discharge in present case if debtor received a discharge in a prior case filed under Chapter 7, 11, or 12 within four years, or a prior Chapter 13 case filed within two years of present case.
Effect of nondischargeable taxes, alimony, child support, or liability for personal injuries arising from drunk driving or boating.	Does not affect eligibility to wipe out other debts. Owing these types of debts makes it easier to pass the Means Test.	Potential to indirectly affect eligibility because plan must provide that these obligations be paid in full over a period no longer than five years.

Considering Other Types of Bankruptcy

Although your case almost certainly falls under the Chapter 7 or 13 rubric, a few other potential options bear thinking about.

Chapter 11: Large reorganizations

Whenever you don't qualify for Chapter 13 and you have substantial assets that you want to continue to control, Chapter 11 is worth looking into. But a Chapter 11 proceeding is extremely complicated and expensive and, in all honesty, rarely an option or even a smart choice for a nonbusiness debtor. Still, it makes sense to see whether it works for you.

A Chapter 11 filing is a bankruptcy specialty in its own right. Many lawyers concentrating on consumer bankruptcy don't have much experience with Chapter 11 cases. If you go this route, make sure that your lawyer is an experienced Chapter 11 practitioner.

Chapter 12: Reorganizations for family farmers and fishermen

Chapter 12 is a special type of bankruptcy reserved for family farmers and fisherman. Congress recognizes that those endeavors play a unique role in our culture and economy and deserve special treatment.

If you qualify, Chapter 12 provides most of the benefits of Chapter 13, and then some. Repayment plans aren't restricted to five years, and you have fewer limitations on the your ability to restructure home mortgages. The downside of a Chapter 12 is that dischargeable debts are limited to those dischargeable in a Chapter 7. So, you don't get the super discharge available with a Chapter 13 filing.

To qualify as a family farmer, you must meet each of the following requirements:

- Debts may not exceed $3,237,000.
- Fifty percent of those debts (excluding your home mortgage) must be from farming operations.
- Fifty percent of your income from the preceding year, or from each of the two years before that, must have come from farming operations.

But what exactly is a farmer? One debtor, whose sole income (less than $10,000) for the year, before bankruptcy, came from the firewood he chopped on his land, was deemed a family farmer. As a result, the court approved a repayment plan that actually reduced the mortgage on his home so that it would be paid off in 10 rather than 15 years.

To qualify as a family fisherman, you must meet each of the following requirements:

- ✔ Debts may not exceed $1.5 million.
- ✔ Eighty percent of those debts (excluding the home mortgage) must be from commercial fishing operations.
- ✔ Fifty percent of income from the preceding year must have come from commercial fishing operations.

Chapter 20: Adding Chapters 7 and 13

Although no Chapter 20 appears in the Bankruptcy Code, that term *is* used to describe the practice of filing Chapter 7 to wipe out most of your debts and then following up with a Chapter 13 to reap the benefits of both.

Say that you owe a bunch of credit-card bills and you're under an order to pay restitution for a crime. You can file Chapter 7 to get rid of the credit-card bills and then file Chapter 13 to pay the restitution over three to five years. We take a closer look at Chapter 20 bankruptcy in Chapter 18.

Changing Your Mind

After you're in Chapter 7 bankruptcy, you can't back out without the court's permission, and that's a tough sell. For example, the day after filing Chapter 7, Steve crashed his car into the back of a minivan. When Soccer Dad threatened to sue, Steve asked the bankruptcy court to dismiss his case so that he could turn around and file a new one. That way, Steve figured, he could file a new Chapter 7 and include any claims from the crash.

The bankruptcy court didn't buy it because dismissing Steve's case so that he could turn right around and file another simply wasn't in the best interests of his creditors.

On the other hand, when you file Chapter 13, you can dismiss the case if things don't turn out as expected, or if you just change your mind.

You can also convert one type of bankruptcy to another, if you realize that you're better off taking a different route.

We take a closer look at converting from Chapter 13 to Chapter 7 in Chapter 20.

Chapter 5

Confronting the Means Test

The Bankruptcy Abuse Reform Act, or "BARF," was regurgitated by the 109th Congress in 2005 after previous efforts to tighten the screws on debtors failed. Its main ingredient is a so-called Means Test, which is essentially a formula to determine whether you can really afford to cough up some cash for your creditors. If you flunk the mean test — uh, Means Test — your only option is to repay a portion of your debts over a five-year Chapter 13 plan. Chapter 7, where your debts are simply forgiven in exchange for turning over any non-exempt property, is not an option — at least not at first. In other words, if you flunk the Means Test, you'll file under Chapter 13, although you may be able to switch to Chapter 7 later if it turns out that you can't make your Chapter 13 plan payments.

In this chapter, we reveal that jumping though the Means Test is more of a pain in the butt than a real obstacle to filing Chapter 7.

Putting the Means Test in Perspective

The first thing that you need to know is that odds are that you probably won't have to take the Means Test at all, provided you pass the *Median Test*. If your income for the six months preceding bankruptcy is less than the median income for your state, you're home-free.

"Primarily" consumer debts

The Means Test applies only to debtors whose debts are "primarily consumer debts" within the meaning of the Bankruptcy Code.

Courts disagree both on what "primarily" means as well as the meaning of "consumer debts." Most say that your debts are primarily consumer debts if the *dollar amount* owed on consumer debts exceeds the amount owed on nonconsumer debts, without regard to the *number* of debts.

Say that you owe $25,000 on two consumer debts and only $15,000 on five nonbusiness debts. Then your debts are primarily consumer debts. The Bankruptcy Code defines "consumer debt" as a "debt incurred by an individual primarily for a personal, family, or household purpose." 11 U.S.C.§101(8).

Most courts agree that home mortgages are consumer debts, but income tax liabilities are not. They are about evenly split on whether student loans are consumer debts. It would seem that claims that aren't based on contracts, such as liability for an auto accident, should not be considered "consumer debts," and at least one court has agreed.

The basic theory behind the Means Test is that folks who earn more then the median income should not be able to simply walk away from their debts in Chapter 7 if they can pay a significant amount under a Chapter 13 repayment plan. It's hard to argue with that reasoning, but how will courts figure out how much you can afford to pay? That's where the Means Test comes into play. This brain-twisting set of rules attempts to establish a one-size-fits-all formula for what constitutes income, and how much of it you should be paying for your living expenses.

Don't worry too much about applying these rules — that's your lawyer's problem. Your job is to organize your finances and provide your attorney the information she needs to perform all the necessary calculations. (If you completed the worksheets in Chapter 2, you already have most of the information you need.)

Keep in mind that the Means Test is aimed exclusively at consumers. It doesn't apply at all to folks whose debts are not "primarily" consumer debts. If your debts are not primarily consumer debts (see the sidebar in this section), you can scream "alleluia" at the top of your lungs and skip this chapter altogether.

Taking the Median Test

If you earn less than the median income, you don't have to worry about the Means Test. That's the good news. But the bad news is, well — you don't make a whole lot of money. As a result of political compromises in Congress, Social Security benefits aren't counted as income for purposes of the Means Test, but in the real world, this money may be what's putting food on your table.

Computing your income

First, you have to figure out your average monthly income during the six months preceding bankruptcy and multiply this number by 12 to see how you measure up against the median. The six-month period is determined as ending on the last day of the calendar month immediately preceding your bankruptcy. In other words, if you file in the middle of July, you average your income for the months of January, February, March, April, May, and June, regardless of which exact day in July you file. Table 5-1 sets out a worksheet to help calculate your income.

Income does not include

- Social Security benefits

- Payments to victims of war crimes or crimes against humanity

- Payments to victims of terrorism (such as victims of the terrorist attack on the World Trade Center)

Just about everything else is considered income, whether it's taxable or not, including

- Wages, salary, fees, commissions, and bonuses

- Retirement income

- Tax refunds

- Net income from any business dealings and sales of assets

- Net rental income

- Your share of any partnership income

- Support payments you receive

- Any money that others (including your spouse, if you don't file a joint bankruptcy) regularly contribute toward your living expenses

- Scholarships and other educational benefits

- Insurance payments and reimbursement under health and accident plans

- Prizes and awards

- Compensation for illness or injury

- Gifts and inheritances

Although it's not crystal-clear, we're making an educated guess that income would not include fringe benefits. Many observers think that income also doesn't include unemployment benefits because they can be traced to the Social Security Act; we think that, just to be on the safe side, you should include it unless your lawyer says otherwise.

If your income is equal to or less than the median and you have all the information required, your lawyer should charge you less for handling your bankruptcy.

Having income below the median is important even if you're planning on filing Chapter 13. Reason: If your income is above the median, a Chapter 13 plan must run for five years. Otherwise, a three-year plan is usually possible.

Here are some guidelines for evaluating your income:

- BARF determines "current monthly income" by examining all your average gross earnings for the past six months, not just take-home pay.

- In determining whether your income exceeds the median, your spouse's income is included whether you file bankruptcy jointly or not. Two exceptions to this rule exist. Income of a nonfiling spouse doesn't count if you're legally separated or if you're living separate and apart, unless you split up just to evade the Means Test. Even if all of your nonfiling spouse's income isn't included, your income would include any amounts that she regularly contributes to household expenses. The rule is different when taking the Means Test — when figuring out how much surplus income you have, income from a nonfiling spouse is included only to the extent that she actually contributes toward your household expenses.

- Income taxes and other wage withholdings aren't deducted in determining your income. They're deducted as expense items.

Table 5-1	Average Monthly Income
Calculation of Monthly Income	
1	Special Exclusion for Disabled Veterans
	If you're a disabled veteran whose indebtedness occurred primarily during a period when you were on active duty or while performing a homeland security activity, you aren't subject to means testing of any kind and may skip the rest of this chapter.
2	Marital/filing status.
	a. Unmarried. __ Complete only Column A ("Your Income") for Lines 3–11
	b. Married, not filing jointly. Separated from spouse. __ Complete only Column A ("Your Income") for Lines 3–11
	c. Married, not filing jointly. Living with your spouse. __ Complete both Column A ("Your Income") and Column B ("Spouse's Income") for Lines 3–11
	d. Married, filing jointly. __ Complete both Column A ("Your Income") and Column B ("Spouse's Income") for Lines 3–11

Calculation of Monthly Income

All figures must reflect average monthly income for the six months prior to bankruptcy ending on the last day of the month before filing. If you received different amounts of income during these six months, you must total the amounts received during the six months, divide by six, and enter the result on the appropriate line.

		Column A Your Income	Column B Spouse's Income
3	Gross wages, salary, tips, bonuses, overtime, commissions	$	$
4	Income from operation of business, profession, or farm. Subtract Line b from Line a and enter the difference on line 4. Do not enter less than zero. Do not include any business expenses that were deducted under other categories.		
	a. Gross receipts $		
	b. Business expenses $		
	c. Business income Subtract Line b from Line a		
5	Rents and other real property income. Subtract Line b from Line a and enter the difference on Line 5. Do not enter a number less than zero. Do not include any operating expenses that were deducted under other categories.	$	$
	a. Gross receipts $		
	b. Operating expenses $		
	c. Rental income Subtract Line b from Line a		

(continued)

Table 5-1 *(continued)*

Calculation of Monthly Income

6	Interest, dividends, and royalties	$	$
7	Pension and retirement income	$	$
8	Regular contributions to your household expenses. Do not include contributions from spouse if Column B is completed.	$	$
9	Unemployment benefits. Check with lawyer because they may not count.	$	$
10	Income from other sources. Do not include any benefits received under the Social Security Act or payments received as a victim of a war crime, crime against humanity, or as a victim of international or domestic terrorism.	$	$
	a. $		
	b. $		
	c. $		
	Total and enter on line 10	$	$
11	Subtotal of Current Monthly Income for Median Test. Add Lines 3–10 in Column A and if Column B is completed, add Lines 3–10 in Column B. Enter the total(s).	$	$
12	Total Current Monthly Income for Median Test. If Column B has been completed, add Line 11, Column A to Line 11 Column B and enter the total. If Column B has not been completed, enter the amount from Line 11, Column A.	$	$

Comparing your income to the median

In taking the Median Test, you compare your income with the median income for your state based on U.S. Census Bureau figures. The most current information is available from the clerk of the bankruptcy court or from the United States Trustee at `www.usdoj.gov/ust/bapcpa/means testing.htm`. To give you some idea of where you stand, Table 5-2 lists the national medians. Table 5-3 contains a worksheet so that you can compare your income to the median.

Table 5-2	National Gross Median Income
Size of Household	*Annual Gross Median Income*
One-person household	$37,168
Two-person household	$48,316
Three-person household	$55,624
Four-person household	$63,067
More than four-person household	Add $6,300 for each additional person

Of course, these figures vary depending on where you live. For example, the median income for a four-person household in West Virginia is $51,795, while in New Jersey, it's $88,401! These places are the extremes, though. Median incomes for most states are pretty close to the national medians.

These numbers are adjusted annually after the most recent census to reflect changes in the Consumer Price Index, calculated from the date of the most recent census to the year preceding the year of your bankruptcy.

Table 5-3	Comparing Your Income to the Median	
Calculation of Monthly Income		
13	Multiply the amount from Line 12 by the number 12 and enter the result	$
14	Applicable median family income. Enter the median family income for your state and household size. The most current information is available at `www.usdot.gov/ust` or from the clerk of the bankruptcy court. www.census.gov/hhes/www/income/statemedfaminc.html	$

(continued)

Table 5-3 (continued)

Calculation of Monthly Income

15	If the amount on Line 13 is less than or equal to the amount on Line 14, you pass the Median Test and do not have to take the Means Test.
	If the amount on Line 13 is more than the amount on Line 14, you have to take the Means Test.

Deducting Your Expenses and Taking the Means Test

After you calculate your BARF income, you get to the really hairy part — figuring out what expenses are allowed. Remember, though, that if your income is below the median (see "Taking the Median Test," earlier in this chapter), you've already passed the test, and you can skip the rest of this chapter. Yippee!

The first thing you need to do is adjust the figure used in the Median Test if you included the income of a spouse who isn't filing bankruptcy with you. Under the Means Test, if you and your spouse aren't filing bankruptcy together, her income counts only to the extent that she actually contributes to family living expenses. Table 5-4 will help you adjust your income for the Means Test — which can be different than the income figure used for the Median Test.

Table 5-4	Adjustment for Spouse's Income	
16	Enter the amount on Line 12	$
17	Marital adjustment. If you checked the box at Line 2.c, enter the amount of the income listed in Line 11, Column B that was NOT regularly contributed to your household expenses. If you did not check the box at Line 2.c, enter zero.	$
18	Current monthly income for Means Test. Subtract Line 17 from Line 16 and enter the result.	

The Means Test allows deductions from income for

✔ Amounts specified under IRS National and Local standards, regardless of your actual expenses

✔ Other actual necessary expenses allowed under IRS Standards

✔ Certain expenses specified in BARF

✔ Expenses for repayment of certain kinds of debts

These deductions were cobbled together in a series of compromises among competing creditor interests and, as a result, are confusing, ambiguous, and sometimes contradictory. But they are what they are, and hopefully we can provide some navigational assistance.

IRS National and Local Standards

For years, the IRS allowed certain standard expenses to determine how much a delinquent taxpayer would be forced to come up with to keep the feds off his back. Congress, in enacting BARF, incorporated the amounts specified in these standards without realizing that they didn't quite mesh with other provisions of BARF.

The IRS uses National Standards for living expenses, such as food, clothing, housekeeping supplies, personal-care products and services (for example, haircuts), plus an additional amount for discretionary spending ($100 per month, plus $25 for each additional family member). The allowable amounts depend on a person's gross monthly income and family size and are adjusted annually. Table 5-5 outlines the 2005 allowable amounts.

Table 5-5		IRS Standards for Living Expenses			
Total Gross Monthly Income	One Person	Two-Person Family	Three-Person Family	Four-Person Family	Family of More Than Four
Less than $833	$403	$620	$835	$881	+$134
$833 to $1,249	$428	$630	$851	$967	+$145
$1,250 to $1,666	$460	$636	$867	$971	+$155
$1,667 to $2,499	$494	$744	$882	$981	+$166
$2,500 to $3,333	$577	$794	$908	$990	+$177
$3,334 to $4,166	$649	$857	$1,002	$1,131	+$188
$4,167 to $5,833	$691	$1,020	$1,156	$1,298	+$199
$5,834 and over	$953	$1,280	$1,430	$1,564	+$209

Housing expenses include rent, property taxes, interest, parking, necessary maintenance and repair, homeowner's or renter's insurance, homeowner dues, and condominium fees. Also included are utility expenses, such as gas, electricity, water, fuel oil, coal, bottled gas, trash and garbage collection, wood, and other fuels, septic cleaning, and telephone.

Transportation expenses include vehicle insurance, vehicle lease payments, maintenance, fuel, state and local registration, required vehicle inspection, parking fees, tolls, driver's license, and public transportation.

Housing and transportation standards depend on where you live. You can get the most recent standards from the clerk of the bankruptcy court or www.usdoj.gov/ust/bapcpa/meanstesting.htm#irsdata.

Under BARF, you deduct the amount specified in the National and Local Standards, regardless of your actual expenses for these items.

Other necessary expenses

The IRS standards also allow deductions for necessary or unavoidable items, including

- ✔ Taxes
- ✔ Mandatory payroll deductions
- ✔ Insurance
- ✔ Court-ordered payments
- ✔ Childcare expenses
- ✔ Health care

Table 5-6 shows how to figure the expense you're allowed under the IRS standards.

Table 5-6	Calculation of Deductions Allowed under IRS Standards
Calculation of Monthly Income	
19	National Standards: Food, clothing, household supplies, personal care, and miscellaneous. Enter Total amount from IRS National Standards for Allowable Living Expenses for your family size and income level. $
20	Local Standards: Housing and utilities, utilities/maintenance expense. Enter the amount from the IRS Housing and Utilities Standards: Utilities/Maintenance Expense for your county and family size. $

Calculation of Monthly Income

| 21 | Local Standards: Housing and utilities, mortgage/rental expense. Enter the amount from the IRS Housing and Utilities Standards: Mortgage/Rental expense for your county and family size. Do not include payments on any debt secured by your home included in Line 42. Subtract the amount of Line 42 Average Monthly Payment attributable to such debts from the IRS Mortgage/Rental Expense, but do not list an amount less than zero. |

a.

IRS Housing and Utilities Standards; Mortgage/Rental Expense

$

b.

Average Monthly Payment for any debts secured by your home, if any, as stated in Line 42

$

c.

Net mortgage/rental expense

Subtract Line b from Line a.

$

| 22 | Local Standards: Transportation, vehicle operation/public transportation expense. You're entitled to an expense allowance in this category regardless of whether you pay the expenses of operating a vehicle and regardless of whether you use public transportation. Enter the number of vehicles for which you pay the operating expenses. |

__ 0 __ 1 __ 2 or more

Enter the amount from IRS Transportation Standards: $
Operating Costs & Public Transportation Costs for the
applicable number of vehicles in your region.

| 23 | Local Standards: Transportation ownership/lease expense, Vehicle 1. Check the number of vehicles for which you claim an ownership/lease expense. (You may not claim an ownership/lease expense for more than two vehicles.) |

__ 0 __ 1 __ 2 or more

Enter, in Line a below, the amount of the IRS Transportation Standards, Ownership Costs, First Car; enter in Line b the total of the Average Monthly Payments for any debts secured by vehicle 1, as stated in Line 42; subtract Line b from Line a and enter the amount in Line 23. Do not enter an amount less than zero.

(continued)

Table 5-6 *(continued)*

Calculation of Monthly Income

	a.	
	IRS Transportation, Ownership Costs, First Car	
	$	
	b.	
	Average Monthly Payment for any debts secured by Vehicle 1, as stated in Line 42	
	$	
	c.	
	Net ownership/lease expense for Vehicle 1	
	Subtract Line b from Line a.	
	$	
24	Local Standards: Transportation ownership/lease expense; Vehicle 2. Complete this line only if you checked the "2 or more" on Line 23.	
	Enter, in Line a below, the amount of the IRS Transportation Standards, Ownership Costs, Second Car; enter in Line b the total of the Average Monthly Payments for any debts secured by vehicle 2, as stated in Line 42; subtract Line b from Line a and enter the amount in Line 24. Do not enter an amount less than zero.	
	a.	
	IRS Transportation, Ownership Costs, Second Car	
	$	
	b.	
	Average Monthly Payment for any debts secured by Vehicle 2, as stated in Line 42	
	$	
	c.	
	Net ownership/lease expense for Vehicle 2	
	Subtract Line b from Line a.	
	$	

Calculation of Monthly Income

25	Other Necessary Expenses: Taxes. Enter the total average monthly expense that you actually incur for all federal, state, and local taxes, other than real estate and sales taxes, such as income taxes, self-employment taxes, Social Security taxes, and Medicare taxes. Do not include real estate or sales taxes.	$
26	Other Necessary Expenses: mandatory payroll deductions. Enter the total average monthly payroll deductions that are required for your employment, such as mandatory retirement contributions, union dues, and uniform costs. Do not include discretionary amounts, such as non-mandatory 401(k) contributions.	$
27	Other Necessary Expenses: Life insurance. Enter average monthly premiums that you actually pay for term life insurance for yourself. Do include premiums for insurance on your dependents, for whole life or for any other form of insurance.	$
28	Other Necessary Expenses: court-ordered payments. Enter the total monthly amount that you are required to pay pursuant to court order, such as spousal or child support payments. Do not include payments on past due support obligations included in Line 44.	$
29	Other Necessary Expenses: education for employment or for a physically or mentally challenged child. Enter the total monthly amount that you actually expend for education that is a condition of employment and for education that is required for a physically or mentally challenged dependent child for whom no public education providing similar services is available.	
	$	
30	Other Necessary Expenses: childcare. Enter the average monthly amount that you actually expend on childcare. Do not include payments made for children's education.	
31	Other Necessary Expenses: health care. Enter the average monthly amount that you actually expend on health care expenses that are not reimbursed by insurance or paid by a health savings account. Do not include payments for health insurance listed in Line 34.	$

(continued)

Table 5-6 *(continued)*

Calculation of Monthly Income

32	Other Necessary Expenses: telecommunication services. Enter the average monthly expenses that you actually pay for cell phones, pagers, call waiting, caller identification, special long distance, or Internet services necessary for the health and welfare of you or your dependents. Do not include any amount previously deducted.	$
33	**Total Expenses Allowed under IRS Standards**. Enter the total of Lines 19 through 32.	$

Specific BARF deductions

BARF specifically allows deductions for

- ✔ Health and disability insurance and contributions to health savings accounts
- ✔ Expenses for care and support of needy family members
- ✔ Expenses incurred to protect your family from domestic violence
- ✔ Home energy costs in excess of the IRS standards, if necessary
- ✔ Education expenses up to $125 per child
- ✔ Additional monthly expenses for food and clothing over and above those allowed under the IRS standards
- ✔ Charitable contributions you continue to make

Table 5-7 lists expenses allowed under specific sections of BARF.

Table 5-7   **Specific BARF Deductions**

Calculation of Monthly Income

34	Health Insurance, Disability Insurance, and Health Savings Account Expenses. List the average monthly amounts that you actually expend in each of the following categories and enter the total.
	a.
	Health Insurance
	$
	b.

Calculation of Monthly Income

Disability Insurance

$

c.

Health Savings Account

$

Total: Add Lines a, b, and c

$

| 35 | Continued contributions to the care of household or family members. Enter the actual monthly expenses that you will continue to pay for the reasonable and necessary care and support of an elderly, chronically ill, or disabled member of your household or member of your immediate family who is unable to pay for such expenses. |

$

| 36 | Protection against family violence. Enter any average monthly expenses that you actually incurred to maintain the safety of your family under the Family Violence Prevention and Services Act or other applicable federal law. |

$

| 37 | Home energy costs in excess of the allowance specified by the IRS Local Standards. Enter the average monthly amount by which your home energy costs exceed the allowance in the IRS Local Standards for Housing and Utilities. You must be able to show that the additional amount claimed is reasonable and necessary. |

$

| 38 | Education expenses for dependent children less than 18. Enter the average monthly expenses that you actually incur, not to exceed $125 per child, in providing elementary and secondary education for your dependent children less than 18 years of age. You must be able to show that the additional amount claimed is reasonable and necessary and not already included in the IRS Standards. |

$

(continued)

Table 5-7 *(continued)*

Calculation of Monthly Income

39	Additional food and clothing expense. Enter the average monthly amount by which your food and clothing expenses exceed the combined allowances for food and apparel in the IRS National Standards, not to exceed 5 percent of those combined allowances. You must be able to show that the additional amount claimed is reasonable and necessary.
	$
40	Continued charitable contributions. Enter the amount that you will continue to contribute to recognized charitable organizations.
	$
41	**Total BARF expenses.** Enter the total of Lines 34 through 40 $

Deductions for certain debt payments

BARF also allows deductions for amounts you're obligated to pay on

- Debts backed up by collateral — secured debts that will come due in the future
- Past due amounts on debts secured by your car or home
- Payment past due on "priority debts"

Table 5-8 shows how to figure out which debt payments are allowed as expenses under the Means Test.

Payments on secured debts coming due in the future

You're allowed expense items for payments on secured debts that come due in the next five years. If the obligation has more than five years to go, you simply deduct the full amount of the monthly payment. This situation is typical with your mortgage. If you have less than five years to go on the contract, you add the remaining payments and divide by 60. If, for example, you have 27 monthly payments of $200 left on your car, multiply $200 by 27 and divide by 60, arriving at an allowable amount of $90 per month.

Past due sums owed on home or car

If you're behind on any debts secured by your home, car, or other essential item, you're allowed an additional deduction equal to the amount necessary to satisfy this arrearage over 60 months. For example, if you're $1,500 behind on your mortgage, you're allowed a deduction of $25 ($1,500/60) per month in addition to your regular payment.

Obviously, if passing the Means Test is a concern, it's better to wait until after filing bankruptcy to make up your mind on whether you'll be continuing payments on secured debts. Don't surrender your car or allow completion of foreclosure proceedings without first talking to your lawyer.

How about financing an expensive car on the eve of bankruptcy? Will this reduce your surplus income and make it easier to pass the Means Test? Yep. BARF, however, forbids lawyers from telling their clients that information. But because you're not our client, and John's not a lawyer. . . .

Regular payments on vacation homes, recreational vehicles, timeshares, and similar luxury items aren't expressly forbidden. Nonetheless, courts will probably not allow deductions for payments to keep obviously unnecessary property. Also, deductions for past due payments are limited to debts secured by essential items.

Unfortunately, if you've leased your car, you're at a serious disadvantage. Car lease payments are strictly limited under the IRS standards, whereas payments on financed cars are automatically allowed under specific provisions of BARF no matter how much they are. Similarly, you may not be allowed an expense for cable TV, but you'd get an unlimited deduction for payments on a financed satellite dish.

Payments on priority debts

The most common priority debts are

- ✔ Past due support owed to a child, former spouse, or governmental entity. (See Chapter 17 for more information on marital obligations.)

- ✔ Income taxes that are less than three years old, measured from the date the tax return was due. (See Chapter 15 for more information on taxes.)

- ✔ Liabilities for personal injuries caused by drunken driving or boating. (See Chapter 13.)

You're entitled to deduct the amount necessary to satisfy these priority debts over 60 months. So, if you owe $6,000 in back support, you're allowed an expense deduction of $100 per month ($6,000/60).

Marital obligations that are really property divisions rather than support obligations aren't deductible. (See Chapter 17 for the difference between support and property divisions.)

The more you owe on priority debts, the easier it is to pass the Means Test. Talk to your lawyer before making payments on these types of debts. Also, borrowing money to pay priority debts may be a mistake because payments on the new loan (if unsecured) is not deductible.

Table 5-8	Deductions for Debt Payment

Calculation of Monthly Income

42	Future payments on secured claims. For each of your debts that is secured by an interest in property that you own, list the name of creditor, identify the property securing the debt, and state the Average Monthly Payment. The Average Monthly Payment is the total of all amounts contractually due to each Secured Creditor in the 60 months following the filing of the bankruptcy case, divided by 60. Do not include items you have previously deducted, such as insurance and taxes.
	Name of Creditor
	Property Securing the Debt
	Average Monthly Payment
	a.
	b.
	c.
	Total: Add Lines a, b, and c

43	Past due payments on secured claims. If any of the debts listed in Line 42 are in default, and the property securing the debt is necessary for your support or the support of your dependents, you may include in your deductions 1/60th of the amount that you must pay the creditor as a result of the default (the "cure amount") in order to maintain possession of the property. List any such amounts in the following chart and enter the total.
	Name of Creditor
	Property Securing the Debt
	1/60th of the Cure Amount
	a.
	b.
	c.
	Total: Add Lines a, b, and c
	$

44	Payments on priority claims. Enter the total amount of all priority claims (including priority child support and alimony claims), divided by 60.	$

Calculation of Monthly Income

45	Chapter 13 administrative expenses. If you're eligible to file under Chapter 13, complete the following chart, multiply the amount in Line a by the amount in Line b, and enter the resulting administrative expense. This calculation is extremely complex and probably won't produce a very large deduction. Leave this to your lawyer to compute.

a.

Projected average monthly Chapter 13 plan payment.

$

b.

Current multiplier for your district for Chapter 13 administrative expenses. This information is available at from the clerk of the bankruptcy court.

x

c.

Average monthly administrative expense of Chapter 13 case

Total: Multiply Lines a and b.

$

46	**Total Deductions for Debt Payment.** Enter totals of Lines 42 through 45.	$
47	**Total of all deductions allowed under the Means Test.** Enter the total of Lines 33, 41, and 46.	$

If you have surplus income, but no health insurance, get some. Aside from just making darned good sense, premiums you pay for health insurance can make the difference between passing and flunking the Means Test. So, it's a win-win for you.

Figuring Out How Much of Your Debts You Can Pay

After you figure out whether you have surplus income, the question is whether you can pay a significant portion of your unsecured, nonpriority debts. See Table 5-9 to determine whether you could repay a meaningful amount of your debts. If you can, you flunk the Means Test unless you can show that because of special circumstances, you really can't pay a significant amount of your debts.

Table 5-9	How Much Can You Pay?	
48	Enter the amount from Line 18 (Current monthly income for Means Test)	$
49	Enter the amount from Line 47 (Total of all deductions)	$
50	Monthly disposable income. Subtract Line 49 from Line 48 and enter the result	$
51	60-month disposable income. Multiply the amount in Line 50 by the number 60 and enter the result.	$
52	Initial determination. Check which is applicable and proceed.	
	__ The amount on Line 51 is less than $6,000 . You pass the Means Test.	
	__ The amount set forth on Line 51 is more than $10,000. You flunk the Means Test unless "special circumstances" exist.	
	__ The amount on Line 51 is at least $6,000, but not more than $10,000. Complete the remainder of this table.	
53	Enter the amount of your total nonpriority unsecured debt.	$
54	Threshold debt payment amount. Multiply the amount in Line 53 by .25 and enter the result.	$
55	Secondary presumption determination. Check which is applicable.	
	__ The amount on Line 51 is less than the amount on Line 54. You pass the Means Test.	
	__ The amount on Line 51 is equal to or greater than the amount on Line 54. You flunk the Means Test unless there are special circumstances.	

Passing the Means Test by Showing "Special Circumstances"

Even if you appear to flunk the Means Test, you can still qualify for Chapter 7 if you convince the court that you have *special circumstances,* such as a serious medical condition or a call to active duty in the Armed Forces that justifies additional expenses or adjustments of current monthly income for which there is no reasonable alternative.

Special circumstances may also be available if you just lost your high-paying job and for some reason must file bankruptcy immediately. The fact that you made gobs of money last month doesn't help you put food on the table today, so you may be able to convince a judge to allow you to file under Chapter 7 even if you flunk the Means Test.

Considering Ways around the Means Test

BARF mimics the Internal Revenue Code in establishing very specific detailed rules, which also open loopholes. In our view, debtors should be allowed to arrange their affairs, and time their bankruptcy filing, so as to best navigate around these restrictions and take advantage of loopholes, just as corporations and wealthy individuals typically order their financial affairs to take advantage of glitches in the tax code. But you still have to tell the truth. Lying and intentionally concealing information is cheating. And the price for cheating may be a jail cell. Don't even think about it.

If it appears that passing the Means Test may be a problem, here are a few things to discuss with your lawyer:

✔ BARF doesn't forbid folks from timing their bankruptcy so that their average income is as low as possible. If, for example, you just lost your job, you could wait a few months before filing bankruptcy so that your average income for the past six months falls below the medians.

✔ Although large priority debts have to be paid in full over the life of a Chapter 13 plan, they can actually help you pass the Means Test. But borrowing money to pay priority debts is usually *not* a good idea if you have any concern about passing the Means Test.

✔ If passing the Means Test is a concern and you don't have health insurance, this is a good time to sign up because you can deduct actual amounts paid for health and disability insurance for you and your dependents.

✔ If your income exceeds the state median and passing the Means Test is a concern, you have a better chance of passing if you have high mortgage and car payments when you file bankruptcy.

✔ BARF uses medians for families based on how many people live in your household. The Census Bureau defines *household* much more broadly than *family*. Household consists of all the people who occupy a housing unit, including "the related family members and all the unrelated people, if any, such as lodgers, foster children, wards, or employees who share the housing unit." Someone living alone in a housing unit, or a group or unrelated people sharing a housing unit such as partners or roomers, is also counted as a household. So, a person living alone would be subject to Means Testing if her monthly income exceeded approximately $2,167. If another person lived with her, she could not be subjected to Means Testing unless her monthly income exceeded approximately $3,667.

✔ Starting out in Chapter 13 and then converting to Chapter 7 may be one way to come in through the back door. Courts will probably allow it, if you show that you tried in good faith to make your Chapter 13 work, but just couldn't keep up with payments because of your unique circumstances.

✔ BARF doesn't expressly forbid you from reducing income by

- Ceasing to accept support from someone else (for example, a girlfriend or parent)

- Taking an unpaid leave of absence from work

Getting Kicked Out of Chapter 7 for Abuse

A provision of BARF allows the court to dismiss your Chapter 7 even if you pass the Means Test, if it appears that you're abusing the bankruptcy system. No one is really clear on how the courts will interpret this provision. Some courts may conclude that managing your financial affairs in order to squeeze in under the Means Test amounts to abuse, but just as many might disagree, taking the view that dismissal for abuse is to be reserved for characters who are guilty of really, really bad things, such as lying on paperwork or engaging in some other kind of fraud on the court.

Only time will tell how this one will play out, but your lawyer should have a pretty good idea of where local judges stand on this issue.

Chapter 6

Getting from Here to There: The Bankruptcy Process

*O*kay, you're thinking that bankruptcy just may be in the cards. What now? Although it's a bit of a journey, the process of mapping out your route and knowing where you're going need not be an excursion into a dark cave. Instead, view it as more of a self-guided tour, where you've done your homework, picked up the latest travelogue, and now you know which routes are open, which are closed, and which are littered with pot holes and construction crews. By just taking it one step at a time, you won't feel so overwhelmed.

Consider this chapter your road map, outlining the route for the two most common forms of consumer bankruptcy — Chapter 7 liquidations and Chapter 13 reorganizations — and exposing some goblins and trolls that you may encounter along the way.

Navigating the BARF Maze

The credit industry, in drafting BARF, created a number of obstacles to bankruptcy and laid booby traps for folks who don't successfully negotiate each and every land mine. One of our goals is to guide you safely over, through, and around these obstacles.

BARF has the following requirements:

- ✔ Within 180 days before bankruptcy, you undergo credit counseling from an approved agency and obtain a certificate that you've done so. If you've got to file immediately and can't get counseling within five days, you can catch up within 30 days after filing. Additionally, the court can give you an additional five days if you really need it. Whether you receive counseling in person, over the phone, or online, you still need your certificate — think of it as a diploma — as well as a copy of any repayment plan drawn up during your counseling session. (See the section "Arranging for Credit Counseling," later in this chapter, for more information.)

- ✔ Shortly after filing bankruptcy, you must send copies of your most recent federal income tax returns or official summaries of your returns (transcripts) to the trustee and to any creditor who requests a copy. Further, if any creditor or the trustee so requests, you must hand over to the bankruptcy court all federal income tax returns that you file with the IRS while your bankruptcy case is open. If you don't provide copies of your most recent return, your case can be dismissed. If you don't give the bankruptcy court copies of federal returns filed with the IRS while your case is open, your discharge may be denied, and your debts will follow you like a shadow. (See the section "Supplying Copies of Tax Returns," later in this chapter, for more information.)

- ✔ In Chapter 13, prior to the *341 meeting*, you also must have filed with the taxing authorities all the federal, state, and local tax returns that you should have filed in the past four years. You can get an extension of up to 120 days. If you don't comply, your case can be dismissed. (See the section "Attending the 341 Meeting," later in this chapter, for more information.)

- ✔ You must file with the bankruptcy court pay stubs or other evidence of income you've received in the 60 days prior to bankruptcy. (See the section "Completing the Paperwork," later in this chapter, for more information.)

- ✔ As a condition of having your debts discharged in either a Chapter 7 or 13, you must, after filing, complete a U.S. Trustee-approved course in personal financial management. (See the section "Signing Up for Your Financial Management Course," later in this chapter, for more information.)

- ✔ Every year in Chapter 13, you are required to submit an updated statement of income and expenses. (See the section "Filing annual reports," later in this chapter.)

The consequence of not filling all your pay stubs for the 60 days prior to bankruptcy may be catastrophic, even though this omission may seem (and actually is) a pretty minor mistake. If you don't, any creditor can demand dismissal of your case, and the court — however sympathetic it may be — may have no choice but to go along. You could go all the way though a bankruptcy only to find, because of this seemingly trivial error, that you have as many debts going out as you did going in. Moral of the story: Be *extremely* careful and make sure that your lawyer is as well.

Getting Organized Before Talking to a Lawyer

Just by reading this book, you'll by far be better prepared than a typical bankruptcy client. And although doing some legwork prior to meeting with your lawyer isn't required, your initial consultation will go more smoothly and be more productive if you do.

Doing your financial homework

To the greatest extent possible, calculate

- The amount of any income taxes that you owe and for which years
- How much you're behind on support obligations
- What your home is worth, the amount you're behind on mortgages, and the total balances owed on mortgages
- How much your cars are worth, and the amounts you owe against them
- A rough total of the balances (not monthly payments) that you owe on all your bills

You also need to gather copies of the following:

- Completed worksheets (tables) from Chapter 2
- Your pay stubs for the past 60 days
- Your mortgage documents
- The certificate of title for any motor vehicles you're using. If the vehicle is financed, you'll have to request a copy from the lender.

✔ Your most recent income tax return

✔ Any court papers if a lawsuit is pending against you

✔ Any divorce decrees, support orders, or marital settlement agreements

✔ Any information you provided to, or received from, a credit counseling agency within the past 180 days

In addition, Table 6-1 features some simple questions that your lawyer will ask. Check the appropriate box for each question and bring a copy of this checklist with you for your lawyer to review.

Table 6-1	Checklist to Give to Your Lawyer	
	Yes	**No**
Are you considering marriage or divorce?		
Has your household income changed in the last six months, or do you expect it to change in the next six months?		
Have you lived in this state for less than two years?		
Are you about to be sued for causing personal injuries to someone?		
Is a foreclosure pending?		
Have you been served with a lawsuit in which there's still time to respond?		
Is your driver's license about to be yanked for unpaid fines or judgments?		
Are you facing eviction from your apartment?		
Is your car about to be repossessed?		
Have you repaid debts owed to close friends or family members within the past 12 months?		
Have you repaid debts cosigned by close friends or family members within the past 12 months?		
Has someone recently died, or do you expect that in the next year someone will pass away, leaving you an inheritance or life insurance benefits?		
Are you in the process of getting a divorce?		

	Yes	No
Were you divorced within the past four years?		
Have you made credit-card balance transfers within the last six months?		
Have you made large debt repayments within the past 90 days?		
Do you make the mortgage payments on your home when your mate is not filing?		
Have you refinanced your house within the past 12 months?		
Have you refinanced your car or purchased a car on credit within the past 12 months?		
Do you expect to be paying higher medical expenses in the near future?		
Do you expect a large income tax refund this year?		
Have you been fined as part of a criminal proceeding?		
Are your wages being garnished, or are they about to be garnished?		
Have you filed all the income tax returns you were supposed to?		
Are you current with your mortgage payment?		
Are you current with your car payment?		
Have you ever filed bankruptcy?		
Have you any interest in a trust?		
Have you talked to another lawyer (about any matter) in the last four years?		
Within the last four years, have you made large gifts to anyone?		
Within the last four years, have you transferred any assets or put them in other people's names?		
Within the last 90 days, have you racked up more than $500 to a single creditor?		

(continued)

Table 6-1 (continued)

	Yes	No
Have you any money on deposit at an institution where you owe money?		
Are you entitled to a bonus at work, or can you cash in unused vacation pay or sick time?		
Does anyone owe you money?		
Have you made any unusual contribution to your pension or rolled over one pension into another within the past four years?		
Are you current with your child support and alimony payments?		
Have you paid someone else's debts within the past 12 months?		
In applying for a loan or credit card, have you ever overstated your income or given other false information?		
Is your home a manufactured home or a mobile home?		
Do you use your home for a nonresidential purpose?		

Tracking down your creditors

If you're unsure who all you owe money to, you need to obtain copies of your credit reports. For under $10, depending on where you live, you can order your credit report from

- ✔ Equifax, P.O. Box 740241, Atlanta, GA 30374-0241; phone, 800-685-1111; Web site, www.equifax.com
- ✔ Experian, P.O. Box 2002, Allen, TX 75013; phone, 800-682-7654; Web site, www.experian.com
- ✔ Trans Union, P.O. Box 1000, Chester, PA 19022; phone, 800-851-2674; Web site, www.transunion.com

You can also obtain a free credit report from any of these agencies when you request it within 60 days after being denied credit because of a bad report from that company. Sometimes, people apply for a loan knowing that they'll be turned down so that they can receive a free copy of their credit report.

However, they receive only a copy of the report that was used to deny their loan application, not all three reports, so the document is of limited value.

Under the recently enacted the Fair and Accurate Credit Transactions Act (FACTA), consumers may obtain a free copy of their credit report once every 12 months. Go to `www.annualcreditreport.com` to request your free credit report. To request the report by phone or mail, call 877-322-8228 (toll free) or write to Annual Credit Report Request Service, P.O. Box 105281, Atlanta, GA 30348-5281.

Some creditors may report to one or two of the credit bureaus, but not all three. So ordering a credit report from only one company isn't enough. For about $35, you can obtain a merged credit report, combining information from Equifax, Experian, and Trans Union with addresses for creditors, from

- ✔ Coast to Coast Information Services, 800-877-4033, `www.fullcredit reports.com`
- ✔ True Credit, 800-493-2392, `www.truecredit.com`

Bear in mind that the only creditors who appear on a credit report are the ones that have reported you. These creditors generally include credit-card companies, major department stores, and other large institutional creditors. Smaller creditors — such as your doctor, landlord, or local grocery store — rarely report to the credit bureaus until and unless the account is turned over to a collection agency.

Many bankruptcy lawyers are hooked up to an online service that allows them to get information similar to that provided by credit reports and download it directly into official bankruptcy forms. The service charges about $50 per credit report. Although this service can be a great time-saver, neither you nor your lawyer should rely exclusively on this method. Rather, it should be used to supplement the information you can obtain by yourself. As we said, not all creditors report to credit bureaus, and the addresses listed in these credit reports may not be the addresses that BARF requires.

Whenever you contact creditors or credit bureaus that don't know your whereabouts or phone number, try not to provide that information. Doing so may just give them what they need to hound you for payment.

If, within 90 days prior to bankruptcy, a creditor has sent two or more communications to you that specify an address for correspondence and a current account number, you should list that address and account number on your bankruptcy paperwork. Otherwise, the automatic stay (see the section "Using the Automatic Stay") may not apply to that creditor.

Meeting Your Lawyer for the First Time

Reputable bankruptcy lawyers have different styles of practice, and one isn't necessarily better than the other. Some handle a high volume of cases on an assembly line basis, relying heavily on paralegals. Others opt for a lower volume of cases with more personal contact between lawyer and client. Go with whichever makes you more comfortable.

Lawyers who specialize in personal bankruptcy are usually more efficient and tend to charge less and do a better job that lawyers who just file an occasional bankruptcy case.

By reading this book and being prepared, you aren't the typical bankruptcy client — especially if you're willing to pay a lawyer's hourly fee just to get an unbiased assessment of your options. If you explain how you've done your homework when calling for an appointment, even a high-volume office needs to alter its procedures so that you can meet with the lawyer who is in charge of your case, rather than a nonlawyer intake person. If not, you may want to consider looking elsewhere.

In your first meeting, the lawyer — after reviewing the materials you bring in and asking questions — must be able to tell you whether bankruptcy is your best choice and, if so, which type. If you answered yes to any of the questions in Table 5-1 (earlier in the chapter), expect the lawyer to inquire further. If he doesn't, you want to be sure to bring up any issues.

Arranging for Credit Counseling

BARF requires that you obtain a certificate from an approved credit counseling agency that documents that you received counseling within 180 days of filing bankruptcy. But wait until you talk to your lawyer (who can tell what your best local options are) before deciding whether to go for in-person counseling or doing it electronically and what materials you need to submit to the agency.

Keys to spotting a good bankruptcy attorney

A good bankruptcy attorney must, of course, know the law, but she must also be willing to spend the time and effort to learn about your particular situation and thoughtfully assess your options. Run for the nearest exit if the lawyer (or worse, her paralegal) says that your case is "cut and dried" or "run of the mill." For a conscientious lawyer, there really is no such thing. Every case has at least a few unique features to it.

Completing the Paperwork

After you decide to file bankruptcy, you'll have to provide information for the official documents. Some law offices give you a questionnaire to complete at home. Others help you fill it out on the spot, possibly with the assistance of a paralegal. Either way is fine as long as the information is accurate.

Receiving and reviewing drafts of official documents is a must. We recommend taking the drafts home and going over them very carefully at your own speed. Although documents can be amended after they're filed, your lawyer may charge you for the extra work. Remember, you've got to get it right. Mistakes may come back to haunt you.

One in every 250 bankruptcy cases will be audited, and *yours could be the one*. If significant mistakes are found, your discharge may be revoked, and your debts reinstated. If you intentionally misrepresent something, you may face criminal prosecution as well.

Filing Your Bankruptcy Case

When your paperwork is complete, your lawyer makes a strategic decision on when to actually file the papers with the court. This *petition date* determines which debts and property are included in your bankruptcy and which aren't. Tactical considerations in deciding whether to file this week or next may come into play. For example, if you recently lost your job, you may want to delay bankruptcy for several months to lower your average income for the past six months, making it easier to pass the Means Test. Your lawyer can help you with that determination.

In any case, the instant that your papers are filed, the pressure should be off. No more calls from debt collectors. No more collection efforts. You don't have to dread answering the phone any more. An automatic stay (see the next section) kicks in and, when it does, you'll finally see a glimmer of light at the end of your tunnel of financial distress.

Using the Automatic Stay

The *automatic stay* is one of the more powerful tools of bankruptcy. It kicks in automatically when you file, and results in a federal court order forbidding creditors from taking any action against you without first going through the judge. The judge literally makes a federal case against anyone who ignores the protective stay and comes after you.

Warning aggressive creditors that you've filed

Dan phoned the finance company and left a message that he'd just filed bankruptcy. Any finance company should, and would, know that a bankruptcy filing immediately stops all collection efforts.

But somehow, Dan's message got lost, and that night, the company repossessed his car. When it refused to immediately return the vehicle, Dan asked for help from the bankruptcy court. The judge not only ordered the return of the car but also fined the finance company and made it pay Dan's legal fees.

Sometimes, however, a glitch may occur because the court doesn't notify creditors of your bankruptcy until about ten days after it's filed. So, what if a creditor doesn't know that you've filed and repossesses your car?

Your attorney can probably get your car back, but doing so is likely to be an unnecessary hassle and expense. You can avoid this headache simply by informing any creditor who's likely to take immediate action that you've filed bankruptcy. That way, if they violate the automatic stay, they may have to pay you damages and reimburse your attorney fees. As we mention in the earlier section "Tracking down your creditors," BARF requires that if a creditor has contacted you at least twice during the 90 days prior to bankruptcy, you must list the address and account number indicated in this correspondence when you fill out the bankruptcy paperwork. If you use some other address or don't include the correct account number, you may not be able to recover money damages from that creditor if it violates the automatic stay.

If you're in default on your car loan, we suggest that you don't notify the creditor until after you actually file bankruptcy. Otherwise, the lender may attempt to grab the car before the automatic stay takes effect.

After your petition is filed

- ✔ If a foreclosure sale is scheduled, personally attend and announce that you've filed bankruptcy and that the sale cannot legally continue. Bring a copy of your petition just in case anyone insists on verification.

- ✔ Contact anyone who's suing you and send a copy of the bankruptcy petition to any court where you're being sued.

- ✔ If your wages are being garnished from your paycheck, be sure to notify your employer about your bankruptcy so that no more money comes out of your paycheck. Antidiscrimination laws prohibit your employer from taking any action against you simply because you filed bankruptcy.

Exceptions to the automatic stay

The automatic stay is a tremendous shield, but it isn't entirely bulletproof. It won't protect you from

- ✔ Criminal prosecution. Filing bankruptcy won't prevent you from being tried, convicted, and sent to jail if you've committed a crime.

- ✔ Repossession of personal property where the creditor has a purchase money security interest (for example, your car loan), or where the personal property is leased if you haven't entered into a reaffirmation agreement within 30 days of the 341 meeting. See Chapter 11.

- ✔ Evictions if a judgment for possession has already been entered by a state court *and* state law says that it's too late to reinstate the lease. If you're being evicted or threatened with eviction, see a bankruptcy lawyer immediately. Timing is everything.

- ✔ Deductions from your pay or pension to make regular payments on a loan against your retirement plan.

- ✔ Collection of child support or alimony, or even modifications of those support orders.

- ✔ Proceedings to dissolve a marriage, provided that there is no property to divide.

- ✔ Proceedings to establish your paternity.

- ✔ Government regulatory matters . . . as long as they aren't an end run to collect on a prepetition debt.

Plenty of states automatically suspend your driver's license when you fail to pay a judgment stemming from a car crash. The aim, obviously, is collecting money from you, so the automatic stay therefore applies.

On the other hand, licensing requirements that are designed to protect the public from incompetent nurses, doctors, architects, lawyers, accountants, and so on are not designed primarily to collect revenue. Consequently, the automatic stay won't stop the state from revoking your professional license when you've somehow managed to commit malpractice or violate the standards of your profession.

Situations where the automatic stay does not apply due to a prior bankruptcy

The automatic stay is really not so automatic if you've had a previous bankruptcy dismissed (for a reason other than flunking the Means Test) within a year of refiling under the following rules:

✔ If you had one bankruptcy dismissed less than one year before filing a new bankruptcy, the automatic stay kicks in when the case is filed, but it expires in 30 days unless you persuade the court that it should remain in effect.

✔ If you had more than one bankruptcy dismissed within the year before filing a new case, you have to file a special request for the court to impose the stay.

✔ If you had a bankruptcy dismissed within the past 180 days because you willfully disobeyed a court order or requested dismissal after a creditor asked for relief from stay, no stay goes into effect.

You may wonder what you must do to convince a judge to resurrect the stay if you have to refile within one year of dismissal. Good question.

BARF provides that if your case was dismissed for failing to file documents, you must show a *substantial excuse,* not just negligence or inadvertence. If your earlier case was dismissed because you couldn't keep up with your plan payments, you have to prove that circumstances have changed, and now you're able to make payments. Undoubtedly, your chances of success depends on the attitudes and prejudices of local bankruptcy judges, which may be wildly divergent.

Real abusers — in rem orders

Prior to BARF, some debtors thwarted legitimate foreclosure proceedings by repeatedly filing and then dismissing Chapter 13 cases — a practice that is truly abusive.

The new law authorizes the bankruptcy court to enter an *in rem order,* which provides that any future bankruptcy filed within two years will not interfere with foreclosure proceedings. This order isn't a bad idea, and some courts were doing that before BARF.

Taking quick action to save your driver's license

When the state tried to suspend Felicity's driver's license for not paying a judgment in a lawsuit over an automobile crash, she had her lawyer immediately file a bankruptcy petition. The automatic stay stopped the license suspension proceedings so that Felicity could continue to drive.

Smart move.

Had Felicity waited until her license actually was suspended before she filed her bankruptcy petition, she wouldn't have been able to drive until after the bankruptcy discharge was entered and her license was formally reinstated.

For spouses and relatives

The automatic stay protects pretty much only you and your property. It won't, for example, stop foreclosure on your grandfather's house or preclude repossession of your spouse's car, if he doesn't also file bankruptcy.

However, if you have even a partial ownership interest in an asset, the stay may very well apply.

Some sleazebags have abused the automatic stay by transferring partial ownership interests to a number of pals or siblings. That way, whenever repossession or foreclosure is on the horizon, one of them files bankruptcy just long enough for the automatic stay to take effect and then promptly gets the bankruptcy dismissed. The next time creditors get antsy, another "owner" files and does the same thing. This tactic is crummy, and courts are becoming not only willing but also seemingly eager to impose some pretty nasty fines on people who do it. If you ever decide to play this game, well, don't say we didn't warn you.

For cosigned debts

Ordinarily, the automatic stay in your case wouldn't prevent a creditor from going after someone who cosigned a loan for you.

You can, however, protect cosigners when filing under Chapter 13, if your plan proposes paying off the cosigned debt in full (although over an extended period of time). Known as the *codebtor stay,* it may be just the ticket to protect your sister, cousin, mother-in-law, rabbi, or whoever else may have cosigned for your loan.

Receiving Notice of the Creditors' Meeting

Within about ten days after the filing of your bankruptcy petition, the court sends notice to all of your creditors (using the address you provided in your schedules), informing them of your case, announcing the appointment of a case trustee (who represents the interests of the creditors), and setting the date for a meeting with creditors (the so-called 341 meeting).

Supplying Copies of Tax Returns

At least seven days before the 341 meeting, you must send copies of your most recent federal tax return (or an official summary known as a transcript) to the case trustee and any creditor who requests a copy. If you don't meet this deadline, the case may be dismissed.

In Chapter 13, prior to the 341 meeting, you also must have filed with federal, state, and local taxing authorities all of the tax returns that should have been filed in the past four years. Again, if you fail to comply, your case can be dismissed. However, you may get an extension of up to 120 days to file these returns.

If any creditor or the trustee so requests, you must hand over to the bankruptcy court any federal tax returns filed with the IRS while the case is open. A Chapter 7 debtor's discharge may be denied for failure to file tax returns with the court. Also, a Chapter 13 plan may be dismissed if tax returns are not filed with the court.

Attending the 341 Meeting

The one and only time in most bankruptcies where you and your creditors might come face to face is at what is called the *341 meeting*. Named for a section of the Bankruptcy Code, this session is sometimes referred to as the *First Meeting of Creditors*. That's kind of a misnomer because creditors almost never show up and there's rarely a "second" meeting.

The 341 meetings are generally open to the public, although it's unlikely that anyone would attend just out of idle curiosity. However, you might think about attending a couple just to watch the process unfold. Call either the bankruptcy court or the U.S. Trustee's office to find out when and where 341 meetings are held. Chapter 7 meetings are somewhat different than Chapter 13 meetings, so make sure that you check out the type of meeting that will be held in your case.

Signing Up for Your Financial Management Course

As a condition of getting your debts wiped out in either Chapter 7 or Chapter 13, you must complete an approved course in personal financial management after you file bankruptcy, but before your case is closed. The sooner you get started, the better. In Chapter 7, you have to complete the course within about 60 days of the 341 meeting. You have more time in Chapter 13, but there is not reason to delay. The Coalition for Consumer Bankruptcy Debtor Education is one of the few organizations offering quality debtor education. Check them out at www.debtoreducation.org.

Working Your Way through Chapter 7

The first thing that happens in Chapter 7 is the 341 meeting with creditors, which usually takes place 20 to 40 days after filing. The trustee conducts this meeting that you and your lawyer must attend.

Local practice may require that you bring certain things, such as bank statements, pay stubs, income tax returns, car titles, and the like to the meeting, but ideally you've already provided your lawyer with all these materials, and he just has to bring copies for the trustee.

In addition, you must bring a photo ID, as well as proof of your Social Security number.

The 341 meeting in a Chapter 7 case

At the 341 meeting, the trustee asks whether you were honest in listing all your assets on your bankruptcy petition and whether you have any nonexempt property that can be sold off to satisfy creditors. The trustee may also inquire about any payments you made or property that you transferred before bankruptcy. She won't browbeat you for filing or try to embarrass you. Humiliating you isn't her job or her purpose. You can expect to encounter a professional person acting professionally.

Whenever creditors show up, which is rare, they're permitted to ask a few polite questions, but they won't be allowed to harass you or put you down. Keep in mind that the purpose of the meeting is strictly "just the facts, ma'am" informational. You don't have to explain yourself or justify your spending.

Although attending a 341 meeting is not an act of penance, you still want to keep on your toes.

Keep in mind that getting rid of debt that you rack up knowing full well that you won't be able to pay may be difficult. Sometimes a creditor pretends to be sympathetic, trying to lead you down the path of admitting that you knew you couldn't pay the debt when you incurred it. Don't ever let anybody put words in your mouth! If you thought that you'd be able to pay or just didn't realize how bad things were, stick to your guns. Don't admit to things that aren't true just to be helpful or agreeable. Damning admissions can inspire creditors to file papers attempting to prevent that debt from being discharged on the basis of fraud (see Chapter 16).

Moreover, the trustee asks questions to find out whether you meet local requirements for exemptions that you claimed. You'll probably be quizzed about

- ✓ The value of your home, and whether you actually live there
- ✓ Whether you actually use tools in your trade or business
- ✓ The value of your car
- ✓ Your pension plan

Whether you're asked about your pension plan depends on where you live. Your lawyer should anticipate these questions and review them with you ahead of time.

Whenever you have nonexempt assets, the trustee usually inquires if you'd be willing to pay her the value of the asset so that you can keep it. Say, for example, that you owned a personal watercraft worth $1,500. The trustee would ask you if you'd rather pay $1,500 or surrender it. If you decide to keep it, payments may be stretched out over a few months.

If you can't or don't want to buy back nonexempt assets, the trustee arranges to have them picked up for liquidation. In the case of real estate, she hires a real estate agent who then inspects the property and comes to an independent opinion as to its value. The trustee then decides whether to have the real estate agent offer the property for sale.

This applies only to *nonexempt* property and not your home if it's fully exempt.

The trustee may also make arrangements to receive your income tax refund for the current year or request additional information about your assets, payments, or recent transfers of property. Your lawyer usually can handle these issues simply by sending a letter addressing any unresolved questions. Sometimes, a second meeting is necessary, but that's a rarity.

In the majority of cases, the trustee quickly concludes that you don't have enough nonexempt assets to bother with and declares your matter a no-asset case. In these cases, your involvement with the trustee usually ends at the conclusion of the 341 meeting.

Dealing with secured creditors

Aside from dealing with the trustee, you also must make arrangements with secured creditors within 30 days after the 341 meeting. You may

- ✔ Surrender collateral
- ✔ Redeem some kinds of personal property
- ✔ Reaffirm the secured debt
- ✔ Use avoidance powers to eliminate liens

In Chapter 13, if you intend to keep personal property that is either leased or subject to a purchase money security interest, you must provide the creditor with proof that you have insurance on the item within 60 days of the petition date. See Chapter 11 for a more in-depth look at secured debts and ways to deal with them.

Amending paperwork

If you discover that you've made inadvertent mistakes in the paperwork, the earlier you correct them, the better. Telling the trustee about errors is essential. However, when addressing a significant error, merely telling the trustee isn't enough. If you discover significant errors, you need to file a formal amendment so that the court's records show you've been forthright and truthful. Your attorney probably will charge you extra to amend your paperwork, but getting it right is crucial.

Check out Chapter 19 to get an idea of what types of errors may be considered significant enough to require formal amendment to your papers.

Adding creditors

The general rule is that debts that aren't listed on your official bankruptcy paperwork aren't wiped out. But you still can add them after you've filed, if you do so promptly — and the sooner, the better. Making additions to your list of debts within 30 days after the 341 meeting is preferable, and it's essential within 90 days if assets will be available to creditors in your case. (See Chapter 13 for more information about dealing with unlisted creditors.)

Sweating out key deadlines

The Bankruptcy Code mercifully establishes three deadlines, and you can breathe easier after they pass:

- ✔ **Within ten days after the 341 meeting:** The United States Trustee must file a statement with the court as to whether you passed or flunked the Means Test. If the U.S. Trustee thinks you flunked, she must, within 30 days of filing the statement, ask the court to dismiss your case.

- ✔ **Thirty days after the 341 meeting concludes:** The 30th day is the last day for the trustee or creditors to object to your claims of exempt property. If you've properly listed the asset, you're in the clear after that time. But if you have to amend an exemption claim, the 30-day clock starts running all over again.

- ✔ **Sixty days after the 341 meeting:** The 60th day is the deadline for creditors to claim that certain types of debts — most notably credit-card fraud claims and nonsupport marital obligations — should not be wiped out. If the creditor fails to file in time, it's too late, and you're home-free. The same deadline applies to claims that your discharge should be denied altogether because of serious misconduct.

Attending a discharge hearing

Usually, you have to attend a *discharge hearing* only if you want to reaffirm a debt and your lawyer refused to sign a statement that reaffirmation is in your best interest. Understand that your lawyer's refusal isn't to be mean. She's actually trying to look out for your best interest despite your desires. At the discharge hearing, the judge makes sure that you really understand the consequences of reaffirming a debt and can afford to make the payments on the reaffirmed debt.

Closing no-asset cases

Most no-asset cases close about 60 days after the 341 meeting. At that point, you're done. All assets that you listed on your schedules are yours again when the case is closed.

Laying the foundation for credit repair

Sooner or later, you're going to want to repair your credit rating — and there's no time like the present for getting started. You can do a number of things right now that make the going easier down the road.

For example, some banks won't allow a recent bankruptcy filer to open a checking account. You can avoid this hassle by opening a new account before bankruptcy at a bank where you don't owe any money. Just deposit the minimum amount and don't use the account until after you file.

You may also want to consider getting a new credit card or a charge account. Although it may seem that there's nothing you need less than more credit, getting a new account is a step toward rebuilding your credit, and doing it prior to filing bankruptcy may be easier and cleaner.

Be sure to accurately list all your debts and assets on any application, and if you succeed in getting a credit or charge card, don't use it until after you file. If you don't owe money on an account, you won't need to list it on your bankruptcy petition. Chances are the creditor won't cancel your card, and you'll be able to use the new account to begin restoring your credit history in the future.

Administering asset cases

Asset cases remain open long enough for the trustee to liquidate your nonexempt assets, distribute the proceeds to creditors, and file a report with the court. If the trustee can't sell an asset, she abandons it, which means that you own it again.

This whole process is referred to as the *administration of the estate,* and sometimes it takes quite a while — sometimes even years, depending on the kind of assets that are involved.

If someone owed you money on the petition date, the trustee can sue that person to collect it. If you already were in the process of suing someone, the trustee takes over the case. All these steps take time, and courts are pretty indulgent in giving trustees all the time they need.

Even though an asset case can drag on, your discharge (assuming that there are no complications; see the next section for details) still will be entered approximately 60 days after the 341 meeting. Still, you must cooperate with the trustee in her efforts to convert assets to cash.

Fortunately, fewer than 5 percent of Chapter 7 filings are assets cases.

Anticipating complications

Not every Chapter 7 is routine, however, and complications sometimes develop. The good news is that an experienced bankruptcy lawyer usually can tell, even before filing, whether possible problems are lurking on the horizon. If you've been completely candid with your lawyer, and she's not worried about any potential glitches, you needn't worry either.

Working Your Way through Chapter 13

Aside from the obvious fact that you'll be making payments for the next 36 to 60 months, when filing a Chapter 13 reorganization, you have a few extra hurdles to jump. Procedural requirements are designed to ensure that your plan is feasible, that it satisfies certain technical mandates, and that you do the best you can to repay creditors.

Filing your plan and beginning your payments

Although you have 15 days after your petition is filed to submit your payment plan, having it ready when you file is a better idea. Your first plan payment is due within 30 days, and it may come due even before you meet with the trustee. One concern of the trustee is whether you're willing and able to make timely plan payments. Missing the first payment makes for a dreadful start. Your lawyer should tell you how and where to make plan payments.

The 341 meeting in a Chapter 13 case

Many aspects of the 341 meeting with creditors are the same in Chapter 13 as they are in Chapter 7 cases, but the emphasis is different and some additional concerns exist. (For more on Chapter 7 filings, see the section "Working Your Way through Chapter 7," earlier in this chapter.)

The Chapter 13 trustee scrutinizes your income and expense shown on your bankruptcy paperwork to see whether you are

✔ Likely to meet your monthly payment obligations. You probably won't be able to keep up with payments if you haven't been realistic in estimating your living expenses.

✔ Making a good faith effort to repay your creditors as much as reasonably possible. The trustee questions you to make sure that you listed all your sources of income and carefully reviews your proposed expenses.

In areas where the local practice is to conduct confirmation hearings (see the next section) immediately after the 341 meeting, more creditors may attend and ask questions along the same line as those just listed. In other locations, most creditors do not attend 341 meeting.

Confirming your repayment plan

The court decides whether to approve or reject your repayment plan at what's called the *confirmation hearing.*

In many places, if the trustee supports your plan and your creditors have no objections, you don't have to appear at the confirmation hearing, and the court will probably approve your proposal as a matter of course.

But whenever the trustee or a creditor objects, you and your lawyer have to attend. Your lawyer determines whether to proceed with a hearing and tries to convince the judge that the objections have no merit or tries negotiating with objecting creditors. If the court upholds any objection to your plan, you'll probably have an opportunity to file a modified plan and schedule another confirmation hearing. Occasionally, the judge concludes that the objection is so serious that any attempted plan modification would be futile and simply orders that the case be dismissed.

Going through valuation hearings

Another type of hearing known as a *valuation hearing* is where secured creditors can object to how they're being treated under your plan because the value of their collateral is different than you claim. Your lawyer usually can resolve valuation issues through negotiation, but, if that fails, the judge decides.

Filing annual reports

Every year that you're in Chapter 13, you must file an updated statement with the court showing your income and expenses for the past year. The first one is due 90 days after the close of the first tax year you are in Chapter 13. Subsequent reports are due no later than 45 days before the anniversary date of the plan's confirmation. Your lawyer can help you complete these reports.

Looking at the claims process

Whenever any creditors are entitled to receive money from your bankruptcy — that is, if you filed a Chapter 13 or a Chapter 7 asset case — be sure that the money goes toward satisfying debts that won't be discharged or that will continue to linger because of a lien.

For example, if you file Chapter 13 to catch up on your back mortgage payments, you want the money you pay to the trustee to be used for this purpose — not toward payment of debts that will just be eliminated.

But remember that a creditor can't receive any money from a bankruptcy estate unless a document called a *proof of claim* is filed with the court. Most creditors have 90 days from the 341 meeting to file such a claim. If the creditor doesn't file one, you can lodge a proof of claim on behalf of the creditor up to 120 days from the 341 meeting.

Governmental units get special treatment and are afforded 180 days after the petition date to file a proof of claim.

Certain taxes are *priority debts*. These taxes, which ordinarily would be nondischargeable, can be wiped out in Chapter 13 whenever the taxing authority doesn't file a timely proof of claim. (Obviously, you don't want to file a proof of claim for these debts.)

Comparing the Chapter 7 and Chapter 13 Process

Table 6-2 shows what usually happens, step by step, in Chapter 7 and Chapter 13 cases.

Table 6-2	The Bankruptcy Process
Chapter 7	*Chapter 13*
1. Petition filed.	1. Petition filed.
2. Aggressive creditors notified immediately.	2. Aggressive creditors notified immediately.
3. Court sends notice to you, your lawyer, and all your creditors.	3. Court sends notice to you, your lawyer, and all your creditors.

4. You send copies of your most recent federal income tax returns (or transcripts) to the trustee and to any creditor who requests a copy at least seven days before the 341 meeting.	4. Plan must be filed with first payment due in 30 days.
5. 341 meeting.	5. You send copies of your most recent federal income tax returns (or transcripts) to the trustee and to any creditor who requests a copy at least seven days before the 341 meeting. You also must have filed with the taxing authorities all the federal, state, and local tax returns that were due in the past four years. You can get an extension of up to 120 days.
6. Within ten days of 341, U.S. Trustee decides whether you passed the Means Test.	6. 341 meeting.
7. Deal with secured creditors.	7. Thirty days after 341 meeting, last day to object to exemptions.
8. Complete course in financial management.	8. Within 60 days after the petition date, provide proof of insurance to holders of purchase money security interest or lessors of personal property.
9. Thirty days after 341 meeting, last day to object to exemptions.	9. Confirmation hearing.
10. Sixty days after the 341 meeting is deadline for claiming some debts not discharged, and discharge should be denied or case should be dismissed for flunking the Means Test.	10. Valuation hearing.
11. Discharge hearing.	11. 120 days after 341 meeting last day for proof of claim to be filed on behalf of creditor you want paid. (180 days from petition date for governmental creditors.)
12. Discharge usually entered about 60 days after 341 meeting	12. If any creditor or the trustee so requests, you must file with the bankruptcy court all federal income tax returns that come due or are filed while your bankruptcy case is opened.

(continued)

Table 6-2 *(continued)*

Chapter 7	*Chapter 13*
13. 120 days after 341 meeting last day for proof of claim to be filed on behalf of creditor you want paid. (180 days from petition date for governmental creditors.)	13. You file annual reports of income and expenses.
14. If any creditor or the trustee so requests,you must file with the bankruptcy court all federal income tax returns that come due or are filed while your bankruptcy case is opened.	14. Compete course on financial management.
15. Complete course on financial management.	15. Completion of pay payments.
16. Closing of no-asset case.	16. Discharge hearing elimination of remaining balances.
17. In asset cases, trustee liquidates property, distributes proceeds to creditors, files reports, and closes case.	

Part II
Avoiding Bankruptcy

The 5th Wave   By Rich Tennant

OUT OF BUSINESS

Main Street CHINA SU

"What made you think you were the one to own and operate a china shop, I'll never know."

In this part . . .

With a new bankruptcy law in October 2005, it's tougher than ever to figure out whether bankruptcy spells relief for you. If you think another alternative may be your best bet, this is the part for you. Read on to fully understand the downsides of bankruptcy. In this part, we offer a crash course in successful sparring with debt-collection bullies — to keep them at bay while you make up your mind — and some tips on negotiating the granddaddy of all debt collectors: Good ol' Uncle Sam.

Chapter 7

Considering Alternatives to Bankruptcy

*B*ankruptcy is a fantastically powerful tool for financial rebirth, and one that never should be viewed only as a last resort. Bankruptcy is a tool at your disposal, and you need to measure its usefulness by the simplest of criteria: Do the benefits outweigh the disadvantages? Too many people comply with the advice of less-than-objective debt counselors and sincere-but-ignorant friends and relatives, parting with essential assets like their homes and pensions, only to wind up in bankruptcy (where those kinds of assets may have been protected) anyhow.

But bankruptcy isn't necessarily the best or even the only solution for you. Filing bankruptcy has definite downsides, and sometimes a different strategy is more appropriate for your situation or your personality.

In this chapter, we look at some of the pitfalls of bankruptcy and the alternatives, such as using your home equity or pension to pay your debts.

Appreciating the Negative Consequences of Bankruptcy

Bankruptcy isn't without consequences, and some of them can be painful. You need to fully appreciate what you have to lose if you file bankruptcy, and what you stand to lose if you file at the wrong time.

The drawbacks of bankruptcy

Although the drawbacks frequently are exaggerated, filing bankruptcy *can* (note we say "can" and not "will")

- Hurt innocent people who extended you credit.

- Damage your credit rating.

- Represent the ultimate admission of financial defeat.

- Result in pubic humiliation in communities where newspapers print the names of bankruptcy filers. (Because of the sheer volume, however, many newspapers now limit those listings to businesses and prominent individuals.)

- Subject your personal lifestyle to scrutiny in a public meeting room (rarely, however, do any curiosity-seekers show up).

- Be used against you by prospective employers, particularly if your career involves being bonded (bank teller, jewelry associate, and so on).

- Cause you to lose some of your belongings.

- Preclude bankruptcy as an avenue of relief if you get in even worse trouble in the near future.

Reasons not to file bankruptcy

Bankruptcy may be the wrong solution for you if

- Your debts are small enough that you can probably pay them off in full in a few years without too much trouble.

- You don't owe the money. Just because someone says you owe him money doesn't necessarily mean that you do. If you sincerely believe the debt is an error, and can prove it, fight.

✔ You won't be able to shed your most nettlesome debts by filing. Bankruptcy won't eliminate all your debts. Criminal fines, student loans, most taxes, support obligations, and personal injuries caused by drunk driving usually can't be wiped out in bankruptcy.

✔ You have valuable nonexempt assets that can be taken to satisfy creditors, and you don't want to risk losing them.

✔ Your goal is just to delay a creditor or jerk him around.

✔ Your biggest debts are secured (by your house or car, for example), and your unsecured debts are relatively insignificant.

✔ You have transferred property to or put title in someone else's name to keep it away from creditors.

Reasons to delay filing bankruptcy

Sometimes a successful bankruptcy depends on careful timing. Your lawyer may suggest that you wait if you

✔ Expect to receive a large income tax refund. If you file before receiving the windfall, the money goes toward paying your debts. But if you wait until after you receive your refund, you'll be able to spend it on essentials (like car or house repairs) before filing.

✔ Racked up quite a bit of debt recently. If you wait for a while to file bankruptcy, it will be less likely that creditors would claim fraud and try to prevent elimination of these debts. See Chapters 14 and 16.

✔ Repaid debts to family members during the past year. If you wait for a year to expire after paying debts to family members, you protect them from having to cough up this money to a bankruptcy trustee. See Chapter 19.

✔ Recently suffered a reduction in your income, or expect to in the near future. Remember that the Means Test is only a problem for folks with incomes over the median, and this calculation is based on your average income for the six months preceding bankruptcy. If, for example, you just lost a high-paying job, your average income would decrease for every month you did not receive a paycheck. So, delaying your bankruptcy for several months would reduce your average monthly income and minimize any Means Test problems. See Chapter 5.

✔ Filed bankruptcy before. Your debts won't be wiped out in a Chapter 7 filed within eight years of a prior case or in a Chapter 13 filed within four years of a previous bankruptcy. See Chapter 4.

✔ Are facing large medical bills in the foreseeable future. Remember that if you file bankruptcy, you won't be able to file another one anytime soon. See preceding bullet.

✔ Are contemplating divorce. Deciding exactly when to file bankruptcy when a divorce is looming is devilishly tricky. See Chapters 5 and 17.

✔ Owned your home for less than 1,215 days and live in a state that allows a generous homestead exemption. See Chapter 12 and Appendix A. BARF imposes a $125,000 limit on homesteads acquired within 1,215 days of bankruptcy, even if your state would allow more. In this situation, you might want to delay your bankruptcy for 1,215 days. Say, for example, that you live in Massachusetts and inherited a home worth $350,000. Your home is completely off-limits to creditors unless you file bankruptcy within 1,215 days of acquiring it, in which case only $125,000 would be protected. What a different a day could make!

✔ Owe taxes that wouldn't be dischargeable if you filed bankruptcy right now, but would become dischargeable in the near future.

Looking at Remedies Other Than Bankruptcy

You don't swat a fly with a sledgehammer or use a wrench to drive in a nail — or at least you shouldn't. By the same token, you don't need to file bankruptcy just to solve a trivial financial problem or when a more targeted remedy is available. Although you never should view bankruptcy as a last-ditch solution, you probably shouldn't make it your first consideration either. If you can get out of trouble without filing, that's wonderful! In fact, this section explains a number of things that you may want to consider before deciding that bankruptcy is the way out.

Budgeting

If you can get your financial house in order through discipline and careful budgeting, go for it. The key to realistic budgeting is establishing a reasonable timeframe for immediate and long-term goals and adopting a positive attitude that focuses not on what you're giving up but rather on what you're achieving.

You may also consider looking into an Employee Assistance Program (EAP), if your employer offers one. These plans provide counseling for a variety of issues, including debt problems. The EAP may also suggest ways that your company credit union can help. However, you always need to be leery of attempting to borrow your way out of debt. It's kind of like those diet plans that claim you can eat your way thin.

Allowing your family to bail you out

Frequently, a parent or other family member offers to save your hide, and accepting that generosity often is tempting. Allowing your family to bail you out may be a wise alternative to bankruptcy, but only if your Guardian Angel

- ✔ Is ready, willing, and able to help.
- ✔ Can pay your debts without suffering financial hardship himself.
- ✔ Can truly solve your problem, not just postpone an inevitable bankruptcy. Loaning or giving money to a loved one to relieve the immediate pressure is common, but such actions ultimately are a waste of money when you end up in bankruptcy anyway. The money is gone, the gesture was futile, and far too often, bad feelings linger.

Selling your assets

If you own assets that you'd lose to a bankruptcy trustee, you may want to consider selling your stuff to pay your debts. If that doesn't raise enough money to pay *all* your debts, it at least helps whittle down your debt load.

Every state has laws that make certain essential assets exempt or off-limits to creditors, regardless of whether the debtor files bankruptcy. Note that we're talking about selling *nonexempt* assets — those that a creditor can get. Don't let anyone bully you into selling exempt assets, which in most cases are off-limits even if you don't file bankruptcy. Most states allow you to keep

- ✔ Homesteads up to a specified value
- ✔ Pensions
- ✔ Basic household furnishings
- ✔ A modest vehicle

Practically speaking, here's how exemptions work. Say your home is worth $100,000, and your mortgage(s) total $80,000. The equity in your home is $20,000. If the homestead exemption for your state is $25,000, the only creditors who can take your home are the ones holding your mortgages. The law says that your home is yours — unless you agree otherwise by getting another mortgage or borrowing more on your present one. In other words, selling exempt assets to pay debts is rarely a good idea. Actually, it's often downright foolish.

When selling assets, you need to

- ✔ Sell the asset for a fair price. If you sell to someone you know, be prepared to show how you determined the price.

- ✔ Avoid repaying debts to friends or relatives if there's any possibility of bankruptcy.

- ✔ Tell your bankruptcy lawyer when you've sold assets (actually, it would be better to tell him beforehand if possible) and be sure that the sale is mentioned in your bankruptcy paperwork.

Some department stores take a *security interest* in items that you purchase on their charge accounts. In practical terms, that means you aren't supposed to part with an item you've charged before you fully own it. But if you've already sold it, it's probably not a big deal if you didn't know any better.

Keep in mind that the law does *not* require you to strip yourself of key assets to satisfy creditors. (We describe such exemptions in detail in Part III.) You need somewhere to live. You may need a car. Someday you'll need a pension. Bankruptcy protects all those things.

Transferring credit-card balances

Although trading high interest rates for lower rates is worth checking out, credit-card balance transfers seldom are effective. A *balance transfer* actually is a new loan, with the proceeds going to pay debts that should be pretty far down on your list of priorities. Furthermore, whenever you transfer a balance and then end up in bankruptcy, you may be facing an allegation of fraud, and your creditors may fight to prevent the debts you owe them from being wiped out.

If you do decide to shop around, a Web site at www.getsmart.com can help you find a more favorable credit-card rate. Another Web site, www.bankrate.com, also provides useful information about credit-card rates and mortgage rates.

Keep in mind, however, that creditors have ulterior motives. Even when monthly payments are lower, the longer the creditors continue collecting interest, the more money you'll ultimately pay.

Restructuring home mortgages

You may be able to free up some cash by restructuring your home mortgage. Basically, you can do this in two ways:

✔ By arranging a mortgage workout agreement

✔ By refinancing

If a foreclosure sale is scheduled, keep your eye on that date and, if possible, try to get it postponed. When such a sale goes forward, you're likely to lose any equity that you have in the property. See Chapter 12 to see why bankruptcy must be filed before a foreclosure sale is conducted.

Mortgage workouts

If your only problem is that you temporarily fell behind on your mortgage payments — perhaps because of a layoff, sickness, or family emergency — your mortgage holder may allow you to catch up on back payments over an extended period of time. The bank doesn't want your house, but it definitely wants the money you promised to pay for it (or at least as much as it can get).

The sooner you contact the lender, the better. After a foreclosure begins, the amount that you eventually have to come up with increases by at least $1,000, because you have to pay the lender's attorney fees.

When you've built up significant equity in a property, selling it before a foreclosure is completed usually is better. Foreclosures rarely produce any money over and above the amount owed to the lender, but you may be able to sell the property for more than that amount. That way, you get to keep the extra.

The widespread use of mortgage insurance also offers a glimmer of hope. With this type of insurance, a mortgage insurer agrees to pay the lender any losses that it suffers if you don't pay the mortgage, and after it pays off the lender, it steps into the lender's shoes and takes over the loan.

Government agencies, such as the Federal Housing Administration (FHA), the United States Department of Housing and Urban Development (HUD), the Farmers Home Administration (FmHA), and the Veteran's Administration (VA) insure many mortgages. These agencies have programs designed to help folks avoid losing their homes. When you approach the lender about a workout agreement, ask whether the loan is insured by one of these agencies. If so, call the agency to find out what programs are available.

An often-overlooked defense to foreclosures

The Federal Truth in Lending Act (TILA — U.S. Code, vol. 15, secs 1601–1667) (volume 15, sections 1601 through 1667 of the official compilation of federal statutes known as the United States Code) can be a godsend in stopping foreclosure.

The TILA requires lenders to provide borrowers with certain precise information about the loan, at the time that it's made. If the lenders screw up — and they often do — you can rescind, or cancel, a mortgage on your home, thus ending the foreclosure. At some point, you're supposed to repay the money that you borrowed, but if you

don't, they can't take your home. The time for rescinding expires three years after the loan is made.

Truth-in-lending defenses frequently are overlooked because most lawyers aren't up to speed on the Act. Public-interest law offices and legal aide counselors tend to be the most knowledgeable about this powerful weapon.

The greatest limitation to TILA defenses is that the TILA doesn't apply to mortgages taken to buy the home — probably your first mortgage.

Refinancing

By refinancing your mortgage — in effect, trading an old mortgage in for a new one with a more favorable interest rate — you can significantly cut your monthly payment, perhaps by a couple hundred dollars a month or even more. You can shop around for a better mortgage rate at www.interest.com/mmis.html and www.bankrate.com.

Generally, refinancing makes economic sense only when rates have fallen a full 2 percentage points. Otherwise, closing costs and fees eat up any potential savings. Likewise, be wary of variable-interest mortgages, which fluctuate, usually with the prime interest rate. They have a nasty tendency to go up at the worst possible time.

Home-equity loans

A world of difference exists between refinancing to get a better rate and taking a home-equity loan — which doesn't reduce the amount of your mortgage debt. All you really do with a home-equity loan is, in essence, unbuy your house and then buy it back again.

Many companies aggressively tout home-equity loans, urging you to use the value that you've built up in your home as collateral. They claim that borrowing against your home to pay off credit cards is the greatest thing since canned beer because

- ✔ Interest on home mortgages is tax-deductible.
- ✔ Making a single monthly payment is more convenient than numerous credit-card payments.

✔ The interest rate is lower.

✔ Your monthly payment will be lower than what you're now paying on credit cards.

Sometimes the slick ads also subtly suggest that you may even have enough cash left over after paying off credit cards for you to take a much-deserved vacation or buy an expensive toy.

All this may sound pretty good, but don't forget that your home may be the most valuable and important asset that you have, and you're putting it at risk when you play the home-equity credit game. If paying credit-card bills was a struggle, making payments on a home-equity loan probably won't be much easier. To make matters worse, after your credit-card bills are paid off, your credit-card accounts will be available for more borrowing — the very thing that got you into trouble in the first place.

You also want to keep in mind that home-equity loans usually carry a steeper interest rate than conventional mortgages, so you probably won't save much in interest. And if your plan is to take out a loan so that you can pay a number of smaller bills, you're actually just exchanging many smaller bills for a large one, and probably paying some loan fees to boot.

Furthermore, remember that a home-equity loan creates a lien on your home that survives bankruptcy. Say that after sucking all the equity out of your home to pay your credit-card bills, you still end up in bankruptcy. What you've done is needlessly put your house on the line. The credit-card debts were unsecured and would've probably been eliminated in bankruptcy. But the value of your house secures the home-equity loan. No wonder lenders (and sometimes credit counselors who work openly — or not — for lenders) push home-equity loans!

Whenever you do consider refinancing, be on the alert for hidden costs, such as broker's fees, points (additional interest), and penalties for prepaying your present mortgage. These fees can negate the benefits of using home equity to consolidate your debts.

And watch out for loans that require "balloon" payments. Sometimes, these loans are structured in such a way that you fork over relatively small monthly payments until the final installment is due — and then you get whacked.

Finally, if bankruptcy is even remotely visible on your horizon, consult with an attorney *before* taking out a second mortgage. The sight of folks losing bankruptcy as a viable solution by taking out one of these loans is all too common, so you need to be quite clear about the ramifications of a second mortgage before taking that step. No competent attorney will try to push you into bankruptcy if that isn't your best choice, or if you're just not ready. But a good bankruptcy lawyer needs to be able to give you a clear picture of the potential benefits and drawbacks of your unique situation. Expect to pay a reasonable fee for the lawyer's time (between $100 and $200) and consider it a smart investment. See Chapter 3.

Reverse mortgages

So-called *reverse mortgages* usually target senior citizens (borrowers must be at least 62 years old to qualify), enticing them to tap into their home equity by borrowing money that doesn't have to be repaid until they move or die.

For example, say you're 65 years old, and you own your $100,000 home free and clear. With a reverse mortgage, you'd borrow up to some specified percentage of the home's value, say $80,000, and then receive portions of that money in regular intervals without having to make any mortgage payments.

Sounds like a good deal, doesn't it? Depending on your unique circumstances, it may be. Just don't lose sight of the fact that someday that loan will have to be repaid; otherwise, your house will be turned over to the lender, and that inevitability may come as quite a shock to your heirs.

Be very careful when considering a reverse mortgage and look out for outfits that prey on older people with equity in their homes. Stick with a reputable lender and be sure that you understand all the costs and fees that you'll be charged. Finding out whether and how a reverse mortgage in your particular situation may affect your eligibility for government benefits, such as Social Security or Medicaid, also is a good idea.

Reliable information is available by calling the American Association of Retired People at 1-800-209-8085 or visiting its Web site at www.aarp.org.

Once again, we encourage you to talk to a bankruptcy lawyer before entering into a reverse-mortgage arrangement. Depending on the available homestead exemption, you may be much better off just filing bankruptcy.

Tapping your retirement plan

In most states, creditors can't get at your pension unless you enable them to do so by withdrawing the money or taking a loan against it. Taking either of those routes seldom is a good move. You may face serious tax consequences when you take an early pension distribution or fail to repay a pension loan.

Borrowing against your retirement plan is usually a lousy idea because

- ✔ It gives the lender a claim against your pension. Ordinarily, creditors can't get their hands on your retirement account.
- ✔ Most debts that you'd pay with the proceeds of the pension loan, such as credit-card accounts, can probably be wiped out in bankruptcy.
- ✔ If you don't repay the pension loan, you suffer serious tax consequences.
- ✔ If you lose your job, you may have to repay the loan almost immediately.

In a few situations, tapping into your retirement fund may be a feasible way of solving your problems. But you'd do well to find out your bankruptcy options before risking your retirement nest egg.

Choosing Which Bills to Pay First (If at All)

Chances are you don't have the money to pay all your bills, at least not right away, so you'll need to decide which ones to pay. You obviously need to continue paying current bills for living expenses like food and utilities.

Amid all your personal financial turmoil, debt collectors usually give you crummy advice because all they care about is wringing as much as possible out of you, as soon as possible, and with the least amount of effort on their part. Your decisions must be based on reason and guided by what's best for you and your family, and not on what makes for a happy debt collector.

Keeping that perspective when a bill collector is bullying you isn't always easy. Remember, however, that the most obnoxious collectors act the way they do because they really don't have any other weapon to use against you.

We hope that you plan to talk to a bankruptcy lawyer before making these decisions, but if you're not quite ready to take that step, you may want to start by asking yourself two questions:

- ✔ What can this creditor do if I don't pay?
- ✔ Will I be able to escape this debt altogether if I eventually decide to file bankruptcy?

When you can't pay everyone, you need to invest your money where it does the most good or avoids the gravest of problems. Dribbling out money to the most aggressive collectors without an overall plan is a mistake. The payments at the top of your priority list (in order) should be your

- ✔ Rent, or mortgage, if you intend to keep your house
- ✔ Utilities
- ✔ Essential vehicle
- ✔ Fines, if nonpayment would land you in jail
- ✔ Child support and alimony
- ✔ Income taxes
- ✔ Possibly student loans (but first see whether you're eligible for one of the repayment plans described in Chapter 18)

It's no accident that credit cards, loans from finance companies, and medical bills don't make the cut in this list. That's because these types of creditors must sue you and obtain a judgment before they can take any of your property. In other words, before they can ever cause you any real trouble, they have some hurdles to jump over. Besides, these kinds of debts can be wiped out if you end up in bankruptcy.

If bankruptcy is in your future, you should neither repay any loans to close friends or family members nor loans that are cosigned by any such people. If you file bankruptcy within one year of making these types of payments, the trustee can get the money back. See Chapter 19.

As a general rule, you need to be wary of partially paying creditors just because you think it will get them off your back. It won't. Trust us on this one. And it may cause you additional headaches in the future.

Credit counselors or *consolidators* backed by the lending industry may try talking you into taking a home-equity loan to pay off your credit cards. If you see any possibility at all that you'll eventually go bankrupt (and it is probable that you do), a home-equity loan is a terrible idea. The reason? You'd essentially transform unsecured debts (your credit-card bills) into a debt secured by your home. Then, if you don't pay, they can take your home sweet home. See why the creditors like it so much?

The National Consumer Law Center publishes a guide that helps you decide which debts to pay and generally how to cope with debt outside of bankruptcy. You can obtain this publication, *Surviving Debt* by Jonathan Sheldon and Gary Klein, through many bookstores, or you can order it directly by contacting the National Consumer Law Center, 77 Summer St., 10th Floor, Boston, MA 02110-1006; phone, 617-523-8089.

Deciding whether to pay your mortgage

Although you'll probably want to make your mortgage payments if you decide to file bankruptcy, it isn't necessarily a given.

Whenever your home is worth less than what you owe on it, you may just want to save the money for a deposit on a new place to live, knowing that eventually the mortgage holder will foreclose and kick you out anyway. However, if you intend to keep your home, be sure to maintain insurance and, if possible, pay real estate taxes. If you don't, the lender may be able to foreclose even if you're making your payments.

Considering whether to make car payments

As is true with your house, the question to ask about your car is whether it is worth less than you owe on it. You'll have to make your car payments if you want to keep it. And even if you decide to surrender the vehicle, your problem may not be cured. Most car dealers sell surrendered vehicles at wholesale prices, leaving you liable for any balance due on the loan. You may try selling the vehicle yourself to raise enough to pay the loan in full and satisfy the entire obligation.

Dealing with alimony and child support payments

If at all possible, you also need to get current with your alimony and child support obligations. The consequences for neglecting those obligations are serious, possibly even criminally serious if you're jailed for contempt of court. And many judges have adopted a zero-tolerance approach toward deadbeat parents.

Deciding whether you should pay your taxes

You need to pay current income taxes, and probably those from the last three years. Taxing authorities can make your life miserable if you don't, and penalties for not paying add up at an astonishing rate. (See Chapter 9 for more information.)

Negotiating with Your Creditors

If you can find someone who actually has the authority to negotiate, you may be able to cut a deal that works to everyone's satisfaction. But if your creditor is a large institution, you'll have difficulty getting beyond the bean counters and paper pushers — that is, if you even get past the answering machines. You're more likely to succeed if your creditor is a small organization. Regardless, attempting a nonbankruptcy solution is worth the effort.

Workout agreements

Traditionally, a nonbankruptcy *workout agreement* — where a debtor reaches a negotiated solution with creditors — falls into one of three categories:

- ✔ Composition arrangements, where all creditors agree to accept less than full settlement of the debts

- ✔ Extension agreements, which merely extend the term for repayment in full

- ✔ Combination agreements, where debts are reduced and paid over an extended time period

The problem with these plans is that all your creditors must go along with it, and so, the more creditors you have, the harder it is to get them to agree. In addition, you'll probably need a lawyer to negotiate settlement agreements, and the legal fees may be exorbitant, if not prohibitive.

Strange as it may seem, whenever a creditor writes off a debt outside of the bankruptcy context, the amount of the write-off is taxable income to the borrower unless he was insolvent (owed debts exceeding the value of your assets) when the debt was kissed off. If you're in this situation, consider filing Form 982 with your tax return. You can get it on the IRS Web site at www.irs.ustreas.gov/formspubs/index.html (click forms and publications by number).

Workout agreements are more useful when you have valuable nonexempt assets that are worth enough to pay your debts, but you need some time to sell without having to juggle creditors. In consumer cases, rarely does a debtor have enough assets to pay his debts.

Threatening bankruptcy

If you genuinely are considering bankruptcy, unsecured creditors may agree to settle for a pittance simply because when you do actually file, they'd otherwise receive nothing.

Assume that you borrowed $50,000 to start a business, which never got off the ground. There's no way you can repay this debt, and all you own is a modest home, mortgaged to the hilt, an old car, and a pension. If you file bankruptcy, the lender won't receive one red cent. If you offered the creditor the money that you will otherwise spend on filing bankruptcy, about $1,000, he should (if he's thinking rationally) agree to taken the money and write off the debt. A thousand dollars is still better than nothing. And you avoid having to file bankruptcy.

The success of this kind of strategy depends on convincing your creditor that you're truly prepared to file bankruptcy. The best way to accomplish that is to hire a well-known bankruptcy specialist to handle the negotiation. That way, the creditor knows that you're serious. But, don't ever bluff or threaten bankruptcy unless you're truly prepared to turn in that direction.

Considering Credit Counseling Services

You can find a number of outfits that offer credit counseling. Consumer Credit Counseling Services (CCCS) is the most common. CCCS offices are local nonprofit debt-counseling outfits, numbering about 1,300 and joined under the National Foundation for Consumer Credit.

CCCS acts as an intermediary between you and the creditors. It often gets late fees dropped and wage garnishments revoked. Typically, you and the CCCS counselor devise a repayment schedule, and then you make regular payments to the CCCS, which forwards the money to the creditor.

Creditors pay CCCS a commission on the funds that it collects. Because of this commission, some people claim that CCCS is nothing more than a glorified bill collector. Nevertheless, fees charged to consumers are fairly nominal and usually under $25 a month. Sometimes CCCS even renders its services for free. To find a CCCS near you, call the main office at 800-388-2227, write to the headquarters at 8611 Second Ave., Suite 100, Silver Springs, MD 20910, or check out the National Foundation for Consumer Credit Web page at www. nfcc.org.

CCCS is more helpful to you in either of the following situations:

- ✔ When the total amount of your debts is small enough that you know you can pay if just given enough time.

- ✔ When you intend eventually to file bankruptcy, but need to buy some time. For example, you may be waiting until past-due income taxes become dischargeable.

Terrible advice from a credit counselor

When Joe and Mary's little boy, Ray, was diagnosed with leukemia, they spent all their savings, incurred $50,000 in medical bills, and charged $20,000 on credit cards trying to do the best for Ray. After Ray died, a credit-counseling outfit convinced Joe and Mary to sell the family home and cash in their pensions.

That was bad advice.

Even after surrendering all their assets, Joe and Mary remained $23,000 in the red and still had creditors on their tails. They ultimately ended up in bankruptcy, but, by then, their home and pensions, which would have been preserved had they filed for protection earlier, were long gone.

The credit agency was looking out for creditors and, from Joe and Mary's standpoint, made a rotten situation only that much worse.

Although some organizations like CCCS offer valuable assistance, they're also allied with creditors and have an institutional bias against bankruptcy, even when it's in your best interest.

Some counselors are very good, and, if a person's situation is truly hopeless, they immediately refer that person to a competent bankruptcy attorney. On the other hand, some counselors think that talking people out of filing bankruptcy is their duty. They vigorously push repayment plans, which often are doomed to fail. Additionally, they often fail to have the principal amount of your debts reduced and don't help much in extending payments on secured debts.

Several other organizations offer online debt counseling. Many provide advice about how to get out of debt. As with CCCS, however, you need to be skeptical. Debt-counseling groups, even those with nonprofit status, don't necessarily have your best interests in mind, especially when filing bankruptcy is potentially in your best interest. You may also want to think twice about submitting personal financial information to a stranger.

In any case, here are some of the better known online services and their Web sites:

- **Consolidated Credit Counseling Services:** www.debtfree.org
- **American Consumer Credit Counseling:** www.consumercredit.com
- **Myvesta:** www.myvesta.org

You can also check your local phone book for debt counselors, but be very careful. Many are nothing more than marketing fronts for companies trying to lend you more money. Some are downright crooks. Check out the joint report by the National Consumer Law Center and the Consumer Federation of America at www.nclc.org/initiatives/credit_counseling/content/cc_enforcement.pdf.

Simply Ignoring Creditors

Sometimes doing absolutely nothing makes perfect legal and financial sense, but using that tactic needs to be a conscious and intelligent decision that is not a result of your refusal to face the music.

Whenever you live simply, have little income or property, plan to maintain that lifestyle indefinitely, and don't give a flip about your credit rating, doing nothing may just be the wisest course. You can't go to jail for failure to pay debts (other than support obligations and criminal fines). Creditors can't strip you of basic necessities, such as clothes and food. A good part of your income, as well as Social Security benefits, welfare, and unemployment are inaccessible.

You can be sued, of course, but even bill collectors can't extract blood from a stone.

If you own virtually nothing and plan to own nothing in the foreseeable future, you need to at least consider this option. Creditors recognize the futility of going after some people, don't even bother to sue them, and eventually just give up.

Although the do-nothing strategy may make sense at the moment, this strategy has some limitations.

Your long-lost uncle may leave you a bundle, or maybe you'll win the lottery. If that happens, creditors may find out and try to get a piece of the action.

Even if your ship doesn't come in, you'll always have to be very careful with bank accounts. When a judgment creditor finds out where you bank (and some do periodically check), it can snatch your money. Depositing your money in someone else's account carries its own set of problems, not to mention the danger that a creditor will seize all the money and force your friend to prove just how much belongs to him. So, you may be forced to deal solely in cash or money orders.

In short, before deciding to do nothing, you need to understand and be willing to accept the possible consequences.

Chapter 8

Handling Bill Collectors

*I*t probably seems like yesterday — and it probably was — that credit-card solicitors and hucksters of every stripe were just aching to be your best pal. They just couldn't wait to offer you more and more credit (at higher and higher interest rates).

Well, now that you've missed a few payments, they're singing a different tune. They've turned on you like Brutus on Caesar and unleashed their debt collectors, who play every game in the book to make you feel like a slimeball. They call all the time, suggest that you're going to get sued, and try to squeeze you for whatever they can.

Although some debt collectors are reasonable people just trying to collect what they sincerely believe is legally theirs, many debt collectors, especially the ones working for professional debt collection agencies, are nothing but bullies. They really can't do much of anything, and if you stand up to them, they'll almost certainly back down.

Bill collectors have a grand total of one weapon in their arsenal — intimidation — with all the firepower of a spitball. By comparison, you have an armada in the form of federal and state debt collection laws.

The federal government has provided you with not only a shield but also a sword in the Fair Debt Collection Practices Act, and nearly every state augments that law with its own consumer protection laws.

In this chapter, we take an up close and personal look at bill collectors and review your federal and state remedies for whenever they get nasty.

Taming the Toothless Tiger: The Bill Collector

Creditors with real leverage don't waste time on endless phone calls threatening to sue you or repossess you car; they just do it. Landlords evict. Car lenders repossess. Mortgage holders foreclose. Utility companies turn off the power. Other creditors and their agents huff and puff and try to frighten you with vague promises to take further action (whatever that means), report you to credit bureaus, seize your wages, or turn the matter over to their attorneys.

The key to handling bill collectors is knowing how little power they actually have.

Bill collectors essentially can

- ✔ Cancel your account (big deal)
- ✔ Report you to credit bureaus (they probably already have)
- ✔ Get a lawyer to sue you and get a judgment (easier said than done, which is why some debt collectors put you on hold and pretend to consult with the nonexistent on-site attorney)

But, bill collectors can't

- ✔ Report you to your employer.
- ✔ Publish your name in the newspaper.
- ✔ Embarrass you to family and friends.
- ✔ Take any of your property, at least not until they obtain a judgment by successfully suing you. Even then, most assets are off limits or exempt. A creditor with a judgment may seize your bank account (if you've made the mistake of leaving money in the bank) and roughly 25 percent of your net wages. But the process is complicated, and many creditors don't bother.

When you don't have enough money to go around, the bills to pay first are the ones where creditors can do something (like take your car or foreclose on your house) when you don't pay. Bill collectors are more commonly used to convince you to pay on unsecured debts. They know they're at the bottom of the food chain and are just hoping to get something, anything, out of you.

Giving aggressive bill collectors nothing at all usually is better than giving them a small payment. Whenever they succeed in milking even a few dollars out of you, they're only inspired to keep begging. It's kind of like feeding stray mutts; keep it up, and you'll never get rid of them.

Don't let bill collectors bully you into doing things like calling them at specific times or faxing something to them. These tactics are just an intimidation game. They figure that if they can get you to obey just one command, they've established some weird sort of dominance over you, and the next time, you may come up with a few dollars. In short, you don't have to play games with debt collectors, and you don't have to deal with them at all. So don't.

Invoking Federal Law

Even though bill collectors have no real power, they surely can be a kick in the keister. Congress formally recognized this fact Sept. 20, 1977, when it passed the Fair Debt Collection Practices Act. The FDCPA protects consumers from abusive collection techniques and harassment.

Understanding the FDCPA — and letting your creditors know you understand it — is one of the most effective ways of abruptly putting an end to any overt bullying.

Congress enacted the law after finding abundant evidence that many debt collectors were using abusive, deceptive, and unfair debt-collection practices. It concluded that those kinds of bill-collecting tactics actually increased the number of personal bankruptcies, disrupted marriages, caused joblessness, and invaded individual privacy.

The FDCPA specifies when, where, and how professional debt collectors can contact you concerning a consumer (nonbusiness) debt. It outlaws certain dirty tricks that bill collectors regularly used to employ, and it restricts communications with third persons (such as your boss) concerning your debt.

Under the law, debt collectors can't

- ✔ Call or contact you in any way before 8 a.m. or after 9 p.m., nor at any other unreasonable time or place, without your permission

- ✔ Contact you by postcard

- ✔ Make you accept collect calls or telegrams

- ✔ Use a false name

- ✔ Publish your name and the nature of your debt

- ✔ Threaten to take any action, such as having your wages garnished or initiating a lawsuit, unless they have a legal basis for doing so and truly intend to follow through

  ✔ Threaten to have you arrested

  ✔ Collect any amount greater than your debt, unless specifically authorized to do so by other law

  ✔ Prematurely deposit postdated checks

The FDCPA applies only to those who regularly collect debts owed by others. It doesn't, however, apply to the original creditor.

In other words, if you owe money to the electric company, the collection activities of the electric company aren't restricted by the FDCPA (although they may well be by state statute). And yet, if the electric company hires a collection agency, the Act is triggered. Similarly, the Act doesn't restrain IRS or other governmental employees from acting in their official capacities, but it does apply to private collection agencies hired to collect debts owed to the government.

Additionally, although the original legislation specifically exempted attorneys on the theory that they were only "incidentally involved in debt collection activities," Congress repealed that exemption in 1986. Since then, courts have held lawyers to a pretty high standard. Simply put, attorneys (of all people) must be pretty careful to cross all their T's and dot all their I's when it comes to debt collection. If a collections attorney contacts you, advise him right away that you know your way around the FDCPA. That way, you'll be dealing with a very careful, or a very dumb, lawyer. Either way, you come out on top.

If you believe a debt collector has violated the FDCPA, you can report her to the Federal Trade Commission Correspondence Branch, 600 Pennsylvania Northwest, Washington, DC 20580.

Depending on how badly the debt collector behaved, you may also have grounds for a lawsuit. See the section "Your remedies under the FDCPA," later in the chapter, for more details.

When debt collectors can contact you

Debt collectors can contact you only at reasonable times. They can't contact you any time that they have reason to believe is inconvenient and, in general, may not contact you when they know an attorney represents you. Collectors must tell you that they're calling from a collection agency, and they must identify the original creditor and the amount of the balance. They must tell you that you have 30 days to dispute the debt.

Sending a "bug-off" letter

Under the Federal Fair Debt Collection Practices Act, you can send third-party debt collectors (not the original creditor) what is known as a *cease-and-desist letter* — which is legalese for, "Yo! Take a hike, sucker!"

After receiving this notification, the debt collection agency can't communicate with you further, except to

✔ Advise you that the debt collection efforts are being stopped

✔ Inform you that the collector or creditor intends to do something specific, like sue you

A simple letter, such as this, should do the trick:

Pursuant to the Federal Fair Debt Collection Practices Act, 15 USC§1692c(c), I ask that you stop communicating with me about my account with _____, account number _____. I will take care of this matter when I can.

Although not required, sending your notification by certified mail, return receipt requested, is a good idea, so you have proof that the bill collector received it. Send one copy to the collection agency, one to the original creditor, and one to the Federal Trade Commission.

Sending a cease-and-desist letter does not, of course, eliminate your obligation to repay the debt.

If you tell a bill collector that you're busy and she doesn't terminate the call, or if she calls back when she should realize that you're still busy, she's probably in violation of the law. Ditto if the person answering the phone tells her that you're sleeping. And for the most part, bill collectors can't contact you at all — and that means no calls, no visits, no letters, and no telegrams — if you've notified them in writing to buzz off (see the sidebar, "Sending a 'bug-off' letter" for more information).

Where debt collectors can't contact you

Debt collectors may not contact you at any place that is inconvenient for you or causes you unnecessary embarrassment. They may not contact you at work, if they've been informed that your employer forbids such communication. Furthermore, a bill collector can't contact you at work if she has reason to know that a call would be inconvenient for you, regardless of whether your employer allows such interruptions.

When debt collectors may contact others about your debt

Generally, the FDCPA prohibits debt collectors from contacting *third persons*, or others, about your debt, thus outlawing the once common tactic of trying to shame people into paying a debt. But spouses and guardians aren't considered third persons. So, any time a bill collector contacts you, he can also contact spouses or guardians.

Under the statute, your parents may be contacted only if you're a minor; otherwise, they're considered third persons and are off limits. Others not specifically mentioned in the law — like siblings, uncles, aunts, grandparents, or living companions — always are considered to be third persons.

A debt collector *can* contact your attorney, a credit-reporting agency, and any codebtors. She also can contact any person for the purpose of locating you or obtaining your address, phone number, or place of employment, provided that she doesn't already have that information. But she should never reveal that you owe a debt and generally may not contact the same person more than once. When the collector knows that a lawyer represents you, she must go through the attorney and can't contact others unless the lawyer is unresponsive.

If a creditor has a judgment against you, the collector can also contact others to enforce that judgment.

Dirty tricks are outlawed

The FDCPA forbids debt collectors from engaging in any conduct that tends to harass, oppress, or abuse you. They can't unnecessarily leave messages with a third person for you to return a call, contact you too frequently, imply the use of force against you, use foul language, or threaten to embarrass you.

Additionally, the FDCPA prohibits false, misleading, or unfair practices by debt collectors, including a number of specific practices that creditors have traditionally used to collect debts.

These provisions are especially interesting because they highlight tactics that creditors who aren't subject to the act still may use against you, unless your state has its own law outlawing such ploys.

Of course, the underlying threat of most bill collectors is that you'll be sued if you don't pay up. But a debt collector's threat to sue you can violate this law if the collector doesn't actually intend to do so. With varying success, collectors have tried getting around this rule by saying they "can" sue, or the collector is "authorized" to sue, or recommending that you settle the debt "out of court." One court said that threats to take "drastic action" and engage in "vigorous prosecution," were disguised threats to sue, and the collector violated the law because he never really planned to do so.

ANECDOTE

Collector told to take a hike

Sandy was trying her best to pay her bills but had fallen way behind. Bill collectors were harassing her, calling at all hours, and threatening to tell her employer. Finally, she discovered the Fair Debt Collection Practices Act (FDCPA) and kept a copy of it by the phone.

Whenever bill collectors called, she cited the law verbatim, telling them to take a hike.

That got their attention.

Sandy turned the tables on the bill collectors and sent them running for cover.

Your remedies under the FDCPA

You can sue a debt collector for violating the FDCPA and recover actual damages, punitive damages up to $1,000, and attorney fees. Long shot? Maybe, or maybe not.

Consider this: A Texas jury was so outraged by a credit company's attempt to collect on a $2,000 debt that it awarded the debtors $11 million in damages. Who knows, maybe that pesky debt collector will make you a millionaire! But don't bet on it.

A debt collector still may prevail by proving that he didn't intend to violate the act, and just made an honest mistake.

You must file your suit within one year of the violation.

Tapping State Laws

Under our legal system, laws actually come from two places: legislative bodies that enact statutes, and courts that issue decisions in particular cases that apply to similar situations in the future. This body of court-made law has evolved though the centuries and is known generally as the *common law*. So, although the FDCPA usually doesn't apply to creditors collecting their own debts, state laws may.

State statutes

Almost every state has a statute dealing with abuses by creditors and/or debt collectors.

Although those laws differ greatly from state to state, most states outlaw some or all the conduct that is forbidden under the FDCPA. State statutes, unlike the federal law, generally apply to creditors collecting debts that debtors owe them. You can call your state's attorney general's office or consumer protection agency for a review of local laws.

For a comprehensive analysis, look at Robert J. Hobbs's book, *Fair Debt Collection* (National Consumer Law Center, third edition, 1996). Hobbs's book is the bible for consumer rights lawyers. You can purchase a copy by contacting the National Consumer Law Center, 77 Summer St., 10th Floor, Boston, MA 02110-1006; phone, 617-523-8089.

Common law remedies

Aside from statutory prohibitions, creditors who intentionally misbehave can get into trouble by violating time-honored principles of common decency. In extreme cases, you may be able to sue a creditor or debt collector for things like abuse of process, malicious prosecution, defamation, intentional infliction of emotional distress, and other such wrongs. Talk to a lawyer to find out whether any of these theories applies to your situation, but remember that a creditor's conduct must be pretty outrageous to give rise to a claim under common law.

Keeping Your Dukes Up

Your government — and your society — have determined that overbearing debt collection efforts won't be tolerated. Many debt collectors skirt the law by counting on your ignorance, but when you know your rights and you're ready to exercise them, chances are that overzealous bill collectors will back off in search of easier prey.

If a debt collector can't get any money out of you, she may eventually give up and leave you alone. For that reason, making small payments sometimes is worse than making no payments at all.

You need to be on guard for the following common collections ploys:

✔ Collectors typically use caller ID, so you need to be careful if you want to keep your phone number secret when you call or return a call from a bill collector. You can prevent identification by dialing *67 (1167 for rotary phones) prior to dialing the number, but check with your local phone company because procedures sometimes vary. The *67 remedy, however, won't work when you're calling an 800 or 888 (toll-free) numbers. With toll-free numbers, the only way to evade detection is by using a public phone.

✔ Any FDCPA claim must be listed as an asset in your bankruptcy. In a Chapter 7 liquidation bankruptcy case, only the trustee can prosecute the FDCPA, and any recovery, after paying you the amount of any exemption, would be distributed to your creditors. But when the Chapter 7 trustee doesn't want to bother trying to collect on the claim, she abandons it, and then you're able to prosecute the claim by yourself and keep all proceeds. In a Chapter 13 reorganization bankruptcy, instead of prosecuting the claim herself, the trustee authorizes you to do so. But any recovery you receive is paid into your Chapter 13 plan and distributed to creditors.

✔ Avoid giving a creditor or bill collector a postdated check even (perhaps especially) when they ask you to. Sometimes intentionally writing a check without sufficient funds is a crime and gives the creditor the added leverage of threatening criminal charges or challenging discharge of the debt in bankruptcy.

✔ Be careful not to agree to a payment plan when you're disputing any part of the debt. If a collection notice contains an error, write to the source requesting that the mistake be corrected before formally agreeing to anything. The FDCPA requires debt collection agencies and lawyers to stop collection efforts until they obtain verification of the debt, provided that the consumer's written request is received within 30 days of the collector's giving the consumer notice of the right to dispute the debt. If you don't raise a dispute within this period, you may confront an argument that you've "agreed" that you owe the debt.

✔ If the dispute involves a revolving account, a credit-card account, or an electronic transfer of money, federal regulations provide you 60 days after receiving an erroneous bill within which to send a letter to the creditor indicating a billing error. Even where these laws don't apply, most creditors take a second look at the account whenever the debt is disputed.

✔ Taping a bill collector's call without consent is a dicey proposition. It is, after all, illegal in many states, and unethical for lawyers. But you can refuse to talk to a bill collector unless he agrees to allow you to tape the call. And if a bill collector is dumb enough to leave an abusive message on your answering machine, by all means, save that tape.

Chapter 9

Negotiating with the IRS

*L*ike a lingering cold or an ex-boyfriend, sometimes it seems that you just can't get rid of an old tax bill.

In some situations, bankruptcy may just do the trick (see Chapter 15), but frequently your best shot at relief is negotiating with the Internal Revenue Service (IRS) and hoping it's in a conciliatory mood. You usually can't force Uncle Sam to negotiate, but if he comes to the table, his concessions are legally binding. And, luckily for you, there's never been a better time for dealing with the taxman.

This chapter explains how the IRS goes about getting its (your?) money, describes the logistics and implications of negotiations, discusses how you can negotiate with the IRS while quietly preparing your bankruptcy, and tells you how the government's own taxpayer advocate actually can help you. Ah, your tax dollars at work!

Looking at the Tax Collection Process

The IRS uses three different, and somewhat overlapping, offices to collect taxes:

✔ **Service Centers** are where you file your tax returns. These centers are located in Andover, MA.; Atlanta, GA; Austin, TX; Cincinnati, OH; Fresno, CA; Holtsville, NY; Kansas City, MO; Memphis, TN; Ogden, UT; and Philadelphia, PA.

✔ **Automated Collection System (ACS),** which is a closed-to-the-public command center where scores of clerks sit in front of computer monitors and deal with people only by phone or letter.

✔ **Local offices,** staffed by revenue officers. The people in these offices have some clout, unlike those in the Automated Collection System.

Service centers

If you don't pay the tax due with your return, you are first be sent a polite, nonthreatening letter entitled "Request for Payment" or "Notice of Federal Taxes Due." It's really just a friendly reminder.

When you don't pay within about five weeks of receiving that letter, the Service Center sends the first in a series of four increasingly nasty notices. The first is identified with the number 501, and the last, 504, is a Notice of Intent to Levy (*levy* means "seize your property"). Sending you this series of letters takes about six months. Along the way, you receive Publication 594 (Understanding the Collection Process). If you're heading in this direction, you may want to download the document now from the IRS's Web site at www.irs.gov.

Despite the "Intent to Levy" title of the 504 notice, the IRS probably has no real intention of imposing a levy right away. And although this notice says that it's "final," that just means if you don't pay, your file is transferred to another office. In other words, when you receive a 504 notice, you need to take it seriously without losing a whole lot of sleep.

Automated Collection System (ACS)

ACS has the power to mail further collection notices, negotiate payment arrangements, grab your bank accounts, and intercept your wages. It is essentially faceless. Collectors may not even use their real names, and you probably won't deal with the same official twice.

The ACS is the IRS's notion of efficiency, and its minions try to keep your file within this monument to Murphy's Law whenever possible. However, if you tell them that you don't understand the notices you're receiving, and that you can't agree with what the IRS says you owe, your file should be transferred to a local office. Then, you can deal with a real, honest-to-goodness bureaucrat.

Keeping your eye on the statute of limitations

The Internal Revenue Service essentially has ten years to collect a tax. After that, the tax vanishes. The ten-year clock normally begins ticking shortly after you filed your return when the tax is assessed.

But there's a glitch.

If you don't file a return, the statute of limitations never starts, and a *dummy return,* one that's filed in your name by the IRS, doesn't count.

Figuring out when the statute of limitations begins and expires can be pretty tricky because the clock stops and starts like so many hiccups. For example, a bankruptcy filing *tolls,* or suspends, the statute during the period your case is pending, plus an additional six months.

You also toll the statute of limitations when you

✔ Request a taxpayer assistance order

✔ Make an offer in compromise (see the upcoming section "Submitting an Offer in Compromise")

✔ Sign a waiver of the statute

✔ Ask for a collection due process hearing

Although the IRS has the power to go to court to extend the statute before it expires, it won't; unless you owe a king's ransom or you've been a pain-in-the-butt chronic tax protestor.

Local revenue officers

If the ACS can't collect the tax, or if you've so requested, you hear from a revenue officer. Although looking at a tax collector face to face is a little scarier than just talking with someone on the phone, it may well be preferable to dealing with the ACS, especially when the officer can suspend collection activities by concluding that there's no way you can pay anything.

Making Nice with the Touchy-Feely IRS

Taxpayers and courts long have complained, and with good reason, about the overbearing presence of the Internal Revenue Service. The IRS and its cadre of bureaucrats from you-know-where seemed to relish its guilty-until-proven-innocent-and-even-then-still-guilty attitude.

A few years ago, however, Congress conducted a bunch of hearings and got an earful from constituents who felt like the IRS was treating them like axe murderers. Those hearings resulted in legislation imposing a wide range of restrictions on the collection efforts of the IRS. So now, after years of nurturing its reputation as a bulldog, the Internal Revenue Service is trying to embrace something of a teddy-bear image. It really has become far more accommodating, if not exactly cuddly.

The kinder, gentler IRS is considerably less arrogant and appreciably more humble than it once was. And with all the new procedures, IRS collection efforts have become so burdensome that authorities are more willing to settle than ever before.

As part of its new image, the IRS maintains a very useful Web site (www.irs. gov), where you can find all the official IRS forms, instructions, and other helpful information mentioned in this chapter.

Your due process

One of the reforms, known as *collection due process,* took effect in January 1999 and requires the IRS to give you at least 30 days warning before seizing your property and to notify you of your right to appeal its determinations.

The appeal, which first is heard by the IRS Appeals Office, provides you with an opportunity to claim that you're an *innocent spouse* (where your wife or husband fudged a joint tax return without telling you) or determine the appropriateness of an asset seizure and the correctness of the amount the IRS claims is due. More important, the taxpayer can also propose alternative payment plans such as *installment agreements* or *offers in compromise* (see the upcoming sections in this chapter). If the appeals office turns you down, you can go to federal court and have a judge review the situation. All these new procedural safeguards must take place before any of your property is actually seized.

Negotiating an installment agreement

When you owe less than $25,000, getting the IRS to accept a payment proposal is actually pretty easy. A government that can get what it wants (your money) with a minimum of hassle makes for happy bean counters.

An installment agreement requires that you

- Make all payments on time
- File all future tax returns and pay the taxes due on those returns in full
- Furnish updated financial information whenever requested
- Agree that any state or federal refunds be applied to your unpaid taxes

If your file is still with the Service Center, you can use Form 9465 Installment Agreement Request. This form doesn't require any supporting information about your ability to pay. All you do is plug in the amount you can afford to pay each month and mail it. The IRS normally responds within about 30 days. You may want to take a look at *Taxes For Dummies*, an annual by Eric Tyson and David Silverman (Wiley Publishing, Inc.). It includes a section about filing this form (among other tax pointers).

Your offer is likely to be accepted if the payment you propose takes care of your total tax debt, including interest and penalties that continue to accrue, within 36 months.

If, on the other hand, your file has been transferred to ACS or your local district office, you need to tell the collector that you want to make an installment agreement and indicate how much you can afford to pay. If your offer is rejected, stop! Get professional help.

Knowing when to get professional help

If you owe $25,000 or more or your request for an installment agreement has been denied, we suggest that you hire a lawyer or accountant who is experienced in dealing with the IRS.

At this juncture, the IRS can and does insist on detailed information about all your assets and your family's income and living expenses.

The Service Center and ACS use Form 433-F. Other offices use Form 433-A for individuals and Form 433-B for businesses and self-employed individuals. These forms generally are referred to as Collection Information Statements (CIS).

From the IRS's perspective, the CIS are good for

- ✔ Detailing total household income and expenses

- ✔ Measuring your expenses against IRS guidelines, which the collector may fine-tune to fit your individual situation

- ✔ Telling the IRS where all your assets are located, which facilitates seizure in the event negotiations fall through or you end up defaulting on your agreement

The IRS normally requires payments equal to all your net income minus *necessary living expenses.* Some collection employees have pretty bizarre notions of how much it costs to live and demand completely unrealistic payment plans. But your lawyer or accountant may be able to have such functionaries overruled by the bosses. What's the point in agreeing to a payment structure that you can't meet, especially when you complete a CIS telling the IRS exactly where to get at each of your assets?

If the CIS show that you have any liquid assets — such as cash, stock, or bonds — equal to the amount of tax you owe, the IRS demands immediate payment and may insist that you take cash advances or use credit cards to pay taxes.

Although you can now pay taxes with major credit cards, that's probably not a good idea for anyone considering bankruptcy, because

- ✔ Loans to pay nondischargeable federal taxes also are nondischargeable.
- ✔ Credit-card issuers commonly assess special fees when the card is used to pay taxes.

Gaining "uncollectible" status

If the IRS determines that collecting the tax creates an undue hardship, it may suspend collection efforts indefinitely. (In IRS-speak, the account is "53'd," based on the number of the form the revenue officer must complete when reporting that an account is uncollectible.)

Undue hardship means that you're unable to meet necessary living expenses if required to make installment payments or if the IRS seizes your assets. The agency distinguishes between undue hardship and *mere inconvenience* — usually finding in favor of the former when it thinks pursuing you isn't worthwhile and finding the latter when going after your assets may be worthwhile.

However, even with an undue hardship, your tax isn't abated. Taxes and penalties continue to accrue, and tax liens aren't released. And, of course, the IRS continues to grab your refunds.

The ten-year statute of limitations on collection continues to run, however, and the IRS typically reopens the account right before the statute is about to expire, most likely in an attempt to intimidate you into signing a waiver of the statute of limitations. Don't do it! See a tax specialist!

Planning bankruptcy while pursuing an installment agreement

You and your lawyer need to be keenly aware of how an installment agreement can affect a bankruptcy down the road. You must consider

- ✔ **The statute of limitations on collection:** If the term of an installment agreement expires less than one year before the ten-year statute of limitations, the IRS can insist that you agree to extend it for up to five more years, and that's something you need to consider with extreme care. You may be better off putting up with the IRS for a little longer and letting the statute of limitations expire. Then, you're home free.

- ✔ **The time restrictions for wiping out taxes through bankruptcy:** An installment agreement doesn't extend the various time periods that must pass before taxes are rendered dischargeable in bankruptcy.

✓ **Tax liens:** Taxes may be much more difficult to wipe out or manage in bankruptcy when a tax lien has been filed. Under current policy, if the amount due under an installment agreement is less than $25,000, the IRS won't file a lien (although it may already have done so under previous procedures). In other cases, the IRS can postpone filing a lien as long as you're honoring your installment agreement.

✓ **Allocating tax payments:** When you make installment payments, you designate how your payments are applied. Requiring the IRS to apply payments to the most recent years usually is best. As time goes by, taxes for the earlier years become dischargeable if you end up filing bankruptcy.

Submitting an Offer in Compromise

Unlike a payment agreement, an offer in compromise that the IRS accepts actually results in a reduction in the amount you owe. After getting its wrists slapped by Congress, the IRS is more willing to make a deal than ever before.

Checking out Forms 656 and 656-A (and their accompanying instructions), which you can download from the IRS Web site, gives you a good idea of what's required. However, you need to seek out professional help when actually preparing and submitting an offer. Some accountants and attorneys now specialize in helping folks submit offers in compromise.

The grounds (three exist) for an offer in compromise are

✓ Doubt about whether you actually owe the tax.

✓ Doubt about whether you have sufficient assets and income to pay the tax in full.

✓ Exceptional hardship or unfair or inequitable circumstances caused by payment in-full requirements. (This last one is brand new and its contours will have to be developed.)

When determining how much it will accept in settlement, the IRS looks at your present assets and future earning ability. It calculates how much it would receive from a quick sale of all your assets and adds a lump-sum amount based on what it figures you'd have been able to pay on taxes during the next 48 months.

If you can pay this amount in a lump sum within 90 days, the IRS is likely to accept your offer. If not, you can request up to two years to pay, but the amount increases to whatever the IRS thinks you can pay over 60 months rather than 48 months. However, taxpayers who have less than four years left on the ten-year statute of limitations need offer only the amount they can pay for the period remaining under the statute. Even if you can't pay that amount, don't give up. Given its new attitude and growing backlog, the IRS may accept substantially less, so making such an offer definitely is worth a try.

The disadvantages of making an offer in compromise are

- ✔ It doesn't resolve state tax debts.

- ✔ It may delay the time for filing bankruptcy. One condition for discharging a tax in either a Chapter 7 or Chapter 13 bankruptcy is that it had to be assessed more than 240 days before the bankruptcy is filed. If you file bankruptcy within 240 days of submitting an offer in compromise, the clock stops. In other words, you must wait for a period of time equal to the sum of 240 days, plus the time your offer was pending, plus 30 days before your taxes can be discharged in bankruptcy.

- ✔ If you later default on future tax liabilities, the tax liabilities that were forgiven are revived. The IRS keeps the offered sum, and you have to pay that remaining balance on the original tax along with interest and penalties.

- ✔ Making an offer extends the ten-year statute of limitations by the period that your offer is under consideration plus an additional year.

Getting Help from a Taxpayer Advocate

A taxpayer advocate operates under the IRS Problem Resolution Program. Such an advocate is supposed to act on your behalf whenever you're suffering a *significant hardship* (being treated harshly or unfairly) because of the way the IRS is administering the tax laws. An advocate has authority to issue taxpayer assistance orders, which can, at least temporarily, stop collection activities.

A taxpayer advocate is at your disposal and can be reached by

- ✔ Contacting your local taxpayer advocate office

- ✔ Calling toll free 877-777-4778

- ✔ Sending Form 911 to the local taxpayer advocate office

You can find out the address and phone number of the local taxpayer advocate office and obtain copies of Form 911 by contacting your local IRS District Office.

Disadvantages of a taxpayer assistance order are that

- ✔ It suspends the statute of limitations for whatever amount of time the matter is under consideration.

- ✔ Any time during which a taxpayer assistance order is in effect doesn't count toward tax periods that normally would apply toward discharging taxes.

Part III
Keeping Your Stuff

The 5th Wave   By Rich Tennant

"I bought a software program that should help us monitor and control our spending habits, and while I was there, I picked up a few new games, a couple of screen savers, 4 new mousepads, this nifty pull out keyboard cradle..."

In this part . . .

*I*n the not-so-good old days, creditors could literally take the shirt off your back when you couldn't pay your bills. Those days are gone — despite the best efforts of some mean-spirited folks who drafted the Bankruptcy Abuse Reform Fiasco (BARF) of 2005. Yeah, you may lose some of your property if you go bankrupt and the new law will make it all more of a hassle, but when all is said and done, much of your stuff is strictly off-limits to creditors. This part explains what's yours, what may go to the creditors, and what you can do to keep your most important possessions out of the paws and claws of your creditors.

Chapter 10

Understanding Which Assets Are Off Limits to Creditors

*A*lthough you may lose some of your property by filing bankruptcy, the days when creditors could quite literally take the shirt off your back are long gone. Much of what you need and treasure most is *exempt*, which means creditors can't touch it. So, knowing what's all yours, what isn't, and what is of equal interest to your creditors — who obviously are eager to grab anything they can get their paws on — is really important.

In this chapter, you get the scoop on which assets you can keep, which ones you may have to surrender, and how to make the most of it.

Grasping the Legal Concepts

Gaining an understanding of how bankruptcy affects your possessions means that you need to understand two legal concepts:

- ✔ **Property of the estate,** which includes everything you own on the *petition date* (when you file bankruptcy), some things you acquire later, and other assets that a trustee (the guy who represents the interests of creditors; see Chapter 3) can recover under some circumstances

- ✔ **Exemptions,** which enable you to remove certain assets from the bankruptcy process and take them out of the reach of creditors

The principles behind property of the estate and exemptions are important in Chapter 7 liquidations and Chapter 13 reorganizations.

Even when an asset isn't subject to the bankruptcy process, a creditor with a security interest may cause you grief. (We take a closer look at this problem in Chapters 11 and 12.)

Under Chapter 7 bankruptcy laws, you may lose any asset that is property of the estate unless it is exempt.

In a Chapter 13 reorganization, your minimum payments are determined by the value of your nonexempt property. For example, if the value of your nonexempt property were $7,500, you'd have to pay at least that much during the life of your Chapter 13 plan or sell an individual item and pay the proceeds to the trustee.

If one of your prized possessions is property of the estate and not covered by an exemption, you can be required to give it up or pay its value to the trustee regardless of which way you file — Chapter 7 or Chapter 13. The difference is that in Chapter 7 you must pay for it in a couple of months, but in Chapter 13, you can stretch out payments for up to five years.

By answering the following three general questions about an asset, you can figure out whether a bankruptcy trustee has dibs on it or can make you pay its value:

✔ Is it property of the estate? In other words, do you own it?

✔ What is the value of your interest in the asset? The trustee doesn't care about things worth only a few dollars.

✔ Does an exemption protect the asset? If so, neither trustees nor creditors (unless a particular creditor has a lien; see Chapter 11) can get their mitts on it.

Digging through the property of the estate

The first thing you need to know about an asset is whether it's considered property of the estate. That category includes

✔ Just about every asset you own when you file bankruptcy.

✔ Proceeds from property of the estate. For example, if your rental unit is property of the estate, any rents that you receive, even after you file, are also property of the estate.

✔ Inheritances and life insurance proceeds, if your benefactor dies before bankruptcy or within 180 days after your filing.

✔ Marital property divisions that you become entitled to receive within 180 days after the petition date.

✔ Property you transferred prior to bankruptcy that was recovered when the trustee flexed his strong-arm powers to undo the transfer. See Chapter 19 for more on how trustees have the power to nullify certain transfers of property.

Figuring out your interest in the property

If you own an asset jointly with someone else, ordinarily the trustee can deal only with your chunk — not the half owned by your brother-in-law. But your piece of the pie may well be on the line.

When an asset at issue serves as collateral for a debt, the creditor has ownership rights in the item that are superior to yours or the trustee's. If, for example, your car is worth $10,000 and is subject to an $8,000 secured loan, your interest in the car is only $2,000 ($10,000 – $8,000).

Spouses frequently own their homes jointly, which means each has an undivided one-half interest.

In most states, each spouse's property interests are separate, even though an asset may be jointly owned. If you and your spouse own your home jointly, each of you has a one-half interest. So, if you file bankruptcy, your wife's share of the house won't become property of the estate, unless, of course, she also files for bankruptcy (keeping in mind that you can, but don't have to, file a joint bankruptcy petition).

Do you really own it?

An asset owned by someone else doesn't become part of your bankruptcy just because you have it in your possession, and even an asset titled to you isn't necessarily your property. The pretzel-logic of that concept is easier understood with a few examples:

✔ The chain saw that you borrowed from your neighbor isn't included in your bankruptcy just because it's stored in your shed.

✔ If you're an authorized signer on your elderly uncle's bank account, the account doesn't become part of your bankruptcy when all the money really belongs to him.

✔ Property belonging to your children isn't included in your bankruptcy, but you may be considered to be the real owner of expensive items like a go-kart or motorized toy Jeep that aren't usually owned by minor children.

✔ When your name is on the title to your teenager's car, you can probably convince the trustee that the vehicle doesn't actually belong to you — provided, that is, your kid used his own money to buy it. If you bought it for him, the trustee will insist that you really do own it or, even if you don't own it, that he can go after it.

However, the score's a little different when you happen to live in one of the nine community property states — Arizona, California, Idaho, Louisiana, Nevada, New Mexico, Texas, Washington, or Wisconsin. In those states, all property acquired by either spouse during the marriage is considered community property. Common exceptions are gifts and inheritances received by one spouse during the marriage. Property acquired prior to marriage typically doesn't become community property.

In the community property states, all community property (as well as the individual property of the filing spouse) becomes property of the estate even when only one spouse files bankruptcy. Individual property of the nonfiling spouse doesn't, however, become property of the estate.

Knowing what happens when someone owes you money

If someone owes you money on the date that you file bankruptcy, that debt is considered an asset that is property of the estate, even when it isn't paid until later. So, for example, the income tax refund you're expecting in the current year is considered property of the estate, even if you don't receive it until after the petition date.

Accrued wages likewise are included in the estate, even though you won't receive them until after the petition date. Why? They actually were earned before you filed. It sounds confusing, but thinking it through really isn't that difficult.

Say that you have a job where you're paid weekly. Your paycheck usually covers the previous week's work, not the current one, so the employer is always a week behind. That means that if you file bankruptcy on the day after payday, your employer owes you one week's pay as of that date. For bankruptcy purposes, the wages you have earned before the petition date become property of the estate, even though you haven't yet received them.

Don't sweat it too much. As we point out in the next section, most, if not all, of that money ultimately will be covered by an exemption for wages anyhow.

Understanding how exemptions work

Determining which assets are up for grabs in bankruptcy is pretty tricky — especially under BARF. The Bankruptcy Code contains a list of exemptions, and each state has its own as well. Thirty-four states have opted out of the Bankruptcy Code exemption, so theoretically residents of those states must stick with state exemptions. If you live in one of the 16 states that recognize both state and federal exemptions, you can choose whichever set works best for you.

Lottery winner ends up in bankruptcy

Bennie won $3 million in the state lottery, which was payable in annual installments of $128,000. During the next six years, he spent so much money that he had to file bankruptcy. The court declared the balance of Bennie's winnings property of the estate, including the installment payments that he expected to come due after bankruptcy.

Applying the rules, however, is an easier-said-than-done proposition. Here's why:

✔ You generally apply the law of the state of your permanent home for the two years (actually 730 days) before bankruptcy. If, for example, you lived in the same state two years ago as you do now, the laws of your present state apply.

✔ If you haven't lived in your present home state for two years, the applicable exemptions are those available in the state where you lived for 180 days immediately prior to that two-year period, or for the longer portion of this 180-day period than any other state — at least theoretically. Some state exemption laws say that they're only for residents of that state. Say that Sam moved from Oregon (which limits exemptions to Oregon residents) to Washington and filed bankruptcy in Washington within two years. Under BARF, the Oregon exemptions apply. But Oregon law offers its exemptions only to current residents of Oregon — and Sam the Travelin' Man now lives in Washington. So poor Sammy doesn't get the benefit of either Oregon or Washington exemptions, right? Even the purveyors of BARF didn't think that was fair, so they cobbled together a provision so that people like Sam can use the Bankruptcy Code exemptions even in states that have theoretically opted out of the Bankruptcy Code list. In other words, Sam gets to use the Bankruptcy Code exemptions even though his home state of Oregon says that he doesn't.

You're not legally domiciled in a state just because you live there. *Domicile* is your permanent home, the place you intend to return to after you finish school, your tour of military duty, or your business assignment. Say that you grew up in New York and went off to school in Tennessee, intending to return when your studies were complete. For legal purposes, you were always domiciled in New York, even when you were living in Memphis.

ANECDOTE

Buying Florida mansion nearly backfires on Buffalo boy

The kids were gone and the mortgage was paid off, so Bart decided to leave the ad agency where he'd toiled for 30 years and retire to Florida. He sold the house in Western New York for $315,000 and put the money toward a new home in Daytona Beach. But after four years in Florida, Bart was broke. His lawyer told him that because he had lived in Florida more than two years and acquired his home more than 1,215 days before bankruptcy, the unlimited Florida homestead exemption would protect his home in bankruptcy. But when Bart filed, creditors still tried to have his home liquidated.

It was a close call, but the bankruptcy court sided with Bart. The judge was convinced that Bart planned to retire to Florida before he ran into financial trouble. Otherwise, the court may well have allowed the trustee to sell Bart's new home to pay off creditors. Bart escaped financial ruin by the skin of his teeth.

In addition, even if you've lived in a state more than two years, the maximum homestead exemption you could claim (even if the laws of that state allowed more) would be $125,000 if you acquired your homestead within 1,215 days of bankruptcy — unless you bought the home with money from the sale of a home you owned prior to that 1,215 day period. Example: Say that within 1,215 days of bankruptcy, you sold your first home, which you'd owned for more than 1,215 days, and put $30,000 toward the purchase of your present home. The homestead limit of $125,000 would be increased by $30,000 to $155,000 — provided that your state had a homestead exemption that high — unless the creditor could prove that during the ten-year period preceding bankruptcy, you acquired a homestead for the purpose of stiffing creditors. Honestly, armies of little trolls in Washington lie awake dreaming up this stuff!

Determining the Value of Your Stuff

After figuring out which set of exemption laws apply, you need to calculate how much your property is worth. This calculation must be based not on the cost of replacing your stuff with new items but rather on what it would cost to obtain similar things in used condition. Some things such as an ongoing business or a lawsuit from which you can recover money are extremely difficult to value. Your lawyer should be able to help you in those cases. For the simpler stuff, the following list gives you a basic idea of what your stuff is worth:

✔ **Household goods:** The value of household goods is what a secondhand store would charge or the asking price for similar goods offered for sale in newspaper classified ads. You might also check on www.ebay.com to see whether you can find similar items for sale.

✔ **Automobiles:** You can check all three auto price guides — the *Black Book, Kelley Blue Book,* and *NADA* Guide — by logging on www.cudirect.com. The NADA Guide usually yields the highest price because it assumes that all vehicles are in good condition. Another way to assess the value of your car is to check classified ads in your local newspaper for similar models for sale. Go by the retail rather than wholesale or trade-in value.

✔ **Real property:** Valuing real property depends on where you live. But a good starting point may be finding out the figure used by your local tax assessor — commonly known as the *assessed value*. But in some venues, assessed values are ridiculously inaccurate. If you only recently purchased the property, a better indication is the price that you paid.

Appraisals are great for determining value, but watch out: Appraisals that are completed for loan purposes frequently tend to be high because many lenders encourage appraisers to inflate values to justify making a loan. The same is true of listing prices. Some real estate agents overstate the value of your property to attract your business. We take a closer look at valuing your home in Chapter 11.

✔ **Pensions and life insurance:** You usually can place a dollar amount on your pensions and life insurance policies by calling the company.

Understanding How the Courts View Certain Assets

Special rules govern the way certain property — such as homes, cars, household items, and so on — is treated in bankruptcy. We discuss the most common in this section.

Homesteads

Almost all states have some type of homestead exemption that protects some or all the *equity* in a debtor's home. Additionally, the Bankruptcy Code provides each debtor with a homestead exemption of $18,450. The exemption is doubled ($36,900) for joint owners. This amount (as well as the amount for all the other exemptions specified in the Bankruptcy Code) is adjusted every three years by the government to reflect changes in the Consumer Price Index (CPI). The next change takes effect April 1, 2007. (We discuss homestead exemptions in much more detail in Chapter 12. Chapter 12 can help you figure out the extent to which your home is protected by a homestead exemption.)

Automobiles

Most states allow debtors to exempt at least one motor vehicle, but the amount of the exemption is limited. The federal exemption scheme allows each debtor to claim $2,950 in a motor vehicle.

Whenever the equity in your car exceeds your total exemption, a Chapter 7 trustee can sell the car and pay you the value of your exemption.

For example, when your motor vehicle exemption is $1,500, and your car is worth $2,500, the trustee can sell your car but has to pay you $1,500. You're usually given the opportunity to keep your car by paying the net amount that the trustee would receive from selling the vehicle.

In a Chapter 13, the trustee can't sell the car, but you'd have to pay the amount of nonexempt equity ($1,000 in the previous Chapter 7 example) over the life of the bankruptcy plan.

You also may be able to claim an exemption for your motor vehicle as a *tool of the trade* — if that's what it is. For example, a professional driver's semi rig is likely to qualify, and a specially modified pickup truck used by a carpenter probably fits the bill. But you're really pushing your luck if you try for an exemption on the Mercedes sports car that you use to impress your sales clients.

See Chapter 10 for more on what happens to your car if you file bankruptcy.

Household goods

Most states exempt household goods up to a specified dollar amount. The federal Bankruptcy Code exemption for household goods exempts single items up to a value of $475 and all items up to a total of $9,850.

Occasionally, a question is raised about whether a particular item qualifies as a household good — for example, a firearm. Several courts have said they guns don't qualify; however, another ruling indicates that a pistol used for defense of the family was a household good, but that a shotgun and rifle used for sporting purposes were not.

Tenancy by the entirety

Some jurisdictions recognize an ancient form of husband-and-wife property ownership known as *tenancy by the entirety*, which protects joint property from creditors of only one spouse. The effect of such a rule is that under some circumstances, jointly owned property may be fully exempt when only one spouse files bankruptcy (if no joint creditors are involved) or partially exempt after claims of joint creditors are satisfied.

Jurisdictions recognizing tenancy by the entirety are Delaware, the District of Columbia, Florida, Hawaii, Illinois, Indiana, Maryland, Massachusetts, Michigan, Mississippi, Missouri, North Carolina, Pennsylvania, Rhode Island, Vermont, Virginia, and Wyoming.

Courts also seem to be having trouble deciding whether a computer is a household good. Some courts say that a computer qualifies, and others say the exact opposite. A local lawyer familiar with the courts in your area can be a big help in figuring out what may or may not be exempt.

Inheritances and life insurance benefits

Any inheritance or life insurance benefits left to you by someone who dies before or within 180 days after you file for bankruptcy become property of the estate.

However, if the benefactor passes away before you file bankruptcy, you may be able to find a way of preventing your inheritance from going to the trustee. In some states, you can renounce an inheritance before you actually receive it so that it goes to other heirs. This strategy, however, is very tricky and features many pitfalls. It's definitely something to bring up with your lawyer.

Divorce settlements

Many times, divorce and bankruptcy go hand in hand.

If you become entitled to a divorce property settlement within 180 days after your petition date, the property can be used to pay creditors. These rules apply to property divisions (where a divorce court splits assets and allocates debts) but not to alimony or support, which usually are exempt.

Sometimes filing bankruptcy and then waiting 180 days before filing for divorce is a better strategy. This way, any property you are awarded in the divorce won't be swept into your bankruptcy and liquidated to pay creditors. And, of course, make sure that your divorce lawyer knows about your bankruptcy plans, and your bankruptcy lawyer knows about your divorce. See Chapter 17 for more about divorce settlements.

Spendthrift trusts

A *trust* is a time-honored way for a wise benefactor to make a generous gift to a young or reckless beneficiary without throwing caution to the wind. Legal title to the property is transferred to a trustee (not to be confused with a bankruptcy trustee) with specific instructions so that the beneficiary doesn't blow the entire inheritance.

Typically, the document establishing the trust includes a *spendthrift provision*, which says the beneficiary's creditors can't touch the assets of the trust.

A beneficiary's interest in a valid spendthrift trust doesn't become property of his bankruptcy estate because

- ✔ Creditors of the beneficiary never had any claim against the benefactor.
- ✔ The beneficiary can't force the trust's trustee to distribute trust property to him, and neither can creditors or a bankruptcy trustee.

There are two kinds of trusts:

- ✔ *Intervivos trusts:* Trusts that are effective while a benefactor is still alive
- ✔ *Testamentary trusts:* Trusts that don't go into effect until after the benefactor dies

If you're the beneficiary of a testamentary trust, any distributions you actually receive from the trust within 180 days after filing bankruptcy become property of the estate.

In addition, any distributions you receive from either type of trust are considered disposable income in a Chapter 13 case.

Although courts show considerable deference for legitimate trusts, they're not at all fond of scams or shams. Courts won't honor spendthrift restrictions in trusts that actually are manipulations designed to protect the donor's property from his own creditors. You can't place your own property in a trust for yourself just to keep it away from your creditors. Some self-anointed "experts" touting "living trusts" may tell you differently. Don't believe them. Too often, debtors end up losing property they'd normally keep, except they tried to con their creditors. Don't get cute.

Furthermore, you can't serve as sole trustee and sole beneficiary of the trust at the same time, even when someone else sets it up. The courts aren't going to enable you to shield money when you have sole discretion over how and when it's distributed.

The most important point about trusts is that the rules are technical and extremely tricky. Your lawyer needs to review all trust documents to determine whether you're risking your interest in the trust by filing bankruptcy.

Rent receipts

Any income earned by property of the estate is itself property of the estate. So, be careful if you're a landlord — the trustee may have a claim to any rents received from your property after the petition date.

If you rent out a part of your home, rents coming in after the petition date may be covered by your homestead exemption, but check this situation out with your attorney before spending the money.

When rent comes in from property that is not part of your home, it won't be covered by a homestead exemption. You may, however, be allowed to use rent receipts to make postpetition mortgage payments on the rental property.

You need to receive the trustee's consent or your attorney's approval before using rent receipts to pay the mortgage; otherwise, you may have to reimburse the estate for any rents that you paid out after the petition date. Just imagine the predicament you'd be in if you had already spent the money for something else!

Security deposits

Occasionally, a trustee tries to claim a debtor's rent deposit, contending that the debtor must pay the amount of the deposit into the estate. Doing so, in our opinion, is tantamount to extortion, and courts tend to shoot down the trustee's claim for one of two reasons: Your landlord is entitled to continued possession of the deposit; or, it was protected under the homestead exemption.

However, before taking any action or making any assumptions, talk it over with your attorney.

Wages

As we mention in the "Knowing what happens when someone owes you money" section earlier in this chapter, wages that you have earned, but not yet received, as of the petition date are property of the estate, even when they aren't paid until afterward. Nevertheless, a large portion of your wages is exempt. Under federal law, the estate can't claim any more than 25 percent of the net wages that are due to you on the petition date. In some states, you get to keep even more money.

Sometimes a question arises about whether money that is due to a debtor qualifies as wages. Courts disagree on whether accounts receivable can be considered exemptible wages, even when the debtor is sole owner of the business.

You can minimize the amount of wages that are at risk by filing your petition soon after your payday. Of course, you want to spend this money (your pay) before filing because the funds on hand as of the petition date would also be property of the estate.

Bank accounts

Money in your checking and savings accounts typically is property of the estate, unless you can demonstrate that all or part of the account balance belongs to someone else.

Be careful when dealing with checks that haven't yet cleared when you file bankruptcy. That money technically is still in the bank, and the trustee can make you pay the estate the amounts of any checks that clear after you've filed. For that reason, using cashier's checks or money orders to make payments (like your house payment) right before you file bankruptcy is a good idea.

You may be able to exempt all or part of a bank account, however, when the money in the account is traceable to some exempt source such as Social Security benefits. Most states also allow modest exemptions for cash and bank accounts.

Severance and vacation pay

Other factors to watch out for include whether your job entitles you to severance pay or whether you're entitled to cash in on accumulated vacation time.

The trustee can't, of course, force you to quit your job. However, if you decide to terminate your employment while your bankruptcy case still is open, the trustee may claim these kinds of benefits by arguing that they actually are compensation for services rendered prior to bankruptcy. Nevertheless, a portion of your severance pay may be covered by your exemption for wages.

However, be forewarned that a trustee may be able to cash in your vacation. Courts differ about whether a portion of vacation pay is exempt. In one case, on the petition date, the debtor was entitled to severance pay consisting of accrued wages and vacation pay. The court ruled that the portion of severance pay attributable to accrued wages qualified for the 75 percent wages exemption, but the vacation pay did not.

Sales commissions

A couple of thorny issues arise when the debtor is a commission salesperson.

The first is finding out whether an unpaid commission actually was earned prior to bankruptcy. If so, it's property of the estate even though the debtor doesn't receive it until after the petition date. After the issue is decided, the question turns to whether a portion of the unpaid commission qualifies for exemption as wages. If the court concludes that the commission wasn't earned until after bankruptcy, it's yours and not property of the estate. In this situation, it doesn't matter whether it would be considered as exempt wages.

Real estate commissions

Real estate sales commissions are especially tricky because agents put a great deal of work into their deals, but don't actually receive a commission until the sale goes through. What if a real estate agent files bankruptcy before a deal actually closes?

Some courts say that a commission paid from a sale that closes after the petition date is not property of the estate because the commission wasn't actually earned until after bankruptcy. Other courts would determine whether a commission was earned before bankruptcy by figuring out how much work the real estate agent performed prior to filing the bankruptcy petition. For example, say a real estate salesperson, in putting together a sale, performed 90 percent of the work before bankruptcy. Some courts would say that 90 percent of the commission is property of the estate.

Insurance commissions

Issues similar to those that come up with real estate agents also occur when an insurance agent files bankruptcy. Typically, insurance agents automatically receive a commission every time one of their policyholders renews.

Trustees frequently try to latch on to commissions received by insurance agents that are the result of postpetition renewals of policies they sold before filing bankruptcy. The trustees' argument is based on the premise that all the work was done when the original policy was sold, so they want renewal commissions treated like accounts receivable owed on the petition date.

Insurance agents counter that policyholders won't renew unless the agent continues to service the account. Therefore, renewal commissions, in the view of insurance agents, result from work they perform after the petition date and thus aren't property of the estate.

Some courts accept the trustee's argument, some lean toward the agent's, and others try to strike a Solomonic balance by attempting to figure out how much of a commission is attributable to prepetition work and how much to postpetition efforts.

Under this approach, only that portion of the commissions resulting from prepetition efforts is property of the estate. The rest goes to the debtor.

Similar to real estate commissions, the next question becomes whether renewal commissions are exempt as wages. Again, courts disagree. Some say that the exemption for wages is limited to the classic employer/employee relationship and that commissions are more like business profits. Other courts aren't as strict and say that commissions qualify as wages for exemption purposes.

Suits to recover money

If you had the right to sue someone when you filed bankruptcy, any recovery you receive from that suit is considered property of the estate, even if you didn't receive the money until after bankruptcy.

However, determining whether part or all personal-injury awards qualify for an exemption depends on whether the award is for past earnings, medical bills, pain and suffering, or future earnings. If at all possible, you need to settle the claim before filing bankruptcy. Doing so enables your attorney to structure a settlement that maximizes the amount that you can claim as exempt.

Many exemption statutes say that personal-injury awards for loss of future earnings *are* exempt but yet those for pain and suffering *are not.* Your lawyer can devise a settlement agreement in which most of the award is allocated to items that normally are exempt. Be sure to tell your personal-injury lawyer that you're thinking about bankruptcy and insist that he have a bankruptcy specialist review any settlement documents before you sign them.

Depending on local law, your lawyer may advise you to file bankruptcy after reaching a settlement but before you receive the money. In any event, funds received from the settlement need to be placed in a separate bank account so that they can be identified as the proceeds from your personal-injury claim.

If the claim can't be settled before bankruptcy, a Chapter 7 trustee can conversely take over the prosecution of the suit and thereby control the structure of the settlement so that it maximizes the part that is not exempt.

So, one strategy is to file Chapter 13 to control prosecution and settlement and then dismiss and file under Chapter 7. However, this strategy is pretty tricky and needs to be thoroughly reviewed by your lawyer.

Income tax refunds

An income tax refund attributable to the year in which bankruptcy is filed — and for any tax year ending before that — is property of the estate, even though you don't receive the refund until after the petition date. (Actually, a refund is prorated for the year in which the bankruptcy is filed. If, for example, you filed November 18, which is the 323rd day of the year, ƒ323/365ths of the refund would be property of the estate.)

You can sometimes avoid this problem by delaying bankruptcy until you've received your refunds and spent the money. Another possibility would be to elect, prior to bankruptcy, to apply your refund to the next year's taxes. A few courts have said that doing so prevents the refund from becoming an asset of the bankruptcy estate, but that sentiment isn't necessarily universal. Before relying on this strategy, be sure to check with your lawyer.

If you want to get your refund prior to filing bankruptcy, steer clear of Rapid Refunds outfits or refund anticipation loans offered by many tax preparation services. If you electronically file your return and authorize direct bank deposit of your refund, you can receive your refund within about two weeks and avoid the stiff fees that come with instant refunds. You get your money just as soon, without paying any fees, just by doing it yourself. Unfortunately, things aren't quite as simple here when you owe the government money. They never are.

The IRS has the right to deduct any taxes you owe from your refund. Furthermore, several federal statutes give other government agencies this same right. If you're in default on a guaranteed student loan, the government will try to take your refund. Additionally, if you owe back child support, local support enforcement agencies (such as the district attorney's office) may be able to snatch your refund. In fact, refunds to which you become entitled to for tax years after the petition date may be in jeopardy, unless you're able to eliminate the debt in bankruptcy (see Chapter 15).

Earned income credits

The *earned income credit* (EIC) was designed as an incentive for poor people to work. It creates a refundable tax credit for low-income workers. Whenever you fall into this category, the government essentially pretends that you had more pay withheld than you actually did and then gives some of it back to you. The money is refunded as though it was part of a tax overpayment. So, even if you didn't have any taxes withheld, you still may be able to claim to a refund. Keep in mind that the same brainiacs who came up with that logic wrote the bankruptcy laws.

The courts haven't quite decided how to handle EICs. Although they resemble income tax refunds, EICs are actually a form of government assistance for needy individuals.

Typically, no exemption specifically covers earned income credits. But some courts have applied exemptions for welfare benefits or public assistance. Some have said that EICs are exempt as child support. One court held that an EIC was covered under the state's exemption for personal earnings.

Retirement accounts

The Bankruptcy Code protects most legitimate pensions, including IRAs up to $1 million. Rollovers from one plan to another are also protected if they're made within 60 days of any distribution and otherwise comply with the provisions of the Internal Revenue Code. These protections apply even in states that don't allow other Bankruptcy Code exemptions.

Education savings plans

Funds placed in a tax-qualified education savings plan for the benefit of your child, stepchild, grandchild, or stepgrandchild are excluded from the estate as long as the funds were deposited more than 365 days before bankruptcy. Funds deposited between 720 and 365 days before bankruptcy are protected only up to $5,000

Creating Exemptions

To a limited degree, the law allows some prebankruptcy planning to maximize exemptions.

For example, if you had $1,000 in a bank account, which was not covered by an exemption, you'd lose it to a Chapter 7 trustee. But if you took that $1,000 and made extra payments on your mortgage before filing bankruptcy, the increase in your homestead may be exempt.

Exemption planning is an extremely complicated and unsettled area of the law. If you go too far, the consequences are serious, including denial of discharge, denial of the exemption, or reversal of the transaction.

BARF reduces the amount of a debtor's homestead for any equity accumulated in that property by liquidating other assets that were not exempt if done

  ✔ Within ten years of bankruptcy and

  ✔ With the intent to hinder, delay, or defraud creditors

Prior to BARF, courts often found fraud when someone liquidated all his assets and paid off a mortgage, especially in states with an unlimited homestead exemption.

A number of courts have ruled that a little exemption planning is all right, but the wholesale sheltering of assets that would otherwise go to pay creditors may run afoul of the rule that pigs get fat, while hogs get slaughtered.

Bottom line: Consult a bankruptcy attorney *before* engaging in any prebankruptcy planning.

The difference between converting your property into exempt assets that you continue to own and placing property in someone else's name is a huge one.

Transferring property to someone else is considered fraudulent if the court thinks that you did it just to keep assets out of the reach of creditors. Don't make any gifts or sell any property for less than it's worth before you file for bankruptcy. If you've already done so, be sure to tell your bankruptcy lawyer. (We discuss this topic more in the Chapter 19.)

Chapter 11

Dealing with Secured Debts

. . . .

. . . .

The three people who may have an interest in one of your assets are

- You (obviously)
- The bankruptcy trustee as a representative of unsecured creditors (those who don't have dibs on your car, house, or other belongings)
- A *secured creditor* — one who holds a lien

In simplest terms, a *lien* is a legal claim in which someone else owns a portion of a particular asset that serves as collateral for the debt. You voluntarily create some liens, like your mortgage or car loan. Others are *imposed* against you. For example, if you lost a lawsuit and a judgment was entered against you, that judgment probably created a lien against your home. Similarly, if you fail to pay property taxes, the local government may obtain a lien against your property.

Bankruptcy won't automatically make a lien disappear. So, if you file bankruptcy, you may end up wiping out the debt but still losing assets that have liens on them. Consider your car loan, for example. Filing bankruptcy wipes out your obligation to pay the loan, but the lender can still get the car when you don't pay.

This chapter spotlights liens, the headaches they can cause when they "lien on you," and how, in some instances, you can cast them aside. In Chapter 12 of this book, we explore how this works when the lien is against your home.

Getting the Lowdown on Liens

Generally, you face two types of creditors, unsecured and secured, in bankruptcy cases.

An *unsecured creditor,* such as a credit-card company or medical provider, has no specific claim or right to your property. A *secured creditor* has some leverage. Your debt to him is backed up, or secured, by a specific asset that serves as collateral for the debt. That security interest, in legalese, *encumbers* your property with a *lien.* Put another way, your ownership of the property is conditional — the condition being that if you don't repay the loan, the creditor can go after the *collateral,* or property that secures your debt.

When you finance a car, you and the lender share ownership of the vehicle. As long as you continue making the payments, you're entitled to possession. You don't have the right to sell it out from under the lender, and if you don't make the payments, the lender can take the car. After the debt is paid off, the lender no longer has a claim on the car, the lien is released, and the vehicle is yours free and clear.

Perfecting liens

When a lien is placed on your asset, the law usually requires the lien holder to take certain steps to warn others that it possesses some of the ownership rights associated with the collateral. When these steps are taken, the lien is considered *perfected.* Some sort of public recording or notation is usually required.

For example, your home mortgage isn't perfected until the mortgage document is recorded with the county. Likewise, in most states, a security interest in a motor vehicle isn't perfected until the creditor is listed as a lien holder on the certificate of title.

Perfection is an important concept to understand because bankruptcy trustees have the power to eliminate unperfected liens and take over that creditor's (the lien holder's) ownership rights. (See Chapter 19.)

Seeing liens as double-edged swords

A lien holder's firepower comes from two sources: you and the collateral. By promising to pay the debt, and most likely signing a *promissory note,* you accept personal liability. And by agreeing to a lien, you have given the lender an actual ownership interest in your property.

Putting it into practical terms, if you owe $10,000 on a car that's worth only $7,000, and you don't make the payments, the lender can

✔ Forget about the car and sue you for the full $10,000

✔ Take advantage of the lien and repossess the car

✔ Do both, which, in general, is the most likely avenue of pursuit by the lender

And why not? Then, the lender can repossess the car and sell it for, say, $7,000, apply the money to the debt, and come after you for the balance on the promissory note. Talk about having their cake and eating it, too!

Ordinarily, bankruptcy wipes out your personal liability on the debt, but it won't eliminate the creditor's lien. Although the creditor can no longer go after your personal obligation, it can go after its collateral. Using the example in the previous bulleted list, after you file bankruptcy, the creditor can still repossess the car but can't come after you for the debt itself. So, the cash in your wallet is safe; the car in your garage is not.

The Bankruptcy Code enables you to eliminate liens on household goods and tools of your trade in some situations and to reduce liens in other cases — depending on what kind of lien it is.

Identifying Different Kinds of Liens

Liens can take a variety of forms, including mortgage liens, mechanic's liens, artisan's liens, judicial liens, and tax liens. However, all liens fall in one or the other of two categories — consensual or nonconsensual. And to complicate matters a little more, there are two types of consensual liens — purchase-money liens and nonpurchase-money security liens. These types of liens are typically called purchase-money and nonpurchase-money security interests.

Consensual liens

Consensual liens are liens that you voluntarily grant to someone else. When they involve personal property, such as your car or television, they're called *security interests*. In the case of real property (like your house), they're usually called *mortgages* or *deeds of trust*.

Here's how consensual liens work.

First, start with the understanding that the bank doesn't give you a mortgage to buy a home; rather, you give the bank a mortgage. When you signed your mortgage papers, you gave the lender a lien, thereby giving away some of your ownership rights. You retained the right of possession and granted the lender the right to some of the proceeds if you decide to sell the property. Got that?

Now, by giving the bank a mortgage, you also made your ownership conditional. So, because the bank lent you money, you, in turn, agreed that it could take possession and sell the property if you didn't pay back the loan. As a result, you and the mortgage holder simultaneously have ownership interests, albeit different and sometimes competing ones. Similarly, whenever you grant a lender a security interest on your car, you give up some of your ownership rights.

Consensual liens come in two varieties:

- **Purchase-money security interests,** in which proceeds of a loan are used to purchase a specific item

- **Nonpurchase-money security interests,** which attach to property you already own

When you charge items at some department stores, you often give the store a purchase-money security interest in the merchandise that you buy. Similarly, if you borrow money from a finance company for the express purpose of buying a car that you'll use to secure the loan, it, too, is a purchase-money security interest.

If, for example, you charge a microwave oven on your department store account, you probably agree that the store can take back the appliance if you don't pay off what you owe. On the other hand, if you charged the oven on a general-purpose credit card (such as MasterCard or Visa), to which typically no security interest is attached, neither the store nor the credit-card company can repossess the oven, even if you don't pay for it. You still owe the money, however, and you can surely be sued for what you owe, but nobody can take your microwave or force you to sell it to cover the debt.

Lenders who specialize in relatively small loans to consumers typically require that the borrower give them a lien (security interest) in all their (the borrowers) household goods. This lien is a nonpurchase-money security interest because you didn't borrow the money to purchase the household goods; you already owned them. In theory, this stipulation gives the loan company the right to seize and sell all these items. As you see in the "Freeing your household goods and tools from liens" section later in this chapter, it doesn't usually turn out that way in practice.

Nonconsensual liens

Sometimes the law gives creditors a lien on your property without your consent. The gall! These legal shackles are called *nonconsensual liens.*

Real property taxes, for example, are liens against your property even though you never directly consent. The same is true of a judgment lien. When a judgment is entered against you in some courts, it becomes a lien against your real property, which secures payment of that judgment. (See the "Banging the Gavel on Judgment Liens" section later in this chapter to find out how to eliminate this type of lien in bankruptcy.)

Dealing with Liens in Bankruptcy

Although liens can seem indelible, the Bankruptcy Code provides you with special powers to remove them from exempt household goods, tools, and homesteads. See Chapter 10 for more on exempt assets.

Freeing your household goods and tools from liens

Recognizing the difference between *purchase-money* and *nonpurchase-money security interests* (see the section, "Consensual liens," earlier in this chapter) can help you hang on to your household goods and tools.

Generally, you can't avoid a purchase-money security interest when you file bankruptcy. But you could redeem, reaffirm, or if you purchased the item more than one year (910 days for motor vehicles purchased for "personal use") prior to bankruptcy, pay the value of the collateral over three to five years in a Chapter 13 repayment plan.

On the other hand, you can eliminate nonpurchase-money security interests in some exempt household goods, largely because creditors really don't want your stuff and it's not really worth all that much. Consumer finance companies use these security interests for leverage, so they can threaten to take all your belongings if you don't pay. The Bankruptcy Code allows you to free these items from nonpurchase money security interests:

- Clothing
- Furniture

- Appliances
- One radio
- One television
- One VCR
- Linens
- China
- Crockery
- Kitchenware
- Educational materials and educational equipment primarily for the use of your minor dependent children
- Medical equipment and supplies
- Furniture exclusively for the use of your minor children, or elderly or disabled dependents
- Personal effects (including the toys and hobby equipment of minor dependent children and wedding rings) used by you or your dependents.
- One personal computer and related equipment

You cannot avoid even nonpurchase money security interests in

- Works of art (unless created by you or a relative)
- Electronic entertainment equipment worth more than $500 total (except for one TV, radio, and VCR)
- Antiques worth more than $500 total
- Jewelry worth more than $500 total (except wedding rings)
- A computer (except as provided in the preceding list), motor vehicle (including a tractor or lawn tractor), or a motorized recreational vehicle, water craft, or aircraft.

If a security interest isn't avoidable, the creditor asks you to reaffirm the debt in order to keep your possessions. But you have a couple of other options depending on the size of the debt and value of the collateral. You can

- Pay that creditor the value of the items. For example, if you had several televisions worth about $300 total but owed $1,000, you could pay $300 keep the TVs and wipe out the balance of the debt. In Chapter 7, you have to come up with the money within 30 days of the 341 meeting. In Chapter 13, you pay this sum over the life of the plan. BARF contains a special exception for pawn shops, however. Neither Chapter 13 cram-down (where you pay the value of the item, not necessarily the amount you owe) nor Chapter 7 redemption is available as to property pledged at a pawn shop. In this situation, you have repay the entire debt or give the item back.

✔ Call the creditor's bluff and tell it to come and get its stuff. In many cases, the company simply won't bother.

Redeeming (getting back) your property

If you can't simply remove a lien, you can still *redeem* consumer goods by paying the creditor not the amount of the debt, but rather its value. Personal property depreciates so quickly that its value almost is always less than the amount of the debt. Say, for example, that you charged a $1,000 home entertainment system and gave the store a purchase-money security interest in the unit. Instead of paying the full $1,000 to keep the system, you can pay the store only its value, which, by the time you take it home, is probably half what it was in the store.

In Chapter 7 bankruptcy, this payment must be made in a lump sum and within 30 days of the 341 meeting after your case is filed, unless the creditor agrees otherwise.

Automobiles are usually consumer goods and can be redeemed by paying their value rather than the full amount of the debt. In recent years, a few lenders have come up with the idea of *redemption financing,* where they make you a new loan to redeem your car from the existing lender. This financing may be a good deal because the amount of the new loan is based solely on the value of your car. Say, for example, that you owe $12,000 to ABC Credit Union on a car that's worth only $8,000. You borrow $8,000 from the redemption finance company to redeem the car from ABC, and you then end up owing only $8,000 rather than the original $12,000. Your lawyer can help guide you to a reputable redemption financing lender if one is in your area, or you can check out a company called 722 Redemption Funding, Inc., www.722redemption.com/, 1-888-721-2800.

If you and the creditor can't agree on how much the item is worth, a bankruptcy judge decides.

Reaffirming your debts

If you can't eliminate a lien, don't have the cash to redeem it, and don't want to tether yourself to a Chapter 13 repayment plan, you can reaffirm and promise to pay the debt even though it would otherwise be wiped out during bankruptcy. However, reaffirming means that if you fall behind on the payments after bankruptcy, the creditor can repossess the collateral, sell it, and come after you for any shortfall.

Using the Special Powers Afforded Chapter 13 Filers

In Chapter 13, you can modify some liens and restructure loans that can't be completely eliminated.

If your car loan isn't a purchase-money security interest, you bought the car for some purpose other than personal use (perhaps for your kids or spouse to use or for use in a business), or if you got a purchase-money loan more than 910 days prior to bankruptcy, you can pay the value of the car, not the outstanding loan balance, over the life of a Chapter 13 plan. Say that you borrowed $5,000 from a finance company and pledged a car you owned free and clear as collateral. If the car's retail value was worth only $2,000 when you filed bankruptcy, you could keep the vehicle by paying just $2,000, not $5,000. The same result applies if you acquired the car with the loan, but did so more than 910 days prior to bankruptcy. By contrast, if you got the purchase-money loan less than 910 day before bankruptcy, you'd have to pay the whole loan of $5,000 in order to keep the car.

Similarly, if you bought a washing machine on a department store charge account more than one year before bankruptcy, you could keep it by simply paying its value (the price a secondhand merchant would charge) over the three- to five-year life of your plan. But if you purchased the washing machine within one year of bankruptcy, you'd have to pay the full amount still owed on the purchase price.

We talk about modifying home mortgages in Chapter 12.

Dealing with Rent-to-Own Contracts

Rent-to-own contracts are similar to purchase-money security interests, but they're set up as leases.

With these contracts, you lease a specific item, make periodic rent payments, and, at the end of the contract, end up owning whatever it is you rented.

When a transaction is a true lease, the only way you can keep the item is to make all the payments. You can't redeem the property in a Chapter 7, and you can't just pay its value in a Chapter 13. However, in a Chapter 13, you can make up back payments and make all future payments on time if you want to keep the item.

Lenders know that they make out better if a transaction is a lease rather than one involving a security interest and frequently label transactions "leases" when they actually are security interests. Most courts say that a transaction is not a true lease unless you're allowed to cancel the deal at any time and return the merchandise without further obligation. Your lawyer needs to examine the fine print to see whether a transaction is a true lease or a cleverly disguised security interest.

Banging the Gavel on Judgment Liens

If you lose a lawsuit and the other side is awarded money, a *judicial lien* (a form of judgment lien) may be imposed. Sometimes, a lien is automatically placed on all your real estate the moment a judgment is entered against you. Under the Bankruptcy Code, you can eliminate a judgment lien to the extent that it impairs your homestead exemption.

Consider this example. Assume that your home is worth $75,000, is subject to a mortgage lien of $55,000, and that your state's homestead exemption (which protects at least some of the value of your home) is $30,000. Further assume that you owe $15,000 in medical bills.

If the equity in your home is $20,000, you can file bankruptcy, discharge the medical bills, and keep your home by continuing to pay the mortgage. Neat and clean!

But, say that the hospital sued you before you filed bankruptcy and obtained a judgment lien for $15,000. That lien could cause problems down the road if the equity in your home grew beyond the amount allowed by your homestead exemption. Then if you wanted to sell or refinance your home, you'd have to pay the judgment lien as well as your mortgage.

Congress thought that this consequence was too harsh, especially because a judgment lien is nonconsensual. As a result, the Bankruptcy Code allows debtors to eliminate judgment liens that may impair homesteads. If the debtor in our example took advantage of these provisions, it would be as if no judgment lien had ever hit his property. In other words, to keep his house, all he must do is pay the mortgage even if the value of the house increases above the homestead exemption. The hospital bill gets wiped our along with all the other debts and doesn't come back to haunt you when the time comes to refinance or sell your home.

Beware, however, that the rules about avoiding judgment liens *do not* apply to judgment liens entered by divorce courts for alimony or child support. Forget about avoiding those kinds of judgment liens.

Chapter 12

Saving Your Home

· ·

In This Chapter

▶ Owning and owing — the mixed blessings of home ownership

▶ Discovering the homestead exemption

▶ Addressing jointly owned property

▶ Comprehending foreclosures

▶ Hanging on to your home in Chapter 7 and Chapter 13 bankruptcies

▶ Using truth-in-lending laws to save your home

▶ Watching out for due-on-sale clauses

· ·

*H*ome ownership is an integral part of the American Dream. The Bankruptcy Code recognizes the importance of owning a home and strives to strike a delicate balance between the sometimes competing interests of mortgage companies that finance home purchases, other creditors, and, of course, the homeowners.

In this chapter, we look at what can happen to your home when you file bankruptcy and explain how bankruptcy can prevent *foreclosure* — that nasty situation when lenders take your home.

When you're struggling to make ends meet, refinancing your home or taking out a home-equity loan may seem like a great option — and maybe it is. However, we suggest that you explore your bankruptcy options first. (See Chapter 7 for more about refinancing.)

Your Home, Your Castle — and Sometimes Your Hassle

You probably see your home as a memory-filled place of refuge for you and your family, but others view it through different eyes — cold, calculating ones. Typically, they focus on the *equity* in your house — the difference between its value and the amount owed on mortgages and liens against it.

Three entities that may claim an interest in your home are

- ✔ You
- ✔ Secured creditors — including mortgage holders and other lien holders, such as judgment creditors
- ✔ The bankruptcy trustee, to the extent that its value exceeds the allowable homestead exemption

The three things that you need to know before assessing your options are

- ✔ The value of your property
- ✔ The amount of any mortgages or other liens against the property
- ✔ The homestead exemption that applies to your situation

Figuring out how much your home is worth

Bankruptcy offers various options with regard to your homestead. But before you can figure which works best for your situation, you need an objective appraisal of the dollars and cents value of your home. That can be a tough number to find. If you recently purchased your home, the selling price is some indication of its value. *Some.* Depending on where you live, a good starting point for determining the value of your real property *may* be the tax assessment. Unfortunately, in some parts of the country, values used by tax assessors bear almost no relationship to reality.

Be wary, however, of estimates from real estate brokers who may be more inclined to overstate the value of your home hoping to land a selling job. Similarly, don't blindly accept appraisals made in connection with home-equity loans. Home-equity appraisals routinely are inflated so that the lender can justify giving you a larger loan than you probably can't afford.

If you did not recently purchase your home or if you live in a community where property tax assessments are out of whack, you have to hire a real estate appraiser. This way, you get an expert opinion from someone with no ulterior motives.

Deducting mortgages and other liens that affect your share of the pie

Liens for mortgages, real property taxes, federal taxes, or judgments go against the value of your home, and lien holders have first dibs on any proceeds if you sell the property. They must be paid in full before you or other creditors get anything from the sale of your home. The amounts of any liens need to be deducted from the value of the property so that you can determine how much equity you have. You may want to refer to Chapter 11, where we take an up close and personal look at liens.

Understanding the homestead exemption

Homestead-exemption laws protect a person's home from those creditors who don't have liens against the property. For example, if your home is worth $120,000 and you owe $100,000 on the mortgage, your equity in the home is $20,000. So, if the applicable homestead exemption were $20,000 or more, your home would be protected from the bankruptcy trustee and creditors other than the mortgage holder.

Almost every jurisdiction has some type of homestead exemption; however, notable exceptions include Maryland, New Jersey, and Pennsylvania. Some jurisdictions permit you to choose exemptions contained in the U.S. Bankruptcy Code or those provided by your state law. In other places, you're restricted to the exemptions recognized by your state and the federal exemptions aren't available. (Appendix A summarizes the exemptions state-by-state and provides a list of federal exemptions.)

Arkansas, Florida, Iowa, Kansas, South Dakota, and Texas have unlimited homestead exemptions. If you live in one of those states, your home *may* be sheltered regardless of its value. But it's complicated.

If you acquired your present home within 1,215 days of bankruptcy, your homestead exemption may not exceed $125,000, even if state law allows more. In most cases, this amount isn't a problem because only a few states have such large homestead exemptions. But this restriction is limited to the extent that you used the proceeds of a prior homestead in the same state to purchase your present home — unless, of course, the first residence was also acquired within 1,215 days of bankruptcy.

For example, assume that you moved to Florida in 1995 and bought a home for $500,000 cash. Then, in 2005, you sold this home and used the money to buy a new home in Florida for $500,000. The $125,000 limitation would not apply even if you filed bankruptcy within 1,215 days of acquiring your new home.

There is also an absolute $125,000 cap on homesteads if you've been convicted of certain federal securities law provisions or committed criminal acts or other intentional or reckless acts that caused serious injury or death within five years of bankruptcy.

Although the Bankruptcy Abuse Reform Fiasco law of 2005 is not clear on the subject, we're guessing that if a husband and wife own their homestead together and file a joint bankruptcy, the $125,000 limit may be doubled to $250,000.

But if you don't live in an unlimited-homestead state, the picture may not be so rosy. Although some states have a homestead exemption as high as $500,000 (Massachusetts), homestead exemptions in some states don't amount to a hill of beans. In Michigan, for example, the homestead exemption is a measly $3,500.

The amount allowed for a homestead exemption is reduced to the extent that equity in that home was created with the intent to hinder, delay, or defraud creditors within ten years before bankruptcy. If, for example, a person who was being hounded by creditors liquidated her $25,000 stock portfolio and used the money to either pay down a mortgage on an existing home or purchase a new home with the money, any homestead exemption would be reduced by $25,000. This restriction supplements existing court decisions placing limits on prebankruptcy exemption planning (see Chapter 10).

Sometimes, the effective amount of your exemption may actually be more than the amount specified in exemption statutes. The reason? When the trustee sells your property, he is responsible for paying a commission to any real estate agent he hires. Commissions and other costs of sale can be as high as 10 percent of the selling price of your home and they must be paid from the trustee's share of the sale proceeds, not from the share covered by your homestead exemption.

Occasionally, a court must decide whether an unusual type of residence qualifies for homestead exemption. Not surprisingly, courts frequently disagree. Houseboats, for example, seem to confound the courts. Some judges say they're exempt as homesteads; others say they're not.

Another frequent question is whether you can exempt living quarters where you've rented out part of your abode or used another part of your residence for income-producing activities. Most courts agree that the mere fact that a person rents out a room or portion of his home doesn't impair the exemption. Other courts, however, differ.

Some states require you to actually reside in the dwelling, but others permit temporary absences or require only that a family member live there. Sometimes determining whether someone lives on the property is difficult. For example, does a debtor actually live on vacant land when he's staying in a camper on the property but intends to build a home? Some courts would rule that he doesn't live there; therefore, the land is not exempt.

If you've lived in your present state less than two years, the exemption law of your prior state may be the one that applies (see Chapter 10).

Table 12-1 helps determine if a bankruptcy trustee has any claim to your home — whether you have nonexempt home equity that could be seized for your creditors.

Table 12-1	Applying Your Homestead Exemption
Equity	*Nonexempt Amount*
1. The value of your home	$
2. The costs of selling it (roughly 10 percent of its value)	$
3. Amount owed on mortgages	$
4. Amounts owed on other liens (for example judgments, real estate taxes, federal tax liens)	$
5. Total deductions (add Lines 2, 3, and 4)	$
6. Your equity (subtract Line 5 from Line 1)	$
7. Homestead exemption	$
8. Nonexempt home equity (subtract Line 7 from Line 6)	$

Dealing with Jointly Owned Property

In noncommunity-property states (all except Arizona, California, Idaho, Louisiana, Nevada, New Mexico, Texas, Washington, and Wisconsin), when a married couple jointly owns a homestead, but only one spouse files bankruptcy, the other spouse's interest in the property doesn't come into play in the bankruptcy. Although courts disagree about how to calculate a dollar figure for the interest of one spouse, you can come up with a ballpark figure by deducting mortgages and liens from the value of your property, dividing the remainder by two, and applying your homestead exemption against this figure. The following sections show you what happens in some practical examples.

If you own property solely in your name, don't try to put it in the names of both you and your spouse (without first talking to a bankruptcy lawyer). Doing so can be considered a fraudulent transfer (see Chapter 19).

Example 1: When the homestead exemption is larger than your equity

Assume that your home is worth $100,000 and you owe $70,000 on the mortgage, which means that the equity in your home is $30,000 and your half would be $15,000. If your state's homestead exemption is $20,000, your property is entirely exempt because the amount of your equity is less than the amount of the homestead exemption.

Example 2: When your equity is larger than your homestead exemption

Assume that your property is worth $160,000 and that you owe $70,000 on the mortgage, meaning that the equity in your property is $90,000, with your half being $45,000. If the homestead exemption still is $20,000, you have nonexempt home equity available to creditors.

In the example in the previous paragraph, if a Chapter 7 trustee can find a buyer for your one-half interest for, say $45,000, the buyer can pay you $20,000 and distribute $25,000 to creditors to become a joint owner with your spouse. The trustee must, however, give your spouse a chance to match this offer before actually selling the property.

When a buyer for your one-half interest can't be found, the trustee can ask the court for permission to sell the entire interest in the property, pay the mortgage, give your spouse his or her share, pay you your exemption, and distribute the balance to creditors. In this situation, instead of sharing ownership with a new buyer, your spouse receives cash for his or her share.

As a practical matter, the likelihood that a trustee can find a buyer for a one-half interest in your homestead is minimal, or even less. Furthermore, courts are reluctant to grant a trustee's request to sell a nondebtor spouse's interest in the marital home. So, a nondebtor may be able to buy the estate's interest in the property from the trustee for significantly less than the previous examples suggest, especially when you consider that the trustee has to pay a real estate agent's commission whenever the property is listed for sale.

From a debtor's perspective, things are even better in jurisdictions that recognize a *tenancy by the entireties* exemption. In Delaware, the District of Columbia, Florida, Hawaii, Illinois, Indiana, Maryland, Massachusetts, Michigan, Mississippi, Missouri, North Carolina, Pennsylvania, Vermont, Virginia, and Wyoming, when only one spouse files bankruptcy and no creditors have claims against both spouses, the property is fully exempt. Regardless of its value or whether it qualifies as a homestead, you can keep your home.

The bottom line: One spouse filing for bankruptcy with the other one avoiding it can prove advantageous. Be sure to discuss this angle with your lawyer.

The rules pertaining to jointly owned property are different — and somewhat less favorable — when you live in Arizona, California, Idaho, Louisiana, Nevada, New Mexico, Texas, Washington, or Wisconsin, the nine community property states, where even the nondebtor's interest in community property becomes property of the estate. If the community property isn't fully covered by an exemption, the trustee can sell it. Your home probably is considered community property when it's obtained during the marriage, unless one spouse inherited the property.

Understanding How Foreclosures Work

In weighing your bankruptcy options, you need to know a little about the nitty-gritty of foreclosure. Although procedures vary from state to state, foreclosure typically begins when the lender commences a lawsuit initiating what's known as a *judicial foreclosure* or files documents with the county clerk or another local official and mails copies to you, the borrower, in the case of a *nonjudicial foreclosure.*

But that's only the beginning. State laws require a public auction, referred to as a *foreclosure sale,* and public notice of that auction. In other words, the mortgage gremlin can't just auction off your house to his relatives at a no-contest auction. But even though a foreclosure sale is open to public bidding, the lender typically places the only bid. The time between commencement of a foreclosure proceeding and the actual sale rarely is less than three months and frequently is longer. During this period, you still own the property.

In some situations, depending on the method of foreclosure and requirements of state law, the borrower still may be able to *redeem* the property after a foreclosure sale by paying the full amount bid at the sale. After the foreclosure process is complete, however, the successful bidder can evict the borrower from the premises.

Heading off the Homewreckers

Because holding on to your home may be a number-one priority, evaluating the differences between filing Chapter 7 and Chapter 13 makes sense. We designed the following sections to clarify the distinctions.

Keeping your home in Chapter 7

If you're current with your mortgage payments, and the value of your home is covered by your state's homestead exemption, Chapter 7 bankruptcy may be the way to go. By getting rid of most of your other debts, keeping up with the mortgage will be just that much easier.

Filing Chapter 7 usually is quick, easy, final, and helps you avoid the repayment responsibility that comes with Chapter 13 bankruptcy.

Keeping your home in Chapter 13

If you need time to catch up on back mortgage payments, Chapter 13 is probably the recipe you're looking for because you then can make up late payments over the three- to five-year life of your bankruptcy plan. But remember that you must keep up with all future mortgage payments.

Additionally, whenever your equity is more than your state's allowable exemption, you don't want to file Chapter 7 because you'd probably lose your home to the trustee.

For example, say that your house is worth $100,000, your mortgage balance is $60,000, and the homestead exemption is $25,000. If you file Chapter 7, the trustee can sell your house, pay off the mortgage, hand you $25,000 for your homestead exemption, and distribute the remaining $15,000 to creditors. In Chapter 13, you keep your home and pay creditors the same $15,000 they would have received in Chapter 7, but you have three to five years in which to do it.

Making up back payments: The "cure" for your ailment

A *cure* is the process of paying the amount that you're behind on your mortgage (*arrearage*) over the course of a Chapter 13 case. For example, if you're behind by five $1,000 mortgage payments as of the date of your bankruptcy, you can gradually pay off the $5,000 arrearage over the three to five years of a Chapter 13 bankruptcy plan.

After you file Chapter 13, in addition to chipping away at the arrearage, you must also resume your current payments. Continuing with the previous paragraph's example, say that your mortgage payments are due on the tenth of the month, that you file Chapter 13 on May 15, and that the arrearage consists of payments you missed for January, February, March, April, and May. Under those circumstances, you have to make your regular payments, starting with the one due on June 10, in addition to your payments on the arrearage.

If foreclosure proceedings already were started, you still can proffer a cure by filing Chapter 13 before the property is sold at a foreclosure sale. (See the "Understanding How Foreclosures Work" section, earlier in this chapter.) One problem is that courts disagree on precisely when this sale occurs. A foreclosure, by its very nature, is a public auction. When the bidding stops, the auctioneer declares the property "sold to the highest bidder" (which is usually the mortgage holder bidding all or part of the amount it is owed). However, depending on local procedures, additional steps may be required to complete the process. In some places, a state court judge must confirm that the foreclosure was properly conducted. In addition, a deed must be delivered to the high bidder, who must properly record it in public records.

That said, some courts rule that if you don't file a Chapter 13 before the winning bid is accepted, it's too late for a cure. Others say that cure remains a possibility when a Chapter 13 is filed before all the additional steps are completed.

Filing a Chapter 13 well in advance of the foreclosure sale date usually is best because you're assured that it won't be too late. Filing early also saves you money. Mortgage documents typically require you to pay the lender's costs and attorney fees for the foreclosure proceedings. When you file late in the process, these amounts are added to the arrearage.

Even after a foreclosure sale, you may still have a shot at saving your house if your state provides for a *right of redemption,* an opportunity for you to redeem real property, even after it's sold at foreclosure. Depending on the state and method of foreclosure, you may have a period of time, usually six months to a year, to exercise a right of redemption. *Note:* A right of redemption is not to be confused with the right to redeem personal property under the Bankruptcy Code, which we explain in Chapter 11.

Remember, however, the difference between redemption and cure. When you cure, you only have to make up the missed payments; you don't have to pay the whole loan. And you can take up to five years to make up the back payments.

Redemption, on the other hand, essentially requires you pay the entire outstanding balance of the loan, and you can't stretch payments over the life of the plan. The entire debt has to be paid before the redemption period, which in some states may be only a few months, expires. Your only option in this situation would be to try to find a lender who would advance you the amount needed to redeem the property.

The answer to the question of whether you have redemption rights following a foreclosure depends on local law, so don't count on having the right to redeem without first checking with a local lawyer.

With all this to consider, contacting a lawyer as soon as possible after foreclosure procedures are threatened is essential. Then you and your attorney can discuss the pending deadlines and plan your strategy accordingly.

Modifying home mortgages: Special restrictions

Sometimes you can restructure mortgages in a Chapter 13, but special restrictions sometimes apply when modifying residential mortgages. If they do apply, the only modification allowed is making up back payments under the plan and continuing to make all future regular monthly payments after the petition date.

The following mortgages aren't entitled to special residential mortgage protection:

- ✔ **Loans secured by other property in addition to your home:** For example, a lender may take a security interest in your $100 junk car in addition to the mortgage. That decision — and it's not all that unusual — can cost the bank a bundle. If your home was worth $75,000 and you owed $100,000 on a mortgage that was not entitled to protection as a residential mortgage, a Chapter 13 can enable you to reduce the principal amount of the loan balance to the value of your home ($75,000). If the mortgage were entitled to protection, you'd eventually end up paying the entire $100,000 to keep your home.

  Sometimes lenders, sensing an approaching bankruptcy, discover their blunders and magnanimously offer to release collateral like the junk car. Don't let them without first talking to a lawyer.

- ✔ **Loans that are due, or will come due, during the next five years:** This is common with home-equity loans requiring *balloon payments* where you make really small payments for a few years, basically covering only the interest, and then have to pay off the entire balloon portion of the loan in a lump sum.

✔ **Loans that in reality are completely unsecured because the property is fully encumbered by prior mortgages:** Lenders of first mortgages usually won't approve loans that are more than the property is worth. Lenders of second mortgages, on the other hand, are more inclined to gamble, often stupidly. These home-equity lenders are so blinded by the prospect of making a highly profitable loan that they don't seriously consider whether the property already is fully encumbered.

When your home isn't worth more than the first mortgage, many courts conclude that a second mortgage isn't protected and may be eliminated. But if your property is worth as little as a buck more than the amount due on the first mortgage, the entire second mortgage is protected and must be paid if you want to keep your home. For example, if you owe $75,000 on a first mortgage and $25,000 on a second, you can eliminate the second mortgage if your home was worth $75,000 or less, but if it was worth $75,001, the second mortgage is protected. *Note:* Courts disagree on whether the property should be valued as of the time the loan was made, or as of the petition date.

Your options when the restrictions on modifying home mortgages don't apply

In situations where the restrictions on modifying home mortgages don't apply, you can actually restructure and possibly reduce your mortgage. You can

✔ Propose to suspend payments until you can sell the property to pay off the secured claim

✔ Restructure the debt and reduce the interest rate

✔ Reduce the balance of the loan through *bifurcation* (also known as cramming down)

In Chapter 11, we explain the concept of *cram-down,* a process in which a Chapter 13 debtor pays the value of collateral rather than the full amount of the debt.

When the collateral is real property, this technique is frequently called *bifurcation,* which means "division into two parts," a secured claim equal to the value of the property and an unsecured claim for the balance of the debt.

The practice of reducing the secured claim to the value of the collateral is sometimes referred to as *stripoff.* Paying the value of the collateral under a Chapter 13 plan is known as *cram-down.* For our purposes, stripoff, cram-down, and bifurcation mean the same thing.

Here's a practical example of bifurcation:

> Assume that your property is worth $30,000 and is encumbered by two mortgages. You owe $25,000 on the first mortgage and $20,000 on the second. The first mortgage is fully covered by the value of the property, so it's considered fully secured and can't be reduced. But after you deduct the $25,000 owed on the first mortgage from the value of the property, only $5,000 in value remains. As a result, you can strip off or eliminate all but $5,000 of the second mortgage. If you pay the holder of the second mortgage $5,000 over the course of your Chapter 13 plan, that mortgage goes away even though you owed $20,000!

Not bad! Too bad that this option is available only in situations where the special restrictions on modifying home mortgages don't apply.

Comparing Chapter 7 and Chapter 13

Table 12-2 provides a bird's eye view to help you decide whether a Chapter 7 or Chapter 13 is the best way to save your home.

Table 12-2	Saving Your Home — Chapter 7 versus Chapter 13	
Situation	*Chapter 7*	*Chapter 13*
Mortgage payment current, equity within the exemption.	Home shouldn't be affected Regular payments continue.	Home shouldn't be affected. Regular payments should continue, outside the plan if possible to avoid trustee's commission.
Mortgage payments behind, equity within the exemption.	The trustee won't assert an interest, but you'll will have to make up all the back payments immediately unless the mortgage company agrees otherwise.	Must resume regular monthly payments and make up back payments over the life of the plan. (The Bankruptcy Code requires that back payments on residential mortgages be brought current within a "reasonable time" under the Chapter 13 plan. Some courts have said that back payments must be brought current in the early stages of the plan, but most say that they can be stretched over the full three to five years of the plan.)

Situation	Chapter 7	Chapter 13
Equity is greater than exemption.	Trustee can sell your home, pay you the amount of the exemption, and pay the rest to your creditors.	Trustee can't sell your home. However, plan payments will be higher to cover the amount of your nonexempt equity over the life of the plan.
No equity, mortgage is more than property is worth and is in default (you're behind in payments).	Temporarily stops fore-closure. Chapter 7 won't save home, but it will extinguish personal liability on the loan.	If mortgages don't qualify for dential mortgages, bifurcation is an option. (Despite the rule against modifying residential mortgages, many courts have allowed bifurcation in cases where the creditor has other collateral in addition to your home, where no equity is securing the loan, where the home is other than a single family residence, or where the entire loan balance will come due within the next five years.)

Preserving your homestead isn't always a simple matter, and you can unwittingly lose your exemption if you're not excruciatingly careful. Consult a bankruptcy lawyer before refinancing your home, renting it out, moving, signing a contract to sell, making improvements, or allowing a judgment or tax lien to be filed. And keep in mind that while a Chapter 13 bankruptcy is open — that is, while you're making payments — moving, renting your home, or entering into a contract to sell your home are risky steps to be taking.

Chapter 13 saves the day after injury

Grant and Nicole lived from paycheck to paycheck the way many couples do. When Grant fell off his bike and broke his shoulder, he couldn't work for three months. Nicole's salary wasn't enough to put food on the table and pay the mortgage, so they fell behind. Later, when Grant got back on his feet, they dutifully resumed their payments, but the bank still wanted to foreclose because of the three missed payments.

Like a growing number of people, Grant and Nicole were virtually pushed into bankruptcy by the foolish policy of their mortgage holder. As would be expected, they filed Chapter 13 bankruptcy, and the court protected their home and allowed them to make up the missed mortgage payments over three years. The lender got its money, Grant and Nicole kept their house, and, thanks to sensible bankruptcy laws, everybody's happy.

"Due on sale" — A snake in the grass, and a pain in your . . .

Most mortgages contain a *due-on-sale clause* that says if the property is sold or liens are attached to it, the entire loan becomes due now . . . right now. Generally, nobody pays any attention to these clauses — not even the lender — and they're routinely ignored. In fact, just about everyone who obtains a second mortgage violates this provision. Regardless, it's a hazard lurking in the tall grass, like a venomous snake.

Although most lenders won't bother attempting to enforce these clauses, a few mortgage creditors scour loan documents searching for due-on-sale clauses whenever a borrower files Chapter 13. If you bought your house subject to an existing mortgage and the seller didn't obtain the mortgage company's consent, or if you have allowed other liens to attach to the property, the mortgage company may claim that the loan is in default and can't be remedied, even in a Chapter 13. Many courts are siding — rather unhappily — with creditors on this issue.

When Archie and Edith bought their home from Fred and Ethel, they didn't get their own mortgage. Instead they just started making payments on the existing mortgage. Although the mortgage company accepted payments from Archie and Edith, it never gave its official consent to their purchase of the home. The bank neglected to complain until after Archie and Edith filed Chapter 13, and then it asked for court permission to foreclose on the grounds that the due-on-sale clause had been violated. Although acknowledging that most courts would go the other way, the bankruptcy court in this case ruled against the bank, so Archie and Edith kept their home.

It was, however, a close call.

So far, only a few mortgage companies have made this argument, but you still should have your mortgage documents carefully examined by a lawyer for possible violations of a due-on-sale clause so that a strategy for dealing with the issue can be developed if it ever comes up.

Using Truth-in-Lending Laws

Another federal law gives you the power to cancel liens on your home. It's called the Truth-in-Lending Act (TILA), which is doubly powerful when used in conjunction with a Chapter 13 filing.

When you borrow money against your home, the TILA gives you a three-day cooling off period in which to cancel the transaction. The lender must give you written notice that you have this right. The TILA also requires the lender to provide you with written disclosures of finance and other charges related to your loan.

If a lender doesn't disclose the required information in connection with a *non*purchase-money loan, you can cancel the transaction at any time within the following three years or whenever you sell your home, whichever comes first.

ANECDOTE

The Truth-in-Lending Act: An arrow in your quiver

When Claude received a $22,000 home-equity loan, he agreed to pay a $3,000 fee to the lender's agent for arranging the loan. The lender violated the Truth-in-Lending Act by not including this fee in the finance-charge category on the disclosure statement. Two years later, when the lender called the loan, Claude's lawyer gave notice he was *rescinding* the loan and filed a Chapter 13 bankruptcy for Claude. The bankruptcy court canceled the mortgage and wiped out the debt.

Likewise, if you want to cancel a lien against your home under TILA without bankruptcy, you must return the money to the lender. However, if you were to file bankruptcy, some courts allow you to cancel a lien without returning the money. That's a great deal — if your local court will play ball. Some do, some don't. So don't make any assumptions.

In addition to the TILA, your state's truth-in-lending law may cover you. If your state has such a law, your rights are likely to be greater under the state statute than they are with the federal provision. Some states enable you to cancel a lien even though it may be too late to do so under the TILA. Others aren't quite so forgiving. Your lawyer can advise you on the best course of action for your particular case.

Coping When Your Dream Home Becomes a Nightmare

Regrettably, more and more people are discovering that they can't handle their mortgage payments because they were suckered into taking second mortgages (home-equity loans) to pay off their credit cards. Paying the first mortgage and the home-equity mortgage is just too much. They may also realize that they've used up all the equity in their home and now owe more on mortgages than their houses are worth.

If you're in this predicament, you have our sympathy. You may have used your life savings to buy the home, put down roots, and enrolled your children in the schools of your choice, but now you must think about giving it all up because you were conned into taking a second mortgage.

So, now it's time to bite the bullet and be brutally honest with yourself. If you try to keep your home when you really can't afford to make your mortgage payments, keeping your home may not put you on the road to financial recovery. Struggling to keep up with overwhelming mortgage payments will likely drag you down again.

Your best choice may be to file under Chapter 7 and allow the mortgage holder to foreclose. What's the point in making further payments, provided that you have someplace to go and the funds to do so? Instead, use the money that you'd normally pay on the mortgage to find a new place to live or to pay for moving expenses.

Granted, for a few years, you'll have trouble getting another mortgage at conventional interest rates, but it will probably take you this long to save up for a decent down payment. See Chapter 21 for more on repairing your credit.

Creditors sometimes are willing to pay you something for a *deed in lieu of foreclosure* so that they can avoid the expenses of foreclosure. In that situation, you relinquish your interest in the property in exchange for a modest payment, perhaps $1,000, and agree to move out within a specific period of time. Although this arrangement may be a good deal, don't take it without first exploring the income tax consequences (capital gains taxes) of making such a transaction (or sale).

Nevertheless, you may still want to keep your home even though you have no established equity, especially if you think its value will appreciate or if you're worried about finding a place to live after your bankruptcy. (We explore ways of saving your home without filing bankruptcy in Chapter 7.)

Part IV
Getting Rid of (Most of) Your Debt

The 5th Wave   By Rich Tennant

"...and don't tell me I'm not being frugal enough. I hired a man last week to do nothing but clip coupons!"

In this part . . .

Your aim is to get rid of your debts, and to a large extent, bankruptcy does that, even with the more stringent rules of the law enacted in the fall of 2005. For the most part, debts incurred before you file bankruptcy are eliminated, and debts that arise after you file are not. But when you're dealing with credit cards — and who isn't? — the game's a little different. Ditto with taxes, fines, child support, and student loans. This section reveals those nasty debts that linger like a February flu and helps position you to get the most relief possible.

Chapter 13

Lingering Obligations

. . . .

In This Chapter

▶ Distinguishing debts from other obligations

▶ Living with the 60-day bar date

▶ Borrowing to cover nondischargeable debts

▶ Knowing about reaffirmation agreements

▶ Watching out for the ultimate bankruptcy bummer — denial or revocation of discharge

. . . .

*B*ankruptcy may not provide an escape route for each and every one of your financial obligations. Some debts are much like fly paper. They seem to stick to you no matter what. Your left foot gets stuck, and when you try to free that one, the right gets stuck. Try pushing away with your hands, and your tootsies come free, but now your paws are snared.

Escaping some debts would defy even the talents of Harry Houdini. But escape from others is possible if you just have the key. This chapter is that key. In it, we identify obligations that are just plain immune from bankruptcy and others that you may be able to shuck. You also discover rare situations in which *all* a person's debts survive because his bankruptcy discharge is denied or revoked.

Recognizing (Possibly) Indelible Debts

In Chapter 11, we look at *secured debts,* such as those backed up by your house or car, and explain that auto finance companies and mortgage lenders can still repossess or foreclose after you file bankruptcy. A handful of other obligations also survive bankruptcy and stick to you like hot tar, including

✔ Those that are *not* technically "debts"

✔ Debts arising *after* bankruptcy

✔ Specific types of debts that the Bankruptcy Code preserves — *nondischargeable debts*

(We devote entire chapters to the most common of these: fraud and credit-card abuse — Chapters 14 and 16; taxes — Chapter 15; divorce obligations — Chapter 17; and student loans — Chapter 18.)

✔ Some debts that were not properly listed on bankruptcy documents

✔ Any debt you reaffirmed (or reagreed to after bankruptcy)

✔ All your debts if the court denies or revokes your bankruptcy discharge

However, you can escape some of these sticky debts in some cases:

✔ By successfully completing a Chapter 13 repayment plan

✔ By watching for creditors who are asleep at the switch in a Chapter 7 case and miss the deadline (the *60-day bar date*) for challenging your bankruptcy

✔ By filing a proof of claim (a document that must be filed with the court before a creditor can receive any payments from the trustee) so that at least part of the nondischargeable debt is paid by the trustee

But before going on, you must get a handle on the nature of the debt beast so that you're better able to tell when you have a real tiger, which bankruptcy can't tame, or only a paper feline, which merely requires a little special handling.

Confronting obligations enforceable by court orders

Start with this premise: Courts usually don't force people to perform most contracts; they merely assess damages for nonperformance. For example, courts won't order you to pay a loan under penalty of contempt. They simply enter a judgment against you for some amount of money.

Monetary damages are inadequate where some contracts are concerned. For example, if you sold someone your business and signed a *noncompete covenant* (agreeing not to open a new competing business) and then turned around and set up shop across the street, the court may grant an *injunction,* which is just a court order where the judge says, with a bit more tact, "Yo, wise guy, get outta town, or I'm gonna slap you with a fine or toss your butt in jail!"

Similarly, famous performers and prizefighters often agree to work exclusively for one promoter — a promise, enforced by an injunction, not to work for anyone else.

Rock star can't use bankruptcy to dump record company

Rock star Demonic Dan signed with Moon Records, even though he was under an exclusive contract with Star Recordings. When Star asked a court to enter an injunction forbidding Dan from performing for Moon, Dan filed bankruptcy to discharge the recording contract with Star.

The bankruptcy judge said, "No dice!"

The bankruptcy court ruled that Dan's obligation to Star under the exclusive recording contract wasn't a debt subject to discharge in bankruptcy. So, despite his bankruptcy, Dan must still honor his commitment and can only perform for Star Records.

Most courts say promises that are enforceable by injunctions can't be avoided by bankruptcy because no debt — as the law defines it — needs to be wiped out.

Debts arising after bankruptcy

For the most part, bankruptcy wipes out debts that arise prior to bankruptcy, but not those arising afterward. Therefore, you need to carefully decide not only *whether* you need to file bankruptcy, but also *when*.

Debts arise when the events causing the liability occur and not when you get the bill. When you buy something on credit, the debt *arises* at the moment of purchase, not when your credit-card statement comes in the mail. Similarly, if you cause a car wreck, your liability arises when the accident occurred, even though claims aren't made against you until much later.

Occasionally, people discover that they filed bankruptcy too soon. For example, if you file bankruptcy right before undergoing extensive medical treatment, the medical bills resulting from your treatment won't be included in the bankruptcy. Most of the medical bills, it is hoped, are covered by insurance, and you'll be able to pay the balance. But you can never be sure. In a situation like that, postponing bankruptcy until the dust settles and you know exactly where you stand may be best.

Postpetition charges on prepetition contracts

Charges arising after bankruptcy (*postpetition charges*) under a contract that you made prior to bankruptcy (a *prepetition contract*) are usually wiped out. For example, if you surrender your car to the finance company before bankruptcy and the lender sells it at auction after bankruptcy but doesn't receive the total amount owed, tough beans. The lender can't come after you because the debt was discharged as a prepetition debt because you borrowed the money when you signed the loan papers. See Chapter 6 for an explanation of how events occurring prior to a bankruptcy filing (prepetition) frequently have different ramifications than those occurring after the filing. In Chapter 10, we describe how and why most things you acquire after the day your bankruptcy is filed aren't affected by your bankruptcy.

However, courts disagree about when certain contractual debts arise.

Say, for example, that prior to bankruptcy, your dad let you use his credit card because you promised to make the payments and *indemnify* (reimburse him) if the credit-card company ever came after Pop. When you file bankruptcy and stop making the payments to the credit-card company, your dad has to step up and pay off the card. In this case, your promise to indemnify kicks in after bankruptcy. Does that mean your promise to reimburse Dad is nondischargeable? Most — but definitely not all — courts will let you off the hook because the actual promise was made prior to bankruptcy.

Divorce awards

Sometimes divorces are pending when bankruptcy is filed. Divorce decrees commonly require one spouse to pay certain bills and indemnify the other for any losses. The final divorce decree, however, is often not entered until after the bankruptcy petition date. This delay raises the question of whether the obligations created by the divorce decree are pre- or postbankruptcy. See Chapter 17 for more on that chicken-and-egger.

Condo charges

Folks who live in a condo or co-op are assessed fees to maintain common areas. In most cases, these fees are secured by the property.

If you intend to keep your residence, simply continue to pay these fees, just like property taxes or your mortgage. But if you intend to surrender your residence, watch out for a trap. Remember that debts arising after the petition date aren't discharged? Well, condominium or co-operative fees assessed against your property after the petition date and up the point you relinquish any interest in the property are nondischargeable. So, if you intend to surrender a condo or co-op, you should do it as soon as possible after filing bankruptcy; maybe even before filing, if you have somewhere else to live.

Unlisted debts

Sometimes, folks forget to list all their debts on their bankruptcy papers.

In a Chapter 13, debts not listed on your bankruptcy papers aren't discharged unless you amend your filing to include the creditor within 90 days of the 341 meeting. (For more about the 341 meeting, see Chapter 6.)

In a Chapter 7 *asset case* (where assets are sold and proceeds are paid to your creditors), an unlisted debt isn't discharged unless you can prove that the creditor had notice or actually knew about your bankruptcy in time to file a proof of claim — generally within 90 days of the 341 meeting.

Most courts say that debts not listed in *no-asset cases* (where no assets are actually liquidated: This category accounts for 96 percent of all bankruptcies) are discharged because the creditor wouldn't receive any money even when the debt was listed. Keep in mind, though, that this stipulation isn't an invitation for sloppiness.

When the time comes to clean up your credit reports after bankruptcy, you can easily show credit bureaus that a particular debt was included in bankruptcy by providing a copy of your bankruptcy schedules. In the case of unlisted debts, you have to prove that in your jurisdiction, unlisted debts in no-asset cases are eliminated and that yours was a no-asset case. Sometimes you even have to hire a lawyer to make this point.

Another reason to be as careful as possible when listing all your debts is to obtain the benefit of the *60-day bar date*. See the "Sweating Out the 60-Day Bar Date" section, later in this chapter.

Debts preserved under sections of the Bankruptcy Code

The Bankruptcy Code specifies that certain types of debts are nondischargeable. There are two kinds of nondischargeable debts: priority debts and nonpriority nondischargeable debts.

Priority debts

The most common are priority support obligations, some taxes, and claims for personal injuries caused by drunk driving or boating. Your Chapter 13 plan can and must propose to pay these types of debts in full.

This requirement may work to your advantage because your Chapter 13 plan can devote a large portion of the payments to paying off debts that would otherwise haunt you after bankruptcy, while paying much less to debts that bankruptcy will eliminate.

If a nondischargeable debt doesn't have priority status, a Chapter 13 plan cannot pay more on it than on ordinary dischargeable debts, so most of the money you pay into the plan goes to pay off debts that would be wiped out. For example, student loans are nondischargeable, but they're not priority debts. A Chapter 13 plan may not pay more to student loan creditors than to holders of dischargeable claims, such as credit-card companies (see Chapter 18). So, if your plan payment is $300, only a small portion goes toward paying off the student loan, which remains after your other debts are discharged.

In contrast, support obligations are *priority* nondischargeable debts, and it's okay for the plan to pay these claims more than others.

To recap, if your plan payment is $300, you can devote almost all the money to extinguishing your support obligations while paying virtually nothing on your credit-card debts. The downside of priority status is that because you must pay these claims in full over the life of any Chapter 13 plan, you may be effectively ineligible for Chapter 13 if your priority debts are more than you can pay over a five-year plan. By the same token, large priority debts may give you a better chance of passing the Means Test (see Chapter 5).

Nonpriority nondischargeable debts

Most nondischargeable debts are nonpriority debts. These debts can't be given preferential treatment in Chapter 13 and won't help you pass the Means Test (see Chapter 5).

This chapter discusses most of the nonpriority nondischargeable debts. However, we devote separate chapters to credit-card debt (Chapter 14); taxes(Chapter 15); intentional misdeeds (Chapter 16); divorce obligations (Chapter 17) and student loans (Chapter 18).

Nondischargeable Debts in Chapter 7 versus Chapter 13

Some debts that aren't dischargeable in Chapter 7 can still be discharged if you complete a Chapter 13 and get a *super discharge*. Table 13-1 lists which debts are nondischargeable in Chapter 7 and which are nondischargeable in Chapter 13.

Table 13-1 **Nondischargeable Debts Chapter 7 versus Chapter 13**

Types of Debts	Chapter 7	Chapter 13
Income taxes.	(See table in Chapter 15.)	(See table in Chapter 15.)
Employment taxes.	Not dischargeable unless barred by the ten-year statute of limitations.	Same as Chapter 7 and also must be paid in full under Chapter 13 plan.
Loans to pay nondischargeable taxes.	Not dischargeable.	Dischargeable unless borrowed fraudulently (for example, while planning on filing bankruptcy).
Debts from fraud (including credit-card charges made with no intention of paying and those made on the eve of bankruptcy).	Not dischargeable.	Same as Chapter 7.
Welfare and unemployment benefits wrongfully received.	Not dischargeable if benefits received fraudulently. Even if dischargeable, may be deducted from future benefit payments.	Same as Chapter 7.
Real and personal property taxes.	Not dischargeable if assessed against the property owner rather than just the property and were incurred less than one year before bankruptcy.	Same as Chapter 7 and also must be paid in full under Chapter 13 plan.
Claims for willful and malicious conduct.	Not dischargeable.	Dischargeable except for claims for personal injuries assessed by a court or administrative agency.
Claims for theft or embezzlement.	Not dischargeable.	Same as Chapter 7.
Criminal fines and criminal restitution.	Not dischargeable.	Same as Chapter 7.

(continued)

Table 13-1 (continued)

Types of Debts	Chapter 7	Chapter 13
Noncriminal restitution.	Dischargeable unless restitution is considered to be a fine.	Dischargeable unless willful conduct causing personal injury or conduct was fraudulent or involved theft or embezzlement.
Noncriminal fines and penalties (other than tax penalties).	Not dischargeable.	Dischargeable, but nonpayment may result in criminal prosecution.
Personal injury claims from drunk driving, boating, or flying.	Not dischargeable.	Not dischargeable, and claims for drunk driving and boating must be paid in full under a Chapter 13 plan (they're priority claims). Claims for drunk flying are nondischargeable, but do not have to be paid in full under the plan.
Marital property divisions.	Not dischargeable.	Dischargeable unless fraud or some other intentional misconduct involved.
Marital and domestic support obligations.	Not dischargeable.	Not dischargeable and must be paid in full under Chapter 13 plan.
Student loans.	Not discharged unless undue hardship can be proved.	Same as Chapter 7.
Motor vehicle tickets and fines.	Not dischargeable.	Dischargeable if offense was a minor infraction, such as a parking ticket or equipment violation. But local authorities may give you grief for wiping them out. Nondischargeable where the conduct was criminal (for example, driving with a suspended license).

Types of Debts	Chapter 7	Chapter 13
Pension loans.	Not discharged.	Discharged in Chapter 13, but the amount you owe can still be deducted from your pension account.
Unlisted debts.	*Might* be dischargeable in a no-asset case.	Not dischargeable.

Sweating Out the 60-Day Bar Date

Some debts listed in Table 13-1 are actually only *potentially* nondischargeable. A creditor with one of these types of debts must file an *adversary proceeding* — a minilawsuit filed in the bankruptcy court — within 60 days of your 341 meeting with creditors. (Don't confuse an adversary proceeding with filing a *proof of claim,* which requests funds from the bankruptcy estate.) An adversary proceeding to except a debt from discharge seeks to keep the debtor on the hook for the debt despite bankruptcy.

If a creditor wants to use any of the grounds in the following list to try to keep its debt from being discharged, that creditor must meet the 60-day deadline:

- Fraud
- Embezzlement or theft
- Willful and malicious conduct

When the creditor misses this deadline, you're off the hook, provided that the creditor

- Was properly listed on your bankruptcy papers, or
- Knew of your bankruptcy in time to file an adversary proceeding

Avoiding the Urge to Borrow to Pay Nondischargeable Debts

Most loans are dischargeable. So, some people are tempted to take out a bank loan or a cash advance on a credit card to pay a would-be nondischargeable debt, with the aim of discharging the new loan in bankruptcy and essentially trying to replace nondischargeable debt with dischargeable debt.

Bad idea.

If the lender can prove that was your plan all along, the new loan wouldn't be discharged in either a Chapter 7 or Chapter 13 — because of fraud — and may be grounds for dismissing any Chapter 13 filing on bad faith grounds.

Funds borrowed to pay nondischargeable taxes aren't dischargeable in a Chapter 7, even though you weren't planning to file bankruptcy when you took out the loan. But the loan would be dischargeable in Chapter 13 unless you borrowed the money without intending to pay. And remember that if the nondischargeable debt is a *priority* debt, leaving it unpaid as of the petition date can make it easier to pass the Means Test.

See Chapter 15 to find out which taxes are nondischargeable.

Remember that the trustee can also recover some kinds of payments made before bankruptcy and distribute the funds among all your creditors (see Chapter 19). So, not only do you risk the lender's wrath, but also the nondischargeable debt you intended to pay is revived — a double whammy!

Understanding Reaffirmation Agreements

Any debt that is reaffirmed is not eliminated.

Reaffirmation is a process by which you agree to pay all or part of a debt that otherwise is wiped out in bankruptcy. It's as if you never filed bankruptcy on that particular debt; the creditor has all the remedies available before bankruptcy. He can sue you, repossess collateral . . . whatever.

In the old days, creditors used a number of ploys to trick people into reaffirming their debts. Sometimes, if a debtor merely acknowledged the existence of the discharged debt, it automatically was revived. The 1978 Bankruptcy Code sought to put an end to those shenanigans by requiring that reaffirmation agreements be in writing, filed with the court, and subject to cancellation by the debtors for 60 days. In addition, the bankruptcy court must conclude, based on information from the debtor or the debtor's attorney, that reaffirmation doesn't impose an undue hardship and is in the debtor's best interest.

Reasons to reaffirm

Why on earth would someone file Chapter 7 to wipe out her debts and then turn around and reaffirm? Isn't that the ultimate hair-of-the-dog? Good point. But people do reaffirm, and sometimes for good reasons. The reasons folks typically reaffirm are so that they can

- ✔ **Keep collateral that secures the debt.** See Chapter 11.

- ✔ **Maintain credit privileges.** Creditors often offer to extend new credit when you agree to reaffirm a portion of an existing account. Accepting such credit rarely is a good idea. By recognizing that the amount you reaffirm is essentially a finance charge for the new loan, you can see how ridiculously expensive the new credit is. Besides, you probably won't have that much trouble getting new credit anyway.

- ✔ **Compromise a debt to a creditor claiming to have grounds for declaring the debt nondischargeable.** Often, a creditor will go away if you reaffirm just a portion of the disputed debt rather than the whole thing. Reaffirming to settle a potentially nondischargeable debt makes sense only if a creditor has a good case. Your lawyer will know when the creditor is bluffing.

Changing your mind

Even when you sign a reaffirmation agreement, you still can change your mind if you write to the creditor before your discharge is entered or within 60 days after the agreement is filed with the bankruptcy court, whichever is later.

Some creditors don't bother filing reaffirmation agreements with the court, so be sure to find out whether a reaffirmation agreement was filed whenever a creditor tries to sue you on a reaffirmation agreement after bankruptcy. If the agreement was never filed with the bankruptcy court, you still can cancel it.

Having Your Discharge Denied or Revoked

The bankruptcy court has the power in a Chapter 7 case to deny your discharge altogether so that *none* of your debts are erased. That's obviously a stinker. You already surrendered any nonexempt property, your credit record is besmirched with a bankruptcy, and you still owe all your debts. And, to make matters worse, you can never file Chapter 7 on these debts. Now why would a judge do such a nasty thing?

Prior to BARF, as we and other objective observers refer to the bankruptcy reform bill enacted in 2005, discharge denial was reserved for serious, intentional misdeeds. But now, some minor slip-ups can result in your debts not being wiped out.

Under BARF, all debtors are required to complete a course in financial management as a condition of receiving a discharge unless no courses are available in your area. These courses must be approved by the United States Trustee. For many folks, this requirement may seem like a demeaning and unnecessary exercise, and in many cases, it is. Just the same, if approved courses are available in your area, you must complete the program. Otherwise, your bankruptcy was for naught.

Also, under BARF, a party in interest may insist that any federal income tax returns that you file with taxing authorities while your bankruptcy is open also be filed with the court. If you don't, you won't receive a discharge. Finally, after you've made all the payments under Chapter 13, any prepetition support obligation must be paid in full and all support obligations arising after the petition date must be current. If not, no discharge — even though you may have made every payment under your plan.

Instead of providing creditors with copies of your actual tax returns, you can send them *summaries* (transcripts) of the returns. Generally, transcripts contain less personal information than actual tax returns. The IRS usually mails you copies of transcripts if you call the IRS-centralized Priority Hotline at 800-860-4259.

Grounds for denial of a Chapter 7 discharge

A Chapter 7 discharge can be denied if you

- ✔ Received a Chapter 7 discharge in a case filed within eight years of your present filing, or in a Chapter 13 case filed within six years of your present filing (unless creditors were paid at least 70 percent of their claims in the earlier Chapter 13)
- ✔ Consciously fail to list an asset on your bankruptcy schedules
- ✔ Intentionally give false information in your schedules
- ✔ Lie to the trustee at the 341 meeting
- ✔ Refuse to cooperate with the trustee
- ✔ Disobey an order of the bankruptcy court
- ✔ Fraudulently transfer property within one year before bankruptcy
- ✔ Fail to complete a course in financial management after filing your bankruptcy

✔ Don't file all the federal tax returns that should be filed with the court. See Chapter 6.

✔ Act too aggressively in converting nonexempt assets into exempt assets (see Chapter 10).

Grounds for denial of a Chapter 13 discharge

A Chapter 13 discharge can be denied if you

✔ Received a discharge in a prior case filed under Chapter 7, 11, or 12 within four years of your present filing or in a previous Chapter 13 filed within two years

✔ Have not kept up with your postpetition support payments

✔ Don't file all the tax returns that should be filed with the court (see Chapter 6).

✔ Failed to complete a course in financial management while your bankruptcy was pending

Protecting your discharge

The best way to ensure that you receive a discharge is to be completely truthful and make a full disclosure to your lawyer before you file.

If you put property in someone else's name, money into someone else's bank account, or otherwise try to protect any assets from creditors, be sure to tell your lawyer. These errors usually can be repaired when action is taken *before* you file bankruptcy. Afterward, it may be too late. So, remaining silent and hoping that no one finds out about these kinds of transfers is very dangerous. Don't risk it.

Your lawyer needs to give you copies of all the schedules filed with the bankruptcy court. Review them to make sure that all your assets are listed. Innocent mistakes can easily be fixed if you act promptly, especially when you correct your bankruptcy papers before the 341 meeting with creditors. If someone else points out the error, you may have trouble claiming that the mistake was an innocent one.

Revoking your discharge

Although extremely rare, a Chapter 7 or Chapter 13 discharge may be revoked whenever it's obtained by fraud, and the party asking for the revocation did not know about the fraud prior to discharge. *Note:* We're referring to fraud in the bankruptcy case, *not* fraud in incurring the debt in the first place.

A Chapter 7 discharge may also be revoked if you

- ✔ Fail to report or surrender property of the estate
- ✔ Intentionally refused to obey an order of the court

Under BARF, a Chapter 7 discharge may be revoked if the U.S. Trustee chooses your case for a random audit and you

- ✔ Don't satisfactorily explain any mistakes in your bankruptcy paperwork
- ✔ Don't cooperate with the audit

Chapter 14

A House of Cards: Wiping Out Credit-Card Debts

In This Chapter

▶ Drowning in a plastic sea

▶ Looking at your motivation when you incurred debt

▶ Recognizing bogus charges of fraud

▶ Turning the tables on credit-card bullies

▶ Avoiding the pitfalls of credit-card balance transfers

Almost every consumer who faces bankruptcy has some credit-card debts, and most are up to their gills in it. You'd think that credit-card companies, instead of perpetually whining about the relatively meager losses that are attributable to bankruptcy, would instead dispense credit more responsibly.

And you'd be wrong.

Although bankruptcies force some lenders to be a little more careful, most continue dispensing credit with reckless abandon. Because credit-card debt is such a pervasive element in bankruptcy, understanding the fact, fiction, nuances, and implications surrounding it is important. In this chapter, we reveal how creditors play the game, how they sometimes try to pin you for fraud, and how you can avoid getting stuck with the Old Maid card.

Playing the Credit-Card Game

Credit-card lending is the most profitable segment of banking — which is no surprise, given the heads-we-win/tails-you-lose way lenders play the game.

Credit companies: Their home is your hassle

Did you ever wonder why most credit-card companies claim Delaware or South Dakota as their home state? No? Well, maybe you should. It's pretty clever.

In 1978, the U.S. Supreme Court opened the floodgates for consumer lending with its decision in what's known as the *Marquette Case*. The Court ruled that national banks can export the interest rate of the state in which the bank is located to its out-of-state customers and credit-card holders without running afoul of the usury laws of the customers' home states. This decision, in effect, deregulated control of interest rates by individual states and emasculated state usury laws.

Delaware and South Dakota figured they could attract big lenders by eliminating interest rate restrictions in the wake of *Marquette*.

They were right.

All too often, people accept unsolicited, preapproved credit-card offers that, simply put, make getting into credit trouble all too easy. Borrowers max out their credit cards but find themselves making only the minimum monthly payments at interest rates of around 15 percent (and often higher). Fifteen percent is the average. With this kind of dutiful payment practice in place, credit-card companies happily skim off profits of double, triple, or even quadruple the prime-lending rate. Oh, happy days!

And these unsolicited, preapproved credit-card offers never seem to stop coming (even when your credit report tanks), tempting people to apply for *another* credit card that promises an *additional* credit limit and *increased* borrowing power with which they can cover the monthly minimum payments on their first credit card. Ah, yes, this vicious circle truly is how the credit-card game works. And, you know what? Consumers rarely win.

Whenever you find yourself on the losing side of the credit-card game, consult a bankruptcy lawyer to explore your options and develop a comprehensive plan for handling the problem before it gets worse.

Don't give in to the temptation of paying off your debts by using the equity in your home. Sure, the interest rate on a home-equity loan may be lower and the interest you pay may be tax-deductible, but when you're struggling to make only minimum payments on credit cards, you'll probably have the same kind of trouble making payments on a home-equity loan and face losing your most important asset in the process. Before taking a home-equity loan, your homestead may well be off-limits to credit-card lenders, even if you don't file bankruptcy. When you take out a home-equity loan, you put your house on the line for debts that probably can be eliminated in bankruptcy, or maybe just ignored.

Similarly, think long and hard before dipping into your IRA or 401(k) to pay off credit cards. You'll get socked with hefty tax penalties and may not even be able to solve all your credit-card woes. You get to keep most types of retirement plans in bankruptcy (see Chapter 10), so check with a bankruptcy lawyer *before* raiding your retirement plans.

Watch out for debt-consolidation outfits that may try to convince you to make futile attempts at repaying your debts without clearly informing you that your creditors are paying them a percentage of the money they collect from you. Some borrowers succeed in paying their debts through consolidation, but many people make payments for years only to eventually end up in bankruptcy.

Seeing What Judges See

Bankruptcy judges are growing increasingly unsympathetic with credit-card predators who have the gall to come into their courts and claim that *they* were the ones defrauded. Although your odds of finding a sympathetic judge seem to be increasing, the rule of law reigns, and few judges will violate their legal and ethical obligations to apply that rule just because they don't like the way a credit-card company operates. That said, what you need is an understanding of the legal framework so that you can judge for yourself whether a credit-card company has a legitimate complaint against you. Creditors argue that when someone uses a credit card, he implies that he has the ability and intent to pay. If it turns out that the customer couldn't afford to pay the charges, he's guilty of fraud . . . or so goes the theory of creditors.

Some courts buy this argument, but most find it simplistic and, absent additional circumstances, not terribly persuasive, for reasons that are all but self-evident: Although a customer's use of a credit card may imply that he *intends* to pay, it should not imply that he has the present *ability to pay*. After all, many folks use credit cards precisely because they're short of cash —which is precisely what credit-card companies encourage in their endless solicitations. Remember, debts from fraud are nondischargeable in either Chapter 7 or Chapter 13.

Until recently, debtors could avoid the so-called credit-card fraud issue altogether by filing under Chapter 13 instead of Chapter 7. Even credit-card abusers were given absolution if they were at least willing to pay as much as they could afford over three years.

Not surprisingly, BARF, the alleged "reform" law largely written by the credit-card industry, changes all that. Now there's no escape for credit-card fraud, even if you file Chapter 13. The problem is, fraud very much is in eye of the beholder, and you may find yourself so-labeled even though you did not intend to cheat and merely acted foolishly.

Examining Your Mind Set When You Incurred the Debt

Figuring out whether you acted fraudulently, or just foolishly, takes something of a mind-reading act for the court to accomplish. The court isn't really looking for an excuse to slam you, but if you give the judge a reason, there's a good chance you'll get whacked with a fraud judgment. In addition to the obvious subjective element, a number of objective questions come into play. You may want to ask yourself:

✔ **Did I make a bunch of charges right before bankruptcy?** It's obvious that the closer to bankruptcy that the charges occur, the more likely that a judge may think that you never intended to pay.

A number of small charges within a very short time when an account is in default or over the limit may suggest that the customer purposely kept charges below levels where a merchant is likely to check the card (knowing that the lender would never authorize them). Particularly damning are multiple small charges on the same day. Changes in your charging habits may also indicate an intention not to pay. If, for example, you typically charged about $150 per month, and then a few months before bankruptcy you started charging like crazy, a court may be inclined to think that you bought things on credit while planning to file bankruptcy.

✔ **Did I make charges after talking to a bankruptcy lawyer?** Whenever you charge purchases after talking to a bankruptcy attorney, appearances point to your already having decided to file bankruptcy when you bought the stuff on credit. However, courts realize that many people visit a bankruptcy attorney just to find out their options, and many never end up filing or, at best, wait as long as possible before doing so. So, the mere fact that you charge some purchases after talking to a bankruptcy attorney is not conclusive evidence of a fraudulent mental state.

✔ **What was my financial condition when I made the charges?** The fact that a person is in dire financial straits when incurring debt is relevant as to whether he intended to pay but, again, it isn't definitive. If you honestly believed that things would turn around, that a new job would come through, that you'd be able to refinance your home, that your business would take off, and yes, even that your luck would turn around at the gambling casino, you're probably not in trouble.

In the eyes of most judges, the key determination isn't whether you realistically expected to come up with the cash, but whether you honestly (even if foolishly) believed your ship would come in.

✔ **Did I buy luxury items?** The concept here is that someone buying necessities is more likely to repay the debt than someone who purchases luxury items. But a luxury for one person is a necessity for another.

Forcing the Credit-Card Company to Prove Its Case

Courts don't merely consider whether a debtor was at fault in making excessive credit-card charges: They also consider the degree to which creditors irresponsibly push credit cards on folks who can't afford to pay. In keeping you from wiping out the debt, the creditor must prove that it had no reason to know that you were drowning in debt at the time it authorized the charges.

Several courts have ruled that creditors who issue cards to people whose lack of creditworthiness would have been revealed by an ordinary credit report can't claim that the cards they issue were used fraudulently. These judges say that if the credit-card company had exercised just a little prudence, it would have known that the last thing that person needed was yet another credit card.

The same is true for many creditors that rely on statistical credit scores like the ones prepared by the three national credit bureaus — Equifax, Trans Union, and Experian. Each company has a protocol for its scoring system, but all are based on a computer credit model called the Fair, Isaac credit bureau score, sometimes called FICO. Like it or not, anyone who uses credit cards has a FICO score.

Courts have observed that FICO scores reveal little more than whether a prospective borrower has made timely minimum payments on his account and have disputed whether a creditor is justified in basing its decision to extend credit solely on those scores. These courts are less than understanding in cases where credit-card companies conduct no meaningful investigation into creditworthiness before issuing cards. Only when the debtor files bankruptcy does the creditor come up with so many reasons why it wouldn't have extended credit if had it only been aware of the debtor's financial condition — and argues, therefore, that the court should not allow the debtor to wipe out this particular debt.

Explaining Presumptively Fraudulent Charges

Luxury purchases totaling more than $500 to a single creditor within 90 days of bankruptcy or cash advances totaling more than $750 to a single creditor within 70 days of bankruptcy are presumptively fraudulent. *Presumptively fraudulent* means that instead of the usual situation where a creditor must prove fraudulent intent, the debtor has the burden of convincing the court that he intended to pay for these charges.

However, different judges may understandably have different ideas on what constitutes a "luxury." But you can still rebut the presumption of fraud by showing that you really did intend to pay the charges when you made them.

A prudent bankruptcy attorney attempts to sidestep any problems with presumptively fraudulent charges by simply waiting at least 90 days from the last significant credit purchase before filing the bankruptcy. But there may be reasons why other considerations require an immediate filing. For example, if a foreclosure sale is imminent, you probably can't afford to wait, and your recent purchases may be called into question.

Defending Against False Financial Statement Allegations

Occasionally, a creditor, seeking to prevent its account from being wiped out by bankruptcy, claims fraud on the grounds that the customer obtained credit privileges through the use of a false financial statement.

Most modern credit-card applications ask for little more than a name, address, Social Security number, and income. As credit companies request less and less information on their loan applications, claiming that you committed fraud by not revealing what wasn't asked becomes more and more difficult for them.

The creditor doesn't necessarily win just because your income was not as high as you indicated on the credit-card application. The creditor must also establish that you knew that your statement was false, that you intended to deceive the company, and that it would not have approved credit privileges if it otherwise had known about your actual income. This gambit is next to impossible to prove, especially when a creditor made its decision based on credit scores and not on the credit application.

Using Credit-Card Advances for Gambling

Many people who get into credit-card trouble are gamblers and, for many problem gamblers, the credit-card industry behaves like an all-too-eager-to-please bartender in a room full of binge drinkers. Some creditors even put ATM machines in gambling casinos, thereby encouraging customers to gamble with cash advances. Then, when a customer ends up in bankruptcy, these same companies try to keep the advances from being wiped out by alleging that the debtor was guilty of fraud for using cash advances for gambling — the very thing that the company encouraged them to do in the first place.

If your only hope of paying your debts was to hit the jackpot, you may be looking at an allegation of credit-card abuse. However, the criteria employed by most judges is not an objective analysis of whether your dream of hitting the big one made sense, but rather is a subjective analysis of whether that scenario made sense to you. Your case would be even stronger if, in the past, you used winnings to pay debts.

Bottom line: Even if you used credit cards for gambling, most courts would still allow you to wipe out the charges provided that you honestly believed that you would win enough to repay the charges.

Bullying the Credit-Card Bullies

Creditors are well aware that many debtors are essentially broke and that the last thing they want to do, or are able to do, is pay extra for their bankruptcy attorney to defend them against an allegation of fraud. Sometimes creditors claim fraud in a bankruptcy case regardless of whether the claim has merit, hoping that the debtor settles by agreeing to repay part of the debt.

The Bankruptcy Code, however, provides you with a measure of protection against this sort of arm-twisting. If you put up a fight and win, the creditor can be ordered to pay your attorney fees and, in extreme cases, be fined.

ANECDOTE

Credit-card company pays the price for bullying

As her credit report duly noted, Claire was buried in debt when a credit-marketing company sent her a preapproved line of credit. Not surprisingly, Claire used the new line of credit in a desperate and misguided attempt to pay off her older bills. When she ended up filing bankruptcy, the credit-card company that extended the credit line tried to prevent the debt that was owed from being wiped out by alleging that Claire fraudulently accepted and used the loan knowing full well she could not pay. Because Claire certainly couldn't afford to pay any more money to her bankruptcy attorney to defend against the fraud, she figured that she'd just have to settle.

Not so fast!

Claire's attorney promptly directed the court's attention to the fact that the credit-card company initiated a frivolous fraud claim in an attempt to extort a settlement from his client. The court not only dismissed the fraud allegation, but it also ordered the credit-card company to pay Claire's legal bills.

Transferring Credit-Card Balances

Just about everyone with a mailbox is constantly bombarded with pleas from credit-card lenders to use their low-interest cards to pay off balances on competitors' cards. Odd that these solicitations avoid using words like "borrow" or "loan," isn't it? Instead, they euphemistically label these transactions "balance transfers." Predictably, many people fail to fully realize that the "transfer" actually is a new loan — but that's exactly what it is.

If you're excruciatingly careful and diligent and able to essentially juggle your books without dropping any balls (and if you were that good at financial gymnastics, you probably wouldn't be reading this book), it is possible to play the transfer game to your advantage. For example, you can pay off one loan with another loan that carries a lower "teaser" interest rate and save money as long as you pay off the second loan before the interest rate jumps, which it will. In our experience, however, most people who play this game lose, and the people who promote these transfer gimmicks obviously know the odds are against you. In fact, they literally bank on it.

Recognize balance transfers for what they are and fully explain to your attorney any transfers you've made so that he can decide whether delaying your bankruptcy for a few months would be better.

There are two reasons to delay bankruptcy:

- ✔ Because a balance transfer is a loan, if you file within 90 days of the transfer, the debt might be presumed to have been fraudulent. See the section "Explaining Presumptively Fraudulent Charges," earlier in this chapter.

- ✔ Because a balance transfer is also a payment on an existing debt, if you file bankruptcy within 90 days of the transfer, the trustee could recover the money and thereby complicate your bankruptcy (see Chapter 19).

Chapter 15

Give unto Caesar: Using Bankruptcy to Deal with Tax Debts

Sometimes you can get rid of your tax obligations through bankruptcy, but doing so isn't an easy task. Taxes generally can't be discharged in a Chapter 7 bankruptcy and must be paid in full over the life of a Chapter 13 repayment plan. Nevertheless, under a complicated set of rules and court decisions, you may be able to escape paying taxes, if enough time passes between the time you incurred the tax liability and the time that you file bankruptcy.

In this chapter, we explain the circumstances under which you can wipe out your federal and state income taxes and certain other kinds of taxes. In Table 15-1, we provide a detailed reference to how bankruptcy deals with federal income taxes. We also look briefly at the tactic of borrowing to pay your taxes. See Chapter 9 for nonbankruptcy solutions to your tax problems.

Getting a Handle on What Happens to Taxes in Bankruptcy

Figuring out what will happen to your tax obligations in bankruptcy can be a real bugger. Debts can fall into three categories:

✔ Dischargeable debts that get wiped out.

✔ Nondischargeable *priority* debts that don't get wiped out and must be paid in full under the terms of any Chapter 13 plan. The upshot to priority debts is that having them will make it easier to pass the Means Test. Also, in Chapter 13, you can pay priority debts while paying little or nothing on other types of debts that will be wiped out even if not paid.

✔ Nondischargeable *nonpriority* debts that don't get wiped out, can't be paid ahead of other debts in Chapter 13, and don't help you pass the Means Test. The upside is that you're not required to pay them in full under a Chapter 13 plan.

Tax obligations can fall into any one of these categories.

Wiping Out Dischargeable Income Taxes

As a general proposition, if you filed a timely, nonfraudulent income tax return and haven't engaged in tax evasion other than simply failing to pay the tax, your debt to Uncle Sam is dischargeable in a Chapter 7 or a Chapter 13 — assuming, that is, that the taxes are more than three years old and were assessed more than 240 days before bankruptcy. Simple, right? Of course not.

Nothing is simple when dealing with that veritable monument to Murphy's Law — the good 'ol tax statutes.

For example, if a tax return for 2000 was due April 15, 2001, you may reasonably think that if you filed bankruptcy after April 15, 2004, the taxes would vanish, right? But reasonable thinking doesn't necessarily apply. After all, you're dealing with the Internal Revenue Service. If you received an extension of time to file your return, the three-year period starts on the date that the extension (or extensions) expires. It doesn't start on the date the return originally was due.

Besides extensions, certain events can also interrupt the three-year period, giving the IRS even more time to collect your taxes. For example,

✔ If you filed a bankruptcy case prior to your current bankruptcy, the time that the earlier case was open isn't counted, and 90 days are added to the three years.

✔ Any time that the IRS was prevented from collecting taxes because of a request for a due process hearing (see Chapter 9 for more on due process hearings) does not count, and an additional 90 days is tacked on.

✔ Any amount of time during which a *taxpayer assistance order* (where a taxpayer advocate tells the IRS to lay off you for a while) is in effect doesn't count toward the three years. See Chapter 9 for more information on the taxpayer advocate and taxpayer assistance orders.

Bottom line: If you neglected to file a return, filed it late, submitted a fraudulent return, or otherwise evaded taxes, you've really confuzzled things. But, depending on what you did and why you did it (not paying because you were broke is less of a problem than flat-out lying), bankruptcy may be able to help.

Paying Nondischargeable Priority Income Taxes

Nondischargeable priority taxes are income taxes less than three years old (as calculated in the preceding section) and also taxes assessed within 240 days of bankruptcy.

Although these taxes have to be paid in full under any Chapter 13 plan, priority taxes have several advantages over other nondischargeable debts that do not enjoy priority status:

- ✔ They can help you pass the Means Test (see Chapter 5).

- ✔ In Chapter 13 bankruptcy, you pay these taxes in full (so that they don't haunt you after completion of the plan), while paying little or nothing on dischargeable claims such as credit-card debts.

- ✔ Postpetition interest does not accrue on these claims. (unless a notice of tax lien has been recorded).

- ✔ If the IRS doesn't file a proof of claim in time (180 days after the petition date), these taxes get wiped out even if they're not paid.

Coping with Nondischargeable Nonpriority Income Taxes

Nondischargeable nonpriority taxes are those due more than three years ago and assessed more than 240 day before bankruptcy where you

- ✔ Never filed a return (although the IRS can, and often will, file a *dummy return,* which is a return filed by the feds in your name so that the government can assess a tax. This type of return doesn't count unless the return was filed with your cooperation and assistance).

- ✔ Filed a late return less than two years before bankruptcy. Example: Your 2000 income tax return was due on April 15, 2001. But you didn't actually file the return until July 21, 2003, so the taxes would not be dischargeable in a bankruptcy before July 21, 2005. A growing number of courts say that a return filed by a taxpayer after the IRS has already prepared a dummy return doesn't count. So taxes for this year would be nondischargeable nonpriority taxes even though a debtor filed a return more than two years before bankruptcy.

- ✔ Filed a fraudulent return or intentionally tried to evade taxes.

Claiming too many dependents was tax evasion

Joe told his employer he had eight dependents, but he really had only one. As a result, Joe took home more money from each paycheck. When tax time rolled around, Joe discovered that he couldn't pay his whopping tax obligation because he'd already spent all his extra take-home pay. And yet Joe still properly filed his income tax return; however, he didn't pay the taxes.

Four years later, when Joe filed Chapter 7 bankruptcy, the court refused to wipe out his taxes, saying that Joe was guilty of tax evasion for claiming too many dependents and spending the money on other things.

These taxes are more troublesome than priority taxes because

✔ They don't help you get past the Means Test.

✔ Interest on these taxes continues to accrue.

✔ You can't give them preferential treatment in Chapter 13.

Confronting Unfiled Tax Returns

If you want to file Chapter 13, prior to the 341 meeting, you have to file with the appropriate taxing authorities all federal, state, and local tax returns for the past four years. If you don't, your case may be dismissed. However, you may get an extension of up to 120 days to file these returns.

Although you should have all your returns *prepared* prior to filing bankruptcy, you should consult with a bankruptcy lawyer before actually filing the returns with taxing authorities. Remember that taxes assessed within 240 days of bankruptcy are priority taxes. It may be to your benefit to file tax returns and have the tax assessed within this 240-day period. On the other hand, bestowing priority status on nondischargeable taxes may render you ineligible for Chapter 13 if the tax liability is more than you can pay under your Chapter 13 plan during the maximum five year life of the plan.

If any interested party so requests, you also have to file with the bankruptcy court copies of any federal returns that are filed with the IRS while your bankruptcy is open.

Table 15-1	Discharging Federal Income Taxes	
	Chapter 7	*Chapter 13*
Taxes less than three years old (no IRS Notice of Tax Lien). Measured from the date the return was due, which usually is April 15 of the following year, unless you got an extension to file. If you had a prior bankruptcy, the time period during which the automatic stay was in effect doesn't count. Also, any period when a taxpayer assistance order was in effect or the federal government is barred from collection because of a request for a due process hearing doesn't count. In both situations, an additional 90 days are added on.	Not discharged. Must make payment arrangements with IRS after bankruptcy is closed.	Not discharged, *unless* the IRS fails to file a proof of claim. But the taxes can be paid over the life of the plan without further penalties, and without postpetition interest (unless a Notice of Tax Lien has been filed), can be given preferential treatment.
Taxes more than three years old (returns filed late, and within two years of the petition date, no IRS Notice of Tax Lien). If you had a prior bankruptcy, the time period during which the automatic stay was in effect doesn't count. Also, any period when a taxpayer assistance order was in effect or the federal government is barred from collection because of a request for a due process hearing does not count. In both situations, an additional 90 days are added on.	Not discharged.	Not discharged even if IRS fails to file a proof of claim, can't be given preferential treatment, and postpetition interest accrues *unless* the taxes are assessed within 240 days of the petition date.

(continued)

Table 15-1 *(continued)*

	Chapter 7	Chapter 13
Taxes more than three years old (returns never filed, no IRS Notice of Tax Lien).	Not discharged.	Not discharged even if IRS fails to file a proof of claim, can't be given preferential treatment, and postpetition interest accrues *unless* the taxes are assessed within 240 days of the petition date.
Taxes more than three years old (fraudulent taxes filed or other intentional tax evasion, no IRS Notice of Tax Lien).	Not discharged.	Not discharged even if IRS fails to file a proof of claim, can't be given preferential treatment, and postpetition interest accrues *unless* the taxes are assessed within 240 days of the petition date.
Taxes assessed within 240 days. This 240-day period is extended by a prior bank-ruptcy the same way that the three-year period is extended. Also, any time that a taxpayer assistance order is in effect doesn't count. In addition, any period during which an IRS offer in compromise was pending, plus 30 days, is added to the 240-day period. Also, any time that the fed-eral government was barred from collection because of a due process hearing request does not count and 90 days is added. Taxes are usually assessed shortly, after the return is filed. Taxes assessed later are usually those arising from an audit.	Not discharged.	Not discharged, unless the IRS fails to file a proof of claim. But the taxes can be paid over the life of the plan without further penalties and without postpetition interest (unless a Notice of Tax Lien has been filed). Can be given preferential treatment.

	Chapter 7	*Chapter 13*
IRS Notice of Tax Lien filed.	Even if the taxes are discharged, any property owned on the petition date, including exempt property, remains subject to the tax lien. If the taxes are discharged, any property acquired after the petition date would not be subject to the lien.	*Regardless* of whether the taxes are discharged, a Notice of Tax Lien gives the IRS a secured claim up to the value of all your property on the petition date. The secured claim must be paid, with interest, over the life of the plan. (Instead of paying the lien for taxes that would otherwise be dischargeable, your Chapter 13 plan can propose to surrender everything you owned on the petition date to the IRS, in full satisfaction of the lien. If all you owned were household goods and a car, it's unlikely that the IRS would actually bother taking the items.)
Prepetition interest.	Discharged *only* if the underlying taxes are discharged.	Discharged *only* if the underlying taxes are discharged.
Postpetition interest on prepetition taxes.	Continues to accrue on nondischargeable taxes.	Accrues on nonpriority but not priority taxes. However, if you filed a joint return for these taxes, but your spouse did not join you in filing Chapter 13, the IRS can still come after her for interest that accrued during the Chapter 13 case. If the Chapter 13 case is dismissed or converted, interest that would have accrued is revived. If a Notice of Tax Lien have been filed, interest may accrue, even on priority taxes.

(continued)

Table 15-1 (continued)

	Chapter 7	Chapter 13
Prepetition penalties.	Discharged if *either* the underlying tax is discharged, or the event giving rise to the penalty occurred more than three years before the petition date. But if a Notice of Tax Lien has been filed, the penalties are covered by that lien.	Discharged if they relate to dischargeable or nondischargeable *priority* taxes, but not penalties for nonpriority nondischargeable taxes. But if a Notice of Tax Lien has been filed, the penalties are included in the amount of the government's secured claim.
Postpetition penalties on prepetition taxes.	Not assessed if the tax is discharged. Not assessed while the case is open (usually about four months).	Possibly, but not definitely, assessed if the case is dismissed. Not assessed if the plan is completed.

Coping with Interest and Penalties

The government charges interest and imposes heavy penalties when you don't pay your taxes on time. Sometimes, interest and penalties add up to more than the tax itself.

Interest is treated differently than penalties in bankruptcy. In addition, different rules exist for interest and penalties accruing before you file for bankruptcy ("prepetition") and those arising after you file ("postpetition").

Prepetition interest charged on unpaid taxes is, for the most part, treated the same as taxes in both a Chapter 7 and a 13. When the tax is nondischargeable, so is the interest. Penalties, on the other hand, are discharged in a Chapter 7 if they are more than three years old. In a Chapter 13, however, prepetition penalties are dischargeable regardless of when they arose.

Postpetition interest on nondischargeable taxes continues accruing during and after a Chapter 7 case. Interest stops accruing in a Chapter 13 case when it's filed. And yet, whenever a Chapter 13 bankruptcy is dismissed or converted to a Chapter 7, interest is added as if no Chapter 13 had been filed.

Here's a wrinkle: If you filed a joint return for taxes included in your Chapter 13 case, but your spouse didn't join you in filing Chapter 13, the IRS still can come after her for interest that accrues while your Chapter 13 case is open.

Penalties on nondischargeable taxes aren't assessed while a Chapter 7 or a Chapter 13 case is open. Keep in mind that a Chapter 7 case is usually not open very long — typically just a few months — unlike a Chapter 13, which ordinarily lasts for at least three years.

Managing Federal Tax Liens

If you owe taxes, the IRS can record a Notice of Tax Lien in the pubic records. Doing so gives it a lien (see Chapter 11 for the lowdown on liens) on all your earthly belongings. Although the IRS periodically issues guidelines as to when a Notice of Tax Lien should be filed, the decision rests largely with the tax collector handling your case.

If a Notice of Tax Lien has been lodged before you file bankruptcy, the rules in the previous section don't apply and discharging taxes becomes even more difficult.

Taxes due, together with associated interest and penalties, are secured by all your prepetition assets (including your retirement plan, which is usually protected from most other creditors). Even when these obligations are dischargeable, they still encumber prepetition assets. If you suspect that a tax lien is about to be filed, contact a bankruptcy specialist immediately.

Making the Trustee Pay Your Taxes

If you think that you'll owe federal income taxes for the current year, and you have assets that will be liquidated in your bankruptcy, you may be able to get the trustee to pay the taxes.

The Tax Code enables Chapter 7 debtors to divide the year in which they file bankruptcy into two short years. For example: If you filed Chapter 7 bankruptcy September 2, 2005, you can elect to divide the tax year 2005 into two parts — the first running from January 1, 2005, to September 2, 2005, and the second running from September 3, 2005, to December 31, 2005. Consequently, liabilities that accrued up to September 2, 2005, are considered prepetition priority claims, which the trustee must pay ahead of other creditors.

This *short-year election* must be made shortly after filing bankruptcy. So, discuss this with your lawyer before you ever file. In addition to making the election, you or your lawyer need to make sure that a timely *proof of claim* is filed by or on behalf of the IRS. See Chapter 6 to find out more about the claims process.

Keeping on Top of Postpetition Taxes in Chapter 13

If you're paying off taxes under Chapter 13, be aware that income taxes arising after bankruptcy aren't discharged, so you should plan on keeping up with future tax obligations. If you can't pay postpetition taxes immediately, you can submit a payment proposal to the IRS when you file your return. If you propose to pay the postpetition tax within three years, the IRS will probably go along. See Chapter 9 for more on submitting payment plans to the IRS.

In a Chapter 13, if you don't keep up with postpetition taxes, your bankruptcy plan may fall apart. See Chapter 20 to see why it's so important to stay on top of postpetition taxes in a Chapter 13.

Paying Taxes Before Bankruptcy

If you owe nondischargeable taxes, consider selling nonexempt property and paying off the tax debt before filing bankruptcy. If part of your tax obligation is dischargeable, you can force the IRS to apply the payments to the nondischargeable part. However, you lose this option after you file bankruptcy. (See Chapter 9 for more about the benefits of allocating tax payments.) But, as we explain in Chapter 19, paying large debts shortly before bankruptcy sometimes can backfire, so don't pay any taxes without first consulting with your lawyer. Also, you may have a better chance of passing the Means Test if priority taxes remain unpaid at the time of bankruptcy (see Chapter 5).

Using the Statute of Limitations to Escape Taxes

Time heals many wounds, including some tax debts. Generally, if more than ten years go by after income taxes are assessed (which is usually shortly after you filed your return), the taxes vanish even if you don't file bankruptcy. But certain factors suspend or extend the statute of limitations (see Chapter 8).

Facing the Consequences if You're a "Tax Protestor"

The courts are fed up with tax protestors. If you have a history of opposing income taxes on constitutional, religious, or philosophical grounds, don't expect much sympathy. The IRS considers you a CPA — Certified Pain in the . . . — and it's going to strenuously object to the discharging of old taxes in a Chapter 7, arguing that you're guilty of intentional tax evasion. If you file a Chapter 13, it may try to get your case dismissed on *bad faith grounds*. A tax protestor who wants to discharge her taxes in bankruptcy has to prove that she has seen the light, and her protesting days are over.

Dealing with the State Tax Man

For the most part, the same rules that apply to federal taxes also cover state income taxes — with one peculiar glitch. Most, if not all, states require you to file an amended state tax return whenever your federal tax liability for a given year changes (perhaps as a result of an audit). Some courts hold that when you fail to file an amended state return in this situation, your initial state return is deemed "unfiled." The result is that your entire state tax — and not just the amount that would have been added had you amended the state return — can no longer be discharged in a Chapter 7 filing.

Addressing Taxes Other Than Income Taxes

As a general rule, nonincome taxes (with the exception of trust fund taxes, which we discuss in the following section) are dischargeable in a Chapter 7 or a Chapter 13, if whatever caused the tax liability occurred more than three years before the bankruptcy filing date.

Paying trust fund employment taxes

Employers are required to withhold certain taxes, known as *trust fund taxes,* from employees' paychecks and turn them over to the government on a regular basis throughout the year. If these taxes aren't paid, the government can go after the company, the owners of the company, and the company employees who were responsible for remitting the funds to the government and intentionally failed to do so. These taxes aren't dischargeable in any type of bankruptcy unless they're barred by the statute of limitations. Also, they're priority debts that must be paid in full under any Chapter 13 plan.

When a business is going down the tubes, paying trade creditors and letting employment taxes slide to continue to operate is tempting. This strategy almost always is a mistake. Employment taxes should be the *first* thing paid, not the last.

Deciding whether to pay real and personal property taxes

Certain advantages and disadvantages can be realized when deciding between paying or not paying real and personal property taxes, and you need to make a smart decision about what you're going to do.

Real property taxes

Real property taxes — taxes imposed on land and buildings, — are typically a problem only when you want to keep the property. That's because these taxes are assessed against the property, not against the owner personally. Nonetheless, the taxes are liens and must be paid if you intend to keep the property. In addition, failure to pay real property taxes probably constitutes a default under your mortgage, the same as when you fail to make your mortgage payments.

Personal property taxes

Personal property taxes — taxes paid on items that aren't real estate (such as cars) — aren't dischargeable if, under local law, they are assessed against the owner personally rather than against only the property and are less than one year old.

Obtaining Loans to Pay Your Taxes

If you borrow money to pay nondischargeable taxes, the loan is not dischargeable in Chapter 7. But you may be able to get rid of it in Chapter 13, unless you borrowed the money while contemplating bankruptcy. Also, replacing an obligation to pay priority taxes with a nonpriority debt may make it tougher to pass the Means Test — that new test to figure out if you have means to repay some of your debts (see Chapter 5).

The federal government and some states encourage folks to use credit cards to pay their taxes. Paying taxes with your credit cards is seldom a good idea if a bankruptcy is in your future.

In any event, don't pay any large debts prior to bankruptcy before reading Chapter 19 to see how a bankruptcy trustee can sometimes recover this money, which can leave you worse off than if you had never paid the debt in the first place.

Chapter 16

The Devil Made Me Do It: Fines, Fraud, and Other Foibles

*B*ankruptcy is designed to give honest debtors a second chance, not to provide a safe haven for crooks and scalawags. So, for the most part, if you intentionally cheat someone or purposely hurt someone, the U.S. Bankruptcy Code isn't your safety net. Still, bankruptcy law coexists with other laws and balances competing interests — legally, politically, and morally. That's always a difficult balancing act.

For example, society has a powerful interest in seeing you get back on your feet. Only then can you rejoin the productive and taxpaying citizens who serve as cogs in the economic and social engine. At the same time, society has an interest in ensuring that those whom you've harmed don't get short-changed simply because you're now broke. So how can the law put you back on your feet, without kicking the legs out from under innocent bystanders? Sometimes it takes the Wisdom of Solomon — plus a dose of sincere remorse on your part.

Many debts that arise from intentional misconduct can't be wiped out in a Chapter 7 bankruptcy, but you have a shot at getting out from under that cloud by filing a Chapter 13. If you demonstrate your contrition and genuinely pay as much as you can under a Chapter 13 repayment plan, even your debts for intentional wrongdoing may be eliminated.

If you've been convicted of a *crime of violence,* the victim may ask that a Chapter 7 case be dismissed. The definition of crime of violence is quite broad and includes the threat of violence or, in some situations, conduct that carries only the threat of violence, such as burglary.

Also, if you're being sued for intentionally or recklessly inflicting serious personal injuries, a glitch under BARF allows a court to delay discharging your debts. But nobody yet knows how that will play out. So, for now, it's just something to keep in mind and discuss with your attorney.

In this chapter, we look at debts stemming from fraud and other misdeeds and explore your options.

Dealing with Debts Resulting from Fraud

So, what's fraud? It doesn't mean that you're merely unable to pay your debts. Just because you're broke doesn't mean that you committed fraud, or anything of the sort. If that were the case, no one ever would get bankruptcy relief. Still, creditors may accuse you of fraud if they think that doing so prevents the elimination of your debt to them. But they have to prove that

- ✔ You knowingly made a false representation.
- ✔ You intended to deceive the creditor.
- ✔ The creditor actually and justifiably relied on your representation.
- ✔ As a result of your misrepresentation, the creditor suffered damage.

That may be a bunch to prove, but it can be done — as we explain in the following sections.

Debts from fraud are *nondischargeable nonpriority debts*. See Chapter 13 for the difference between priority and nonpriority debts.

Charges on the eve of bankruptcy

Congress and the courts aren't particularly fond of people accumulating new debts right before they file bankruptcy. It just smells like you racked up debts with no intention of paying your bills. Eve-of-bankruptcy spending binges is really bad karma. Don't risk it.

Luxury purchases totaling more than $500 within 90 days of bankruptcy and credit cash advances totaling more than $750 within 70 days of bankruptcy are presumed fraudulent. For that reason, it's not a good idea to put bankruptcy attorney fees on your credit card. (See Chapter 14 for more on credit cards and fraud.)

Chapter 7: No escape for a coverup

When Zeke sold his house to Brenda, he assured her that his humble abode was solid as a rock, but that wasn't exactly true.

Actually, the foundation had shifted and the walls were cracking, and Zeke knew it. In fact, he covered the cracks with paint so that Brenda and her real estate agent couldn't see the evidence. Brenda bought the house and soon discovered she was facing thousands of dollars of repair work. She sued, so Zeke filed a Chapter 7 bankruptcy to escape liability. The judge wasn't about to let Zeke play the system for a sucker and gave Brenda the green light to pursue her fraud claim.

False financial statements

Did you ever wonder why some lenders require such a complicated financial statement even though you own only a few items? The answer is simple: Debts obtained through falsely written financial statements aren't dischargeable. Creditors know this rule, and some try to provide the rope with which to hang yourself in the event you end up in bankruptcy.

Some lenders actually encourage you to exaggerate your income or the value of your assets. Then, if you ever file bankruptcy, they dig out the financial statement, point to any inaccuracies, and claim that their debt isn't dischargeable because you provided false information on your financial statement. Sneaky, huh?

The courts think so, and fortunately they require the creditor to prove that you intentionally lied and that the creditor reasonably relied on the misrepresentation in making the loan. In other words, they must show not only that the information was inaccurate, but also that you knew it was inaccurate and that they wouldn't have given you a loan had they known the truth.

Be on your guard whenever a lender asks for a financial statement. Be scrupulously honest and don't ever let anyone coax you into exaggerating. The loan officer may be setting a trap. (See Chapter 14 for more information on whether the information you put on a credit-card application ever is deemed a false financial statement.)

Bad checks

Writing bad checks is considered fraudulent only when the creditor can prove that you knew, or should have known, that the check would bounce.

Payday loans

Payday loans are an epidemic of New Age loan sharking that are spreading at an alarming rate.

Here's how they work. Outfits accept a post-dated check in exchange for cash, with the understanding that you'll buy back the check for the amount of cash advanced, plus a hefty fee, whenever you receive your paycheck. The effective interest rate on these loans can run up to 500 percent, and even higher!

They make this loan knowing full well that when you wrote the check, you didn't have enough money in your account to cover it. In fact, they hope that you won't be able to redeem your check for a long time because each time

payday rolls around and you don't buy back the check, they charge additional fees. The underlying threat is that if you don't eventually pay, you'll be charged with fraud.

That's baloney! There's no fraud here — at least, not on the customer's part. These loans should be dischargeable in bankruptcy the same as any other debt.

If you think that the only people engaging in this type of lending have thick necks and crooked noses, you're wrong. Some of our nation's largest banks are in the payday loan business. They're in the lobbying and political contribution business, too.

Most creditors won't bother unless the check is a big one. So, as a practical matter, debts from rubber checks frequently are discharged. Just the same, banks blacklist people who don't make good on checks, and you may have trouble obtaining a new checking account. Keeping your checkbook balanced is definitely a good idea.

In any case, never let a creditor talk you into signing a postdated check. If it turns out that you can't cover the check, the creditor may claim that you knew the check was bad and, for that reason, claim that the debt shouldn't be wiped out. Or, even worse, the creditor may file criminal bad-check charges against you and have you carted off to the hoosegow in the paddy wagon.

Receiving undeserved welfare and unemployment benefits

Someone receiving more Social Security, unemployment, welfare, or other government benefits than they should have is not all that uncommon. If the bankruptcy court is convinced that you fraudulently obtained these benefits, you're obligated to repay them.

If getting more than your fair share was just a mistake — theirs or yours — any repayment obligation can be wiped out. The key wrinkle is whether you're still receiving benefits.

Under a principle called *recoupment,* some courts enable the o[...]
ernment agency to effect a reduction in your future benefits to [...]
loss even though any obligation to repay was discharged in ba[...]

Willful and Malicious Behavior

Damages from conduct considered *willful and malicious conduct* are not dischargeable in Chapter 7, but may be dischargeable in Chapter 13 unless they involved personal injuries and were assessed against you by a court or administrative agency prior to bankruptcy. In Chapter 13, you still have to convince the bankruptcy court that you're making your best effort to pay as much of the damages as possible under its plan.

As you may expect, determining whether conduct is so awful that it's willful and malicious usually isn't very easy.

The United States Supreme Court has ruled that simple negligence doesn't rise to the level of malice, even if you really screwed up (*Kawaauhau v. Geiger*, 523 U.S. 57, 118 S.Ct. 974 [1998]). For example, if you were stirring your coffee while driving and accidentally rear-ended a school bus, that's *negligence.* Although you didn't mean to cause an accident, you nevertheless did so because you weren't paying attention. On the other hand, if you intentionally rammed the bus in a fit of road rage, that's *malice.*

Creditors sometimes claim that a debtor was guilty of willful and malicious conduct when she sold or gave away the collateral she used to secure her loans — an allegation known in legal circles as *conversion of collateral.*

Some department stores take a security interest (which gives them the right to repossess if you don't pay; see Chapter 11 for more on security interests) in items purchased on the charge accounts their stores offer to customers. These stores sometimes claim that someone who sells or gives away an item before it's paid off acted willfully and maliciously. Say, for example, that you charged a lawn mower on an ABC Store account, and the store retained a security interest in that item. Sometime later, you sell the mower at a garage sale, even though you haven't paid off your ABC Store account, and spent your proceeds. ABC may later accuse you of acting with malice if you don't pay off the account.

In a situation like this one, most bankruptcy courts reject the store's conversion of collateral claim, unless ABC can prove that you were aware of the fine print in the charge account agreement and knew that you weren't supposed to sell the mower until it was paid for. Few consumers actually have any clue what's in the fine print of their charge-card documentation; however, in exceptional cases where the customer clearly is fully aware that she's doing a bad thing, courts rule in favor of the stores.

Rolex scheme falls through

Brad charged a $14,000 diamond-studded Rolex watch at Acme Jewelers. Because the purchase was so large, the store manager carefully explained to Brad that the watch was collateral for the account. He then had Brad sign papers to that effect.

Three weeks later, Brad sold the watch for $1,500 and used the money to catch up on car payments. Shortly thereafter, he filed Chapter 7. The court found Brad guilty of willful and malicious conduct, and his debt to Acme wasn't discharged.

Even though some liabilities from alleged willful and malicious conduct are potentially dischargeable in Chapter 13, the judge scrutinizes your case, making sure that it's filed in a good faith attempt to repay as much as possible and not just to stiff the victim. Remember, when criminal charges are brought and a conviction results in a fine or restitution, these obligations aren't dischargeable. (See the section "Covering Fines, Penalties, and Restitution Orders," later in this chapter.)

Whenever someone sues you claiming that you're guilty of fraud or other misconduct, see a lawyer immediately. If you do nothing, the person suing you automatically wins, possibly preventing you from later claiming your innocence.

Congress wanted to make doubly sure that thieves can't escape liability by filing Chapter 7 bankruptcy. So, in addition to addressing obligations arising from willful and malicious conduct, Congress enacted a separate provision making debts arising from larceny and embezzlement nondischargeable and nonpriority in both Chapter 7 and Chapter 13.

Covering Fines, Penalties, and Restitution Orders

The courts and Congress are like ships passing in the night when it comes to addressing court-ordered fines, penalties, and *restitution* (monetary compensation paid to the victim of a crime). Neither seems to understand exactly what the other is talking about. Making matters worse is the fact that these types of debts frequently arise from efforts by the states to enforce criminal or regulatory laws, and federal courts generally don't like stepping on a state's toes in these matters. The first problem in figuring out what impact bankruptcy has on these debts is identifying the nature of the obligation as accurately as possible.

Criminal fines

Fines that are assessed upon conviction of a crime can't be wiped out in a Chapter 7 or a Chapter 13.

Although you may propose paying off the fine in full during a Chapter 13 case, you still can be confronted with problems. First of all, because they're not priority debts, most courts won't allow you to pay them off while other unsecured creditors are left holding the bag. Second, prosecutors may seek to incarcerate you for failure to pay a criminal fine, even though it's included in your Chapter 13 plan.

It may be better for you to pay the fine before filing bankruptcy, but don't forget that's potentially dangerous. The trustee may decide that you attempted to play favorites with whatever cash you have (see Chapter 19). Your lawyer's knowledge of the policies of local courts and prosecutors is critical in this situation.

Restitution

Courts commonly require anyone who injures another person or damages property to pay *restitution* to the victim. That simply means that if your neighbor has to shell out $300 for the vet because you kicked Fido in the head, you have to reimburse your neighbor. If you're ordered to pay restitution as part of a criminal conviction, the obligation is treated the same as a criminal fine.

Say, for example, that you're convicted of vandalism in a criminal court and ordered to compensate the victim for damages as part of your sentence. This kind of obligation isn't dischargeable in a Chapter 7 or a Chapter 13. On the other hand, if criminal charges weren't brought against you, but the victim sued you and obtained a judgment, that kind of obligation would not be excepted from discharge (nondischargeable) as "restitution." However, it may be nondischargeable in a Chapter 7 on the basis of fraud, willful and malicious conduct, or embezzlement. Still, you may be able to discharge the claim in a Chapter 13 if you did not cause any personal injuries.

Noncriminal fines and penalties

In most instances, penalties imposed on you for noncriminal wrongdoing — such as watering your lawn during a drought or (in some places) not cleaning up after your pooch — are dischargeable in a Chapter 13, but not in a Chapter 7.

But even when you can wipe out the debt, you still may be in for big trouble with the governmental entity imposing the fine or penalty. Many states have diversion programs where people avoid criminal prosecution by undergoing counseling. They're also expected to eventually pay for the services used in diversion programs. For example, the court may give you a break on a marijuana charge if you agree to undergo and pay for drug counseling. If you don't pay for the program, criminal charges may be revived.

Motor-vehicle fines

Unpaid traffic fines and parking tickets present a couple of questions. The first is whether the obligation is dischargeable, and that depends on whether your local courts consider the violation a crime or merely an infraction.

Parking tickets and equipment violations (broken headlights, a noisy muffler, bald tires, and so on) typically are considered infractions, so fines for them are dischargeable in a Chapter 13, but not in a Chapter 7. Serious moving violations (reckless driving or driving with a suspended license) typically are considered crimes, and fines for them aren't dischargeable in a Chapter 7 or a Chapter 13.

Many states will yank your driver's license for unpaid fines, even those involving infractions. If the fine is dischargeable, the Bankruptcy Code requires that the state restore your driving privileges. But that doesn't mean that the bankruptcy court will order the state to do so. You may find yourself in the middle of a huge power struggle between state and federal authorities.

For those reasons, it's better to file Chapter 13 before your license is actually suspended or revoked. Filing bankruptcy will halt suspension or revocation proceedings (see Chapter 6 for a discussion of the automatic stay), enabling you to keep your license while your lawyer tries to resolve any tug of war between the bankruptcy and state courts. However, if you're dealing with a criminal fine, the state doesn't have to restore your license, and bankruptcy won't interrupt suspension or revocation proceedings.

Accepting Responsibility for Drunken-Driving Injuries

Patience for drunken or drugged drivers is at an all-time low. Getting blasted and mowing down a few mailboxes is no longer considered funny.

If you get drunk or high and injure someone in accident, you're going to pay for any personal damages. Liabilities for injuries caused by operation of a vehicle, boat, or aircraft while under the influence of alcohol, drugs, or other substances cannot be discharged in either Chapter 7 or Chapter 13. Due to what was probably a drafting error, liabilities from *aircraft* accidents are nondischargeable but they're *not* priority claims, while liabilities from driving or boating are nondischargeable *priority* debts.

Chapter 17

Till Debt Due Us Part:
Bankruptcy and Divorce

Financial distress and divorce often go hand-in-hand. Sometimes, financial woes cause the divorce. Other times, divorce leads to financial disaster. In balancing your money concerns with your domestic issues, you need to carefully weigh your options, and their implications, in divorce court and bankruptcy court.

The two main reasons you may want to plow through this rather difficult and dour chapter are

✔ You owe money under a divorce decree that already has been entered and wonder whether bankruptcy can help you escape, or at least manage, these obligations.

✔ You're involved in a divorce right now, or thinking about it, and want to know how bankruptcy will affect things.

This chapter addresses these complicated issues.

Introducing Key Points

Because divorce can really complicate your bankruptcy (and vice versa), you need to know some basics. Although hard and fast rules are awfully hard to come by in this area, several constants to keep in mind are that

✔ Bankruptcy deals only with debts in existence on the day you file. If a divorce decree creates financial obligations after the petition date, they won't be included in bankruptcy.

✔ Property divisions completed prior to bankruptcy aren't debts that you can avoid. For example, if a divorce court enters an order transferring an asset to you, it's yours even when your ex-spouse files bankruptcy. But if the divorce court orders your ex to transfer the property and he hasn't done so prior to bankruptcy, he may be able to escape this kind of debt through bankruptcy.

✔ Some liens imposed by divorce courts may be avoidable by your ex if he files bankruptcy because they're deemed judicial liens impairing his homestead. Insisting that your ex sign a mortgage (which is not avoidable as a judicial lien) to secure the debt is a smart thing to do. See Chapter 12 for more on judicial liens.

✔ The fact that you or even the divorce court calls an obligation nondischargeable support isn't binding on a bankruptcy court, which looks at the underlying situation and makes its own determinations.

✔ If you're entitled to receive support when you file bankruptcy, most, if not all that money is exempt (off-limits to creditors) in your bankruptcy. On the other hand, if you expect to receive a property division, chances are that it won't be exempt. See Chapter 10 for more on exempt property.

✔ If you become entitled to a property division within 180 days of bankruptcy, you can lose it to the trustee.

Planning Your Strategy

If a divorce looms in your future, careful bankruptcy planning can

✔ Reduce tensions between you and your soon-to-be ex-spouse

✔ Make divorce simpler

✔ Help produce a marital settlement that both parties can live with that will hold up in a future bankruptcy

On the other hand, blundering through a divorce without carefully considering the possible effects of bankruptcy may bring results that neither party wants, such as

✔ Unproductive and expensive fights about who's going to pay certain bills, especially when both are better off eliminating the debts in bankruptcy

✔ Hostilities resulting from one party believing he got the short end of the stick

✔ Unnecessary losses of assets to a bankruptcy trustee

Exploring your financial obligations

Basically two types of financial obligations arise from divorce: *support* to sustain the kids and your former spouse (*domestic support obligations* under the new bankruptcy law) and the issue of property that's been divided between the two of you. Bankruptcy handles each commitment differently.

Generally, support obligations aren't wiped out in a Chapter 7 or a Chapter 13, while outstanding property division obligations *can* be wiped out in a Chapter 13 but not in Chapter 7. You need to keep in mind a couple of principles.

First, financial obligations arising from a *divorce decree* (or a marital settlement agreement adopted by the divorce court) may require payment of

- ✔ Money for child support and schooling.

- ✔ Life and health insurance premiums.

- ✔ Alimony or maintenance for your ex-spouse.

- ✔ Your ex-spouse's divorce attorney fees.

- ✔ A sum of money to compensate your ex for his interest in joint property. For example, say that the divorce court awards you the marital residence worth $80,000 but requires you to pay your ex $40,000 for his interest in the property. As part of the deal, the court may actually impose a lien on the home to secure payment of the $40,000.

- ✔ Certain debts so that your ex doesn't have to pay them.

If you're wondering which of these is support and which are property divisions, jump ahead to the section "Figuring out which obligations are in 'the nature of' support," later in this chapter.

Second, the decree may also actually transfer specific assets to your former partner. For example, the court may enter a Qualified Domestic Relations Order (QDRO) that gives your ex-spouse immediate ownership in part of your entire retirement plan. If the court enters a QDRO, your ex-spouse has an immediate ownership interest in your pension. In other words, he owns it. You don't.

Or the divorce court can award jointly owned property to one spouse. Say, for example, that you and your soon-to-be ex jointly own your home plus a rental house. A divorce court can rule that you own the home by yourself, and your ex gets the rental property.

In other words, the divorce court can

- ✔ Order you to make payments in the future that represent either support or a property division. These payments may be secured or unsecured.

- ✔ Actually transfer ownership of certain assets to one party.

A little later in this chapter, in the sections "Understanding How Support Obligations Are Treated in Bankruptcy," and "Understanding How Property Divisions are Treated in Bankruptcy," we talk about how bankruptcy affects support obligations and property divisions.

Doing what's best for both spouses

If you and your mate were struggling financially when living together, things are just going to get worse when you have to maintain two households. Although a substantial emotional element is obvious, you'll both be much better off when you can work toward a financial solution that benefits each of you. Doing so isn't really that hard, assuming, of course, that you can respond rationally rather than emotionally. Work toward structuring a marital settlement agreement that

- ✔ Both parties can live with
- ✔ Actually divides your existing property
- ✔ Ensures that sums to be paid by one spouse to the other will survive the bankruptcy of each and, it is hoped, will be exempt

Sure, you can play hardball and insist that your spouse pay all the bills, but you'll probably find out that you're doing nothing more than cutting off your nose to spite your face. Although the divorce court may order one party to pay the bill, that doesn't necessarily protect the other from creditors. Instead of playing one-upmanship, you and your mate need to reach an agreement where credit-card debts and other bills eventually are wiped out in bankruptcy. If you can do that, your mate will be in a far better position to handle any support obligations — and everyone will be happier.

Nevertheless, you still need to notify all creditors on joint accounts in writing that you won't be responsible for any future charges made by your spouse. Although doing so won't relieve you from charges that already were made, it should keep you off the hook for future charges.

Completing property transfers

If a divorce court actually transfers an asset to your ex-spouse, you don't really have any debt to handle in bankruptcy because you no longer own the property; your spouse does. Sorry. For example, if the court enters a QDRO, (see our earlier discussion of Qualified Domestic Relations Orders in the section "Exploring your financial obligations"), your ex has an immediate ownership interest in your pension. There's simply no debt to wipe out or manage.

ANECDOTE

A success story

Bob and Mabel own a home worth $100,000. It is subject to a mortgage of $80,000 ($20,000 equity). They also own an SUV worth $15,000 free and clear. However, they owe more than $50,000 in credit-card debts they racked up during their stormy marriage. The homestead exemption in their state is $25,000, and the vehicle exemption is $2,000. Their pensions are entirely exempt.

Bob and Mabel agree that because Mabel is getting custody of their two children, she also needs to have the house with its $20,000 equity.

Knowing that they'd lose the SUV in bankruptcy, they sell it, and Bob receives the $15,000 proceeds because he's giving up the house. To make things equal, Mabel gives Bob $5,000 from her pension.

Bob then takes the $20,000 and makes a down payment on a new home and buys a $2,000 car.

Bob agrees to make child support payments of $500 per month.

After the divorce is complete, Bob and Mabel each file separate Chapter 7 bankruptcies. (They can't file jointly even if they want to because they no longer are married.) The credit-card debts are eliminated, neither of them loses any property, and Bob's monthly support payments are manageable.

Timing it right

When bankruptcy and divorce intersect, careful timing can make the difference between success and disaster. Although each situation is unique, as a general rule,

- ✔ When you have no assets to divide, no third-party debts (like joint credit-card accounts) to allocate, and no support issues, you need to file bankruptcy prior to filing for divorce. That way, you can file a joint bankruptcy, getting two for the price of one and making your divorce much simpler.

- ✔ In other cases, filing and completing your divorce before actually filing bankruptcy usually is best.

Although delaying bankruptcy until after the divorce is finished ordinarily is better, starting to make plans for your bankruptcy nevertheless makes sense.

Sham divorces

You may be tempted to agree with your spouse that he gets the mine and you get the shaft so that creditors can't go after your assets. For example, if, as a couple, you have few joint debts and your spouse doesn't have many debts in his own name, it may be appealing to give him everything in the divorce and then file bankruptcy. Maybe you'll eventually settle up later, but, in any event, you'd rather see him get your assets than your creditors.

Don't do it.

When you file bankruptcy after a divorce, the trustee makes sure that any property settlement was a fair transaction in which you received valuable property in exchange for property you gave up. If you didn't, the trustee can recover the property that your ex received. In addition, if you pulled this stunt within one year of filing bankruptcy, you may not be eligible for a Chapter 7 discharge (see Chapter 19).

Understanding How Support Obligations Are Treated in Bankruptcy

Although bankruptcy won't eliminate support obligations, it may ease your distress by erasing your other debts. Additionally, with a Chapter 13 repayment plan, you can gradually catch up with your outstanding support, paying during your three-to five-year plan.

Support obligations in Chapter 7

You can't do much with support obligations in a Chapter 7 liquidation bankruptcy. And the automatic stay doesn't protect you from collection efforts.

Chapter 7 still eliminates your other debts, and that makes meeting your support requirements easier. And if yours is an *asset case* — where property is liquidated and some money is paid to creditors — you can file a *proof of claim*, thus ensuring that the lion's share of the funds go toward your support obligation. Chapter 6 explains the claims process.

Support obligations in Chapter 13

Although you can't wipe out support responsibilities in a Chapter 13, you can at least get your spouse off your back and pay accrued support during the three- to five-year duration of your Chapter 13 plan.

Chapter 13 reduces marital obligations to manageable amounts

George and Donna divorce after seven years of marriage. George agrees to pay $1,000 per month alimony to Donna and $45,000 in exchange for her interest in the couple's vacation home. George then loses his job, and doesn't pay either of these obligations. He even loses the vacation home because he can't make the mortgage payments on it.

After two years, George finally lands a good job, but by then he owes Donna $24,000 in back support, still owes her the $45,000, and he racks up $13,000 in credit-card debts to boot.

George files Chapter 13, and the court approves a plan where he pays Donna the $24,000 over five years and continues making current $1,000 payments to her. If George completes his plan, the $45,000 property division is wiped out along with his credit-card bills.

In a Chapter 13, support obligations are broken down into two categories:

- ✔ Back support that you owe when you file
- ✔ Support that accrues in the future

Back support can — and actually must — be paid in full over the duration of your plan from the payments you make to the trustee. Also, you must keep up with support payments coming due after the petition date. If you don't, your Chapter 13 plan cannot be confirmed (see Chapter 6), none of your debts will be wiped out, and your ex-spouse (or a governmental agency collecting support) can ask the state court to force you to pay and also have the bankruptcy court dismiss your bankruptcy.

Support payments that are due after you file for bankruptcy are treated as a budgeted living expense that you pay directly, just like your rent or utility bill. But beware: The automatic stay doesn't provide much protection against support collection, and you may jeopardize your whole Chapter 13 case by letting postpetition support obligations slide. (For more about postpetition obligations, see Chapter 20.) If your postpetition support payments are unreasonably high, the place to look for relief is divorce court. Bankruptcy courts won't allow themselves to get dragged into the divorce business.

Figuring out which obligations are in "the nature of" support

Determining whether a particular obligation is support or a property division often is difficult.

Here's why: Assume that Grace agrees to accept less alimony because her husband, George, promises to pay all their joint debts (keeping in mind that even if the divorce court adopts this agreement and assigns these debts to George, the creditors can still come after Grace if George doesn't pay). Promises to pay third-party debts frequently are labeled as property divisions by the parties or by the divorce court. But, in this particular case, isn't it actually a form of support?

That depends.

A bankruptcy judge can disregard labels, making up his own mind about the true nature of the obligation. In fact, a bankruptcy court doesn't even need to agree with the divorce judge's decision on the question. If the divorce court characterizes an obligation as being in the nature of support, specifically ruling that it can't be wiped out in bankruptcy, the bankruptcy court can reach the exact opposite conclusion, ruling that the obligation is actually a property division.

Bankruptcy is a federal law, and, under our Constitution, national laws overrule inconsistent state laws.

Focusing on financial conditions at the time of your divorce

Although bankruptcy courts consider a number of factors, they like to zero in on the financial condition of the parties at the time of the divorce.

If the relative financial situation of the parties at that time indicates that support was necessary, bankruptcy courts usually find that an award is in the nature of support, regardless of how it is labeled.

If your spouse is barely able to meet basic expenses and has few job skills while you have substantial earning ability, a bankruptcy court probably will rule that the disputed obligation is support, regardless of whether it consists of a lump-sum payment, periodic payments, or a promise to pay a third-party debt. For example, suppose that Jane supports Dan for ten years while he completes his medical training, and the divorce court orders Dan to make payments to her equal to a percentage of the value of his medical practice.

Few courts ever conclude that the obligation is anything other than support, at least to the extent that such payments are necessary for Jane to support herself.

Certain third-party debts are more likely than others to fall under the support umbrella. For example, when a wife is awarded the marital home and her husband is ordered to make the mortgage payments, the obligation is probably support, especially if the wife has custody of children.

Many bankruptcy courts also deem as support a husband's obligation to pay a car loan on an essential vehicle awarded to his wife if, at the time of the divorce, she can't afford the payments herself. Similarly, courts almost always rule that when one spouse is ordered to pay the other's divorce attorney, this obligation is support, not a property division.

Looking at factors that some courts consider

Because the determination about whether an obligation is in the nature of support isn't always obvious, courts examine the circumstances to make those kinds of decisions. Bankruptcy judges consider a number of factors, including whether

- ✔ Children are involved. Payments to an ex-spouse with custody of the parties' minor children are more likely to be deemed support.

- ✔ Marked differences existed between the relative incomes of you and your former spouse at the time of your divorce. A key question is whether the recipient actually needed (at the time of divorce) financial assistance from his ex-spouse in order to make ends meet.

- ✔ The obligation terminates on death or remarriage of the recipient spouse. Traditionally, support obligations end upon the recipient's death or remarriage, but property divisions don't.

- ✔ The obligation is subject to modification based on changes in circumstances. Support obligations tend to be modifiable, whereas property divisions don't.

- ✔ The parties treat the obligation as support on their income tax returns — with the person making payments deducting them and the person receiving them treating them as income. If the paying spouse claims that payments were tax-deductible support payments rather than nondeductible property division payments, the bankruptcy judge will be skeptical if he changes his tune and tries to claim that they're not support obligations.

Understanding How Property Divisions Are Treated in Bankruptcy

If a marital obligation is a property settlement, you can wipe it out in a Chapter 13, but not in Chapter 7. But you still may have to deal with any lien imposed by the divorce court. For example, if the divorce court orders you to pay $10,000 as a property division and imposes a lien on your home to secure payment, you must deal with that lien even when your personal liability on the debt is canceled.

As we discuss in Chapter 11, judgment liens that impair your exemption can be avoided (unless they secure a support obligation). When it comes to judgment liens securing property divisions, the Supreme Court (see *Farrey v. Sanderfoot*. 500 U.S. 291, 111 S.Ct. 1825 [1991]), in a rather convoluted fashion, has ruled that you can't avoid the judgment lien if it's imposed to secure payment for your half of jointly owned property awarded to you in the divorce.

Suppose, for a moment, that the divorce court awards you sole ownership of an $80,000 home — *owned jointly with your spouse* — and then imposes a lien on the property to secure payment to your spouse of $40,000 for his share of the home. That kind of lien isn't avoidable in bankruptcy.

On the other hand, suppose that the divorce court imposes a lien against property that you own in your own name. That kind of lien can be avoidable in bankruptcy to the extent that it impairs your homestead exemption. See Chapter 11 for more on eliminating judgment liens on homesteads.

Other Grounds for Bankruptcy-Proof Marital Debts

Because more than one reason can exist for making a debt nondischargeable, you may encounter some other situations where a property division isn't dischargeable even in a Chapter 7.

A debtor may be guilty of fraud or some other type of intentional misconduct in negotiating a marital settlement agreement. When one spouse agrees to a marital settlement with no intention of performing, that may constitute fraud. Or if he withdraws and spends money from his pension after it was awarded to his ex-wife, he may be guilty of theft.

Chapter 18

Student Loans and Other Mind Games

A college education is one of the best investments you can make in your future — sometimes. It can also be one of the very worst.

Today's college graduates earn 40 percent more than people with only high school diplomas. But the cost of a college education is well beyond what most people, or their parents, can afford without student loans. So, the lending of money for higher education has evolved into an industry unto itself. Today, one of every 12 Americans owes money on student loans.

This chapter explains the complicated workings of the student-loan industry, your bankruptcy options, and your nonbankruptcy options.

Understanding the Student-Loan Industry

When student-loan programs function as intended, everybody wins. With their enhanced earnings, graduates can pay off their loans without serious difficulty, and, by earning more, they pay more in federal and state income taxes. It's a win-win-win situation for the borrower, the lender, and society — when it works out that way. Unfortunately, that doesn't always happen. When you buy a house, the bank assesses the property, ensuring not only that you're paying a reasonable price, but also that the home is worth enough to cover the loan if you happen to default. But with educational loans, no one seems to care whether a particular course of study has any economic value.

Students often incur a fortune in debt to earn a personally fulfilling but economically worthless degree. After that, they're saddled with enormous debt from their school loans, and an earning potential that's no better than it was before they went to school. Frequently, they're up to their necks in debt and have no realistic prospect of paying it off in the foreseeable future.

Bankruptcy, however, isn't always — or even usually — the best way to deal with student loans. For a number of reasons, some better than others, lawmakers have made discharging student-loan obligations in bankruptcy very difficult.

Members of Congress want to ensure that everyone seeking a college education has that option, and they have a vested interest in appeasing the lending industry, which is ever so generous with campaign donations and lobbying dollars. So, Congress creates and sustains an environment where lenders are willing to make loans because chances are good that they'll make money from them.

If you're to have even a fighting chance of eliminating your student loans, you need a firm understanding of how the process works. The first step is figuring out who holds your loan, which isn't nearly as simple as you may think. You then need to know just what the loan holder can do if you don't pay.

Tracing Your Loans

Student loans frequently are moving targets because they constantly are assigned to various players in a huge and hugely complex industry. Although the guaranteed student-loan program is federal, these loans may originate from any of three sources:

- ✔ Private lenders (Federal Family Education Loans, or FFEL)
- ✔ Schools (Perkins loans)
- ✔ The United States Department of Education (Federal Direct Loans)

After your loan goes into default, figuring out who to deal with can be tough. It could be a guarantee agency, a private collector hired by a guarantee agency, the Department of Education, a collection agency hired by the department, or the school. You need to keep these points in mind:

- ✔ If a private lender makes the loan, it frequently turns right around and sells it to a lender specializing in student loans, such as the Student Loan Marketing Association (*Sallie Mae*).
- ✔ Either the original lender or the purchaser of a loan may hire a loan servicer to receive payments and keep track of how much is owed.

- ✔ When a loan is delinquent for at least 270 days and therefore deemed in default, the loanholder (except where the original lender was the Department of Education) is paid off by state guarantee agencies. The state guarantee agency then goes after you or hires a private bill collector to do the dirty work.

- ✔ If the guarantee agency can't collect, the federal government bails it out and inherits the problem.

- ✔ The Department of Education also hires private agencies to collect the loans it holds, regardless of whether the loans originated with the department or were acquired through the guarantee process.

When the loan isn't yet in default, you may find at least a temporary fix for your student loan burden by checking out repayment plans available from the original lender (or the purchaser of the loan, such as Sallie Mae), the school (in the case of Perkins loans), or the Department of Education, if the loan originated from the government.

If you've recently received a collection letter, that's a pretty good starting point in hunting down the holder of your loan. You can call the Federal Student Aid Information Center at 800-433-3243, which likely will reveal the name and address of the holder of your loan. If your loan came directly from the Department of Education, you can call the Direct Loan Servicing Center at 800-848-0979. If you're still having trouble, you can contact the ombudsman office in the Department of Education at www.ombudsman.ed.gov or call 877-557-2575.

Knowing What They Can Do If You Don't Pay

If you're behind on your student-loan payments, you won't receive any more student loans without reestablishing your eligibility or rehabilitating the loan. (See the section entitled "Requesting a reasonable and affordable payment plan," later in this chapter.) Collection can be enforced by

- ✔ Lawsuits
- ✔ Garnishment (where money is taken from your wages even without filing a lawsuit) of up to 15 percent of your net income
- ✔ Interception of your income tax refunds

Likewise, after your loan goes into default, collection costs of up to 25 percent may be added.

Managing Student Loans with Bankruptcy

The statute of limitations on student loans is pretty much gone. So, no matter how old the loan is, you may still have to pay it back. And, if that isn't bad enough, you can't wipe it out (or *discharge* it) in any kind of bankruptcy without first showing that repayment poses an "undue hardship" — a term Congress left for the courts to define.

Absent proof of "undue hardship," the following educational obligations are considered nondischargeable student loans:

✔ A loan made, insured, or guaranteed by a governmental unit, or made under any program, funded in whole or in part by a governmental unit or nonprofit or for-profit institution

✔ An obligation to repay funds received as an educational benefit, scholarship, or stipend

✔ Overpayments made on grants and other educational benefits

Nevertheless, not every education-related expense is protected from discharge. Some courts have ruled that debts for things like books, supplies, and student housing are dischargeable in bankruptcy. Another court may say that Congress didn't intend "to elevate any garden variety indebtedness that a student may incur to an educational institution, be it cafeteria charges, bookstore charges, parking lot charges, or room and board charges, to the category of excepted educational debt." So, getting to know the views of your local bankruptcy judge is critical.

What if someone else lends you money to pay off your student loan? Is that new debt dischargeable? It may very well be. A couple of courts have said that a loan from an employer to pay off student loans is dischargeable. But this stipulation isn't an invitation to borrow money to pay student loans while intending to bankrupt the new loan. As we discuss at length in Chapters 13 and 16, borrowing money without intending to repay it is fraud, and claims of fraud aren't dischargeable.

Proving your insufferable need for a break

If you want to discharge a student loan in bankruptcy because repayment would impose an undue hardship on you or your family, you have to convince the judge of each of the following:

✔ You can't maintain a minimal standard of living for you and your family if you're forced to repay the student loan.

✔ Your situation is likely to continue.

✔ You've made a good-faith effort to repay the loan.

Here's a closer look at these requirements.

Defining financial hardship

Although you needn't be poverty-stricken to satisfy this requirement, you do have to be pretty severely strapped. One court ruled that a household income of about $45,000 can provide a family of five with more than a minimum living standard, and, as a result, the debtor was able to pay at least $175 per month on student loans.

When determining undue hardship, most courts consider all household income and household expenses. But beware. Many courts won't consider the household expenses for a live-in lover or his children if you have no legal obligation to support them.

Determining whether repayment imposes an undue hardship raises the question of how long a person is expected to pay. Some courts look to the original term of the loan, frequently ten years, to assess whether a debtor can repay a loan over that period of time. But others adopt a much stricter view, saying that debtors need to be required to pay on student loans for up to 25 years and, if that's possible, the loan isn't discharged.

Courts don't just look at how much money you're earning right now; they also look at how much you *could* earn in the foreseeable future if you put your mind to it.

Forecasting that your circumstances are unlikely to improve

In addition to proving your inability to pay the loan, you must also show that your financial plight is likely to continue into the foreseeable future. Temporary hardship isn't enough.

ANECDOTE

Noble intentions aren't enough

Mary chose to use her costly law degree to represent indigent clients who were unable to pay her legal fees. Consequently, she couldn't afford to pay off her student loans. Is bankruptcy the answer?

As noble as Mary's efforts were, the court wasn't willing to cut her any slack on her student loans. The judge flatly rejected Mary's argument that she couldn't afford to repay her loans because she was supporting a 20-year-old daughter attending college.

ANECDOTE

Choosing underemployment doesn't cut it

Edwin had a master's degree from Oxford but gave up teaching because of stress and started a pottery business, earning him less than $7,000 per year. The court said that a person can't qualify for discharge of student loan by voluntarily choosing to be underemployed and adopting a minimalist lifestyle.

Similarly, one court refused to discharge a $19,121 student loan because the debtor, who was a teacher, could earn more if she chose to work during the summertime.

This requirement can be met when the debtor suffers from a permanent physical or mental disability or disease. Several courts ruled that a bipolar condition (manic-depression) qualifies, and at least one concluded that chronic fatigue syndrome is a permanent disability. But not all judges are receptive to claims of mental illness.

Although the fact that the education was worthless doesn't by itself justify discharging the loan, it may be taken into consideration when determining whether a debtor's financial plight is likely to improve.

Demonstrating good faith

The third prong of the hardship test requires proof that you acted in good faith regarding your student loans. Essentially, that means you

- ✔ Made all reasonable efforts to maximize income and reduce expenses
- ✔ Didn't file bankruptcy solely to evade student loans
- ✔ Tried nonbankruptcy alternatives
- ✔ Made some effort, if at all possible, to repay the loans

Good faith is one of those eye-of-the-beholder concepts, and, in bankruptcy, the judge has the beholding eye.

Wiping out part of your student loans

Even if they won't discharge your entire student loan, some judges will eliminate part of the burden and force the creditor to accept a repayment plan. For example, courts have

✔ Examined the debtors' budget, determined that the debtor can afford to pay $10 per month, and discharged the balance of the loan

✔ Reduced a Chapter 7 debtors' student loans by more than 50 percent and instructed the parties to propose a schedule for repaying the balance within six years

✔ Deferred collection for a period of one year

✔ Ruled that repayment of the principal balance would not impose undue hardship, but discharged attorney fees and interest, and ordered the creditor to accept a repayment plan of $50 per month

✔ Held that repayment of the total balance of several student loans imposed undue hardship and discharged all but about one-fifth of the total balance, reducing each loan proportionately

Other judges, however, find nothing in the Bankruptcy Code that would empower them to partially discharge or restructure student loans. In their view, discharge is an all-or-nothing proposition. From your standpoint, that's a double-edged sword. Courts that do not feel free to reduce or restore a loan are often inclined to just wipe out the whole thing.

A few courts say that although student loans may not be restructured, each loan can be considered separately so that one or two of a person's student loans can be wiped out while and the others are preserved. If your local court takes this approach, consolidating all your loans before bankruptcy may be a mistake because doing so can eliminate the possibility of discharging one of your more costly loans. After all, consolidation combines all existing loans into a single loan.

Paying student loans under a Chapter 13 plan

Although student loans can't be wiped out in a Chapter 7 or a Chapter 13, absent proof of "undue hardship," you still can force the student loan creditor to accept payments in amounts you can afford to make through a Chapter 13 repayment plan. However, you need to remember that if the loan isn't paid in full during the Chapter 13, you still must pay the balance when your case is over, and interest on the loan balance continues to accrue during the bankruptcy. So, even if you pay the balance of a student loan in full under a Chapter 13 plan, you're still going to owe some interest after your case is complete.

Judges' ideas of good/bad faith

Case law provides some guidance into what judges are likely to accept, or not accept, as a good-faith argument:

When Joanne tried getting out of her student loans by filing bankruptcy right after graduation, the court not only refused to wipe out the loans, but also scolded her for abusing the bankruptcy process.

Ruby, a single mom living with her mother in public housing, barely earned enough to get by. Although she paid only $180 of $9,000 in student loans, the court found that she acted in good faith by paying as much as she could and waiting for several years to file bankruptcy rather than heading directly to bankruptcy court as soon as her loans came due.

Mackenzie was able to discharge $100,000 in student loans, part of which was for law school. On the petition date, she was working as a law clerk, earning $30,000, and her husband stayed home to care for their children. Their monthly income exceeded expenses by only $71. The court agreed that Mackenzie's husband probably couldn't earn enough to offset child-care expenses and concluded that the situation was likely to continue for six years, when the youngest child would be in school full-time. Finally, the court held that the good-faith test was met even though no payments had been made on the loans because Mackenzie was doing her best to minimize expenses and had found the best job available.

If the remaining term of the student loan is longer than the life of your Chapter 13 plan, you can propose making up all the missed payments on the student loan over the life of your plan and resume regular monthly payments as they come due after the petition date. Of course, the balance remaining when your Chapter 13 is completed still has to be paid. A number of courts have endorsed this approach. One court points out that merely resuming regular payments on a student loan is okay, but paying off the entire debt under the plan improperly discriminates in favor of the student loan.

A downside to curing a student loan and maintaining payments as a long-term debt stems from the fact that long-term debt is excepted from discharge in a Chapter 13 without regard to whether repayment imposes undue hardship. By choosing to treat the loan in this fashion, you may lose the right to claim that it should be discharged on undue-hardship grounds.

Using a "Chapter 20" strategy

One way around the rule forbidding Chapter 13 plans from discriminating in favor of student loans is colloquially known as *Chapter 20 bankruptcy* (filing Chapter 7 and Chapter 13 in succession).

Discharging student loans by stealth and ambush

We (and a number of courts) view one way of getting out of student loans in a Chapter 13 as a dirty trick. Although this ploy has worked in some cases, we most certainly don't endorse it. Still, it is something to discuss with your lawyer who knows the views of your local bankruptcy judge. Here's how it works:

A crafty lawyer sticks a provision in a Chapter 13 plan essentially providing that court approval of your plan constitutes a finding that repayment of student loans imposes an undue hardship and that, as such, the debt will be discharged. A copy of the proposed plan is forwarded to the student-loan creditor. If the student-loan creditor lodges no objection, and the

court approves the plan, voilà! The debt is wiped out.

Keep in mind, however, that your victory here may be Pyrrhic because you and your lawyer may well end up getting fined. Many judges aren't at all amused by what they view as an attempt to slip one past the court, and they often react with a vengeance.

Other courts, however, are more tolerant because they view the Chapter 13 as essentially a bargaining process where the plan is simply an offer to creditors. Under this view, fining a debtor or his counsel for simply making an offer to a student-loan creditor wouldn't seem proper.

For this strategy to work, you first file a Chapter 7 to discharge all debts other than the student loan, and then you file a Chapter 13 case where you propose paying the entire student loan. No discrimination problem exists because you now only have one debt left; the others were discharged in the Chapter 7.

Some courts take a dim view of this strategy, but they're more likely to go along if you don't file Chapter 13 until you first try working out a nonbankruptcy repayment arrangement. Actually, you may get a better deal outside bankruptcy. We cover these options in the "Managing Student Loans without Bankruptcy" section, later in this chapter.

Addressing medical school loans

Loans under the Health Education Assistance Loan (HEAL) program and repayment obligations under scholarships granted by the National Health Services Corporation (NHSC) program are even more difficult to discharge in bankruptcy than other student loans. A waiting period must be satisfied, and a court must decide that requiring repayment would be *unconscionable*.

The waiting periods are seven years for HEAL loans and five years for NHSC obligations. Both are measured from the date the obligation first became due to the date of the bankruptcy discharge.

Here's kind of a weird crinkle: The strict standards for discharging medical school loans apply only to a person's first bankruptcy. If he ends up having to file a second time, dischargeability is determined according to the undue hardship standards applicable to ordinary student loans. See the earlier discussion in the section "Proving your insufferable need for a break."

Getting stuck even when you're only a cosigner

Student loans aren't dischargeable even if you're only a cosigner. If you cosigned for your child's student loan, not only are you liable when he doesn't pay, you probably can't escape it by filing bankruptcy.

Clicking your clock into The Hardship Zone

Everyone's financial situation fluctuates, so timing can be critical. When considering undue hardship, the court tries to predict your future income and expenses, based on your current situation.

Obviously, asking the court to discharge the student loan is a question best posed when your financial situation is at its bleakest. Some courts have even allowed debtors to discharge student loans years after their bankruptcy case had been closed.

Bankruptcy can affect only debts existing at the time you file. Debts arising after bankruptcy aren't covered by the bankruptcy discharge. So, replacing a prebankruptcy student loan with a new consolidation loan (see "Consolidating your loans," a little later in this chapter) may undercut your bankruptcy options because the new loan would arise after you filed.

Bottom line: Check with a bankruptcy lawyer before getting a consolidation loan.

Managing Student Loans without Bankruptcy

If, after reading the earlier section entitled "Managing Student Loans with Bankruptcy," you're thinking that bankruptcy doesn't appear to be the answer to your prayers, other options include loan consolidation, deferment, forbearance, renewal of eligibility, and administrative discharge.

Consolidating your loans

Consolidation actually is a misnomer because you don't need to have more than one loan to qualify. Two programs that may prove helpful to you are

- ✓ Direct Consolidated Loans, which come directly from the federal government
- ✓ Federal Family Education Loans, which, although guaranteed by the federal government, are made by private lenders

Through these programs, your loans are paid off, and a new, consolidated loan is created. Monthly payments are based on family income.

Don't confuse these special educational consolidation loans with ordinary pitches from private lenders to consolidate loans by balance transfers or cash advances on credit cards, which almost never are good ways to address a student loan.

The upside is that the consolidated loan may well carry a lower interest rate than the original loan(s), the monthly payment *probably* will be less, and the time to repay *probably* will be extended. It sounds like a great deal if you qualify: Old loans are eliminated, you're immediately eligible for new educational loans and grants, and you're no longer subject to garnishments or other collection efforts.

However, here are a few downsides to consider:

- ✓ If you think you'll ever want to challenge one of your student loans in court, consult with an attorney before you agree to any form of consolidation. A closed bankruptcy can be reopened to discharge a student loan if your financial condition worsens. You may give up that option whenever you obtain a consolidation loan after bankruptcy.
- ✓ Be aware that the consolidated loan carries an 18.5 percent collection fee, which is added to the loan principal after consolidation. Ouch, that hurts!
- ✓ If you've defaulted on any of your student loans, your credit report continues to reflect the fact that you were, at some point, in default, even when you consolidate the loan.
- ✓ As always, realize that extending your payments increases the total amount you have to pay, just as it does with a car loan or a home mortgage.

In almost every instance, the Federal Direct Consolidation loan is a better deal than a FFEL consolidation loan because Federal Direct loans

> ✔ Don't have the FFEL requirement that you must make three payments to qualify.
>
> ✔ Offer lower interest rates and payments. (In fact, payments can be zero for families living at or below the poverty line. After 25 years, the remaining balance is wiped out.)
>
> ✔ May be easier to postpone if someday you need a deferment.

After obtaining either type of loan, the borrower is eligible for new loans, and no longer is subject to tax intercepts, garnishments, or other collections efforts.

Only you, and perhaps your attorney, can decide whether consolidation is the appropriate route. If you think it may be, you can obtain a loan application and fact sheet by calling 800-557-7392. You can also download forms from the Department of Education Web site, www.ed.gov/DirectLoan/consolid2.html.

Spouses need to avoid combining their individual loans into a single consolidation loan; otherwise, each spouse becomes legally responsible for the other's student loans.

Requesting a reasonable and affordable payment plan

As an alternative to consolidation loans, you can request "a reasonable and affordable" payment plan and renew your eligibility (so that you qualify for more student loans) or rehabilitate your loans (so that your name is removed from the creditor's deadbeat list).

Guarantee agencies or collectors for the federal government are required to offer this type of payment plan, but only when you specifically request it by using the magic words: "renew eligibility" and/or "rehabilitate the loans."

When you make six consecutive payments under such a plan, you renew your eligibility for student loans. When you make 12 consecutive payments, you can request that the loan be rehabilitated. In that case, the loan is essentially rewritten. The disadvantage of rehabilitation is that the amount of your payments almost surely increases.

Guarantee agencies have authority to settle for less than the full amount of the loan by waiving collection fees and agreeing to a discount of up to 30 percent in exchange for a lump sum payment. Before agreeing to a compromise, however, you need to confirm that the Department of Education recognizes the deal and won't later try to collect the balance.

Additional resources

Relieving your student-loan obligations without bankruptcy is extremely complicated, and few lawyers are knowledgeable in this area. The best resource is a book entitled *Student Loan Law.* Written for lawyers by the National Consumer Law Center, you can find out more about this book by calling 617-523-8089, or visiting `www.consumerlaw.org`. The Northwest Justice Project also sponsors a Web site that provides similar information at `www.lawhelp.org/WA/showdocument.cfm /County/%20/City/%20/demoMode/= %201/Language/1/State/WA/TextOn ly/N/ZipCode/%20/LoggedIn/0/doc type/dynamicdoc/ichannelprofile` `id/14044/idynamicdocid/1667/ior ganizationid/1553/iChannelID/7/ Search/1/searchterm/STUDENT %20LOANS.`

You can also obtain information from two very helpful publications. One by Robin Leonard and Shae Irving is *Take Control of Your Student Loans* (Nolo Press). The other, by Jonathan Sheldon and Gary Klein, is *Surviving Debt* (The National Consumer Law Center). The Federal Student Aid Information Center at 800-433-3243 may also be able to help, and the Department of Education maintains a Web site at `www.ed. gov`, which is very informative.

Getting a deferment

Depending on what type of loan you have and when the loan was made, many different grounds exist for justifying deferment of your loan. The most common grounds are that you're still in school, have lost your job, or are suffering economic hardship. Contact the holder of your loan to determine whether you may be eligible.

The nice thing about deferments is that you remain eligible for additional student aid and you won't be subjected to collection activity. The problem is that you're not eligible for a deferment if your loan is in default. Just the same, you can reestablish the right to deferment by renewing eligibility or getting a consolidation loan.

Accepting a forbearance

If you don't qualify for a deferment, the holder of your loan may still agree to a *forbearance,* which temporarily suspends your payment obligation. Forbearances are easier to obtain than deferments, but they aren't as good. If the loan is in default, you can still obtain a forbearance and stop collection activity. However, interest continues to accrue. You can also obtain a forbearance to prevent a loan from going into default, thereby preserving the right to a deferment at some point in the future. As is true for a deferment, contact the holder of your loan to find out whether you qualify.

Going for an administrative discharge

In some situations, student loans can be wiped out without bankruptcy through administrative procedures within the U.S. Department of Education. But the grounds for discharge are quite technical and vary among different types of loans. More information is available through the Department of Education Web site at www.ed.gov/finaid.html and www.ed.gov/offices/OSFAP/DCS/loan.cancellation.discharge.html. Those sites offer information about extinguishing student loans if

- You become permanently and totally disabled.
- You were unable to complete an educational program because the school closed.
- The school admitted you without a requisite high school degree or otherwise improperly allowed you to enroll.
- The school improperly certified your ability to benefit from the training offered.

Or if you are

- Engaged in full-time teaching
- In the military service
- Involved in the Head Start program
- In the Peace Corps

Part V
Strategies for a Successful Bankruptcy

The 5th Wave   By Rich Tennant

"I don't care what chapter of bankruptcy I file for, as long as it doesn't read like a Stephen King novel or end with a cliffhanger."

In this part . . .

Now that you've filed for bankruptcy, or decided to file, you need to know how to function in this brave new world — especially in the age of BARF. Even a little misstep in BARF can send you down a slippery slope. But this part tells you how to sidestep the slush and generally explains how to avoid ticking off the trustee assigned to your case and how to live comfortably and happily within the confines of a Chapter 13 repayment plan.

Chapter 19

Avoiding Troubles with Your Trustee

. . . .

In This Chapter

▶ Protecting your fresh start by telling the truth and not playing games

▶ Appreciating how fraudulent transfers can cause you grief

▶ Anticipating situations where your bankruptcy can affect friends and relatives

. . . .

Creditors can usually get only the benefit of those assets deemed *property of the estate* — which includes not only stuff you own on the petition date, but also property you've transferred just prior to filing bankruptcy (see Chapter 9 for more about transferring assets). Under certain circumstances, the bankruptcy trustee can grab property that you transferred and sell it for the benefit of your creditors.

In this chapter, we tell you some things that you shouldn't do before filing bankruptcy, if at all possible. If you've already done something that we talk about here, your lawyer probably can fix the problem — but only if she knows that the problem exists. You can find yourself in an awful mess when you file bankruptcy if you don't appreciate the trustee's ability to retrieve assets that you've transferred prior to bankruptcy, or if you haven't been completely honest and forthright with your lawyer.

Playing by the Rules and Telling the Truth

Quite simply, playing it straight is the best way to avoid headaches when filing bankruptcy. When you don't, the law arms the trustee with some pretty potent weapons, and you really don't want to stare down the barrel of that gun. Trust us on this one.

Debtor too smart for her own good

Joan thought she was being clever. She transferred her vacation house to her daughter but didn't bother telling her lawyer about the transaction and conveniently neglected to mention it in her bankruptcy papers. Who would know? Anyone who wants to, that's who.

A creditor discovered Joan's little maneuver in public records and brought it to the court's attention. Joan's daughter had to transfer the house to the bankruptcy trustee, none of Joan's debts were wiped out, and she barely escaped going to jail.

If Joan had been upfront with her lawyer from the get-go, a far better strategy could have been developed. For example, she may have been advised to sell the vacation house for a fair price and use the proceeds to fix the roof on her primary home and catch up with back mortgage payments.

Making sure that you play by the rules and that any assets that can and should go to creditors actually do go to creditors is the trustee's job. If you gave your kayak to your buddy right before bankruptcy just to ensure that the credit-card company wouldn't get it, the trustee can go after your pal for the return of the boat or payment of its value. Furthermore, and much more painfully for you, if the trustee in a Chapter 7 liquidation case thinks you're jerking your creditors around, she can ask the court to deny your discharge outright. When that happens, filing bankruptcy was for naught, because

- All your nonexempt property has been surrendered
- A bankruptcy is on your record
- None of your debts are eliminated
- You have no chance to eliminate those obligations through a Chapter 7 bankruptcy

In short, it's a lose-lose-lose-lose situation.

By now you're probably asking how you can avoid that headache.

The answer is real simple: Tell the truth, the whole truth, and nothing but the truth. Your parents were right; honesty is the best policy. And not only does truthfulness make you feel good, it may also keep you on the better side of prison bars.

Most documents filed in bankruptcy must be signed under penalty of perjury. If you intentionally lie on bankruptcy documents, or at the 341 meeting with creditors, you've committed *perjury* — a crime that can land you in prison. Careless disregard for the truthfulness of your statements is the same as lying, so ignorance is not bliss.

Accurately Listing Your Assets

If avoiding criminal prosecution and protecting your discharge isn't enough to keep you on the straight and narrow, there's another reason to list all your assets. If you accurately describe an asset and the trustee doesn't sell it while the case is open, that asset is *abandoned* — meaning it's yours again when the case is closed. Conversely, whenever you omit an asset or don't accurately describe it, your case can be reopened, even years later, with a trustee demanding that you turn over the asset or pay for its value.

In addition, whenever you accurately describe an asset and claim it as exempt in your bankruptcy schedules, the trustee and creditors have only 30 days after the 341 meeting to object. If no timely objection is filed, the property is deemed exempt even though a court would have ruled otherwise had a timely objection been filed.

Sometimes debtors forget to list a pending or potential lawsuit they have against someone (from which they hope to gain some money). Forgetting can prove to be a problem, especially when the debtor remembers the lawsuit after the bankruptcy is closed and tries to pursue the claim. If the party defending the claim is on the ball and discovers that you didn't list the claim, she may be able to have your suit dismissed.

Appreciating the Trustee's Ability to Recover Assets

The bankruptcy trustee has powers designed to help her recover assets and distribute proceeds fairly to unsecured creditors. Although powers wielded by Chapter 7 and Chapter 13 trustees are similar, they're most commonly invoked in Chapter 7 cases.

Debtor loses homestead by trying to save it

Sneaky Pete owned his $75,000 Boston home free and clear, but he was buried in debt and afraid that his many creditors would go after the house. So, Pete gave the house to his mother and then filed a do-it-yourself bankruptcy, figuring his creditors couldn't take what wasn't his.

Pete was wrong. Very wrong.

When the trustee learned of Pete's stunt, she went on the warpath. The trustee sued Pete's mom, recovered the home, and sold it. Adding insult to injury, the trustee convinced the bankruptcy court to deny Pete's discharge. So, in the end, Pete lost the house he was finagling to save and still was up to his eyeballs in debt.

Pete's first (and very costly) mistake was attempting to handle his own bankruptcy. That's often about as sensible as a do-it-yourself appendectomy. Any lawyer worthy of her license would have told Pete that under Massachusetts law, Pete's home already was exempt in bankruptcy, provided that he owned it when he filed. So, Pete had no reason to transfer the house to his mother. Furthermore, if he already had given Mom the deed, the lawyer would've told him to get it back before filing bankruptcy. That way, Pete would keep his home, have his debts discharged, and avoid the embarrassment and indignity of getting his mother sued.

These powers include recovering concealed assets and *avoiding* or undoing

- ✔ Fraudulent transfers
- ✔ Preferential transfers
- ✔ Unperfected liens

Fraudulent transfers

A transfer can be deemed a fraudulent transfer even when no actual fraud is involved. The law distinguishes between transfers that reek so bad that they are "actually fraudulent," and those that are only technically fraudulent. A transfer that wasn't necessarily intentionally fraudulent, but was so far out of line that it may as well have been intentional is called a *constructively fraudulent* transfer.

Actually fraudulent transfers

When you're buried in debt, your first impulse may be to give away your valuable property to friends or relatives so that creditors can't get it. That's an *actually fraudulent* transfer, and it's cheating. If you transfer the property within the year before filing bankruptcy, your Chapter 7 discharge may be denied — leaving you in worse financial trouble than when you started.

Your discharge may be denied even when the actual transfer was more than one year before bankruptcy, if you retained a secret ownership interest in the property within the year before you filed for bankruptcy. Say, for example, that three years before filing bankruptcy, you transferred title to your house to your friend with the "understanding" that you still really owned the property. In that situation, many courts apply a doctrine known as *continuing concealment* to deny your discharge because, within the year preceding bankruptcy, you concealed the fact that your really owned the property.

Whenever you try to conceal transfers or property from your bankruptcy trustee, you may end up in jail.

In addition to having your discharge denied, the trustee can also go after the recipient of a fraudulent transfer to recover the transferred asset or its value. And we're not talking about transfers made just before bankruptcy. When taking this route, the trustee can challenge transfers you made up to six years before bankruptcy!

Constructively fraudulent transfers

In contrast to actually fraudulent transfers (see the previous section), *constructively fraudulent* transfers aren't intentional schemes to shield property from creditors. Instead, they involve gifts or legitimate transfers of assets for values less than they're actually worth. The problem, from the standpoint of creditors, is that these kinds of transfers leave you with fewer assets. For example, if you sell a $10,000 car for $10,000, you still have the same amount of assets to use for paying creditors. You simply transformed the car into another asset — cash. On the other hand, if you just gave the car away, you would have less for creditors. Here are a couple more examples that may help illustrate this rather counterintuitive concept.

✔ **Bob gives his sister $10,000 to help her through a nasty divorce.** This is a constructively fraudulent transfer because Bob transferred valuable assets ($10,000) that could theoretically have been used to pay his debts, but didn't receive anything in return. So, the bankruptcy trustee sued Bob's poor sister for $10,000. But at least Bob got his debts wiped out because he didn't intentionally try to stiff his creditors.

✔ **Mary pays $5,600 on her sister's credit card right before filing.** The court deemed the transfer constructively fraudulent because Mary wasn't getting anything for her $5,600 and ruled that the trustee could get the money back from Mary's sister or the credit-card company.

✔ **Joe pays $100,000 to attend a fund-raising dinner with the President of the United States shortly before filing bankruptcy.** When Joe filed bankruptcy, the court ordered the Republican National Committee to turn the money over to the trustee because the court decided that Joe received "less than reasonably equivalent value" for his investment.

Finding out the hard way

Celeste talked her way into a 60-day jail term and four-month home detention after lying to the bankruptcy court and fraudulently concealing assets — namely, artwork, furniture, and money she was making on the sly through her off-the-books escort service. Celeste now has a criminal record, and she owes $25,000 restitution to her creditors.

George and Rose got into trouble with the bankruptcy court for neglecting to list $200,000 worth of marijuana in their bankruptcy schedules. The court said that even though the illegal drugs had no value to creditors, they should've been disclosed.

Betty had authority to draw on her mother's bank account. Because all the money belonged to her mother, Betty didn't list this account on her bankruptcy papers. Later, an angry creditor yelled "fraud" and asked the court to deny her bankruptcy discharge. Ultimately, Betty prevailed because the funds, in fact, belonged to her mother, but her bankruptcy became much more expensive and complicated than it would have been had she revealed her situation to the court and her attorney.

Moral of the story: Tell your lawyer about every asset you own or control and let your attorney decide how to use that information.

Gambling losses present yet another conundrum. Trustees sometimes go after gambling casinos to recover a debtor's gambling losses for the benefit of creditors. But courts usually accept the casino's argument that a gambler *receives significant value* when gambling — the prospect of winning.

Until recently, whenever a debtor donated to his church, the trustee could retrieve that money for payment to creditors. The theory then was that no matter how laudable a person's motives, his creditors shouldn't subsidize his charitable impulses. That's changed.

In 1998, powerful religious organizations pushed through the Religious Liberty and Charitable Donation Protection Act, which protects good-faith charitable contributions of up to 15 percent of a debtor's gross income during the year before filing bankruptcy, or more when greater amounts are consistent with past practices of the debtor. However, if the bankruptcy court is convinced that a debtor's contributions are made for the purpose of short-changing creditors, the money can be recovered, and the debtor can be denied his discharge.

Preferential transfers

Congress considers it unfair for unsecured creditors to get paid on the eve of bankruptcy when others are left holding the bag. As a result, Congress gave bankruptcy trustees the power to recover these payments, which are called *preferential transfers*, for the benefit of all creditors.

Poor planning brings an ugly surprise

Patti's parents loaned her $20,000 to help get creditors off her back. Although the loan provided temporary relief, Patti still was buried deep in debt. A few months later, her parents needed their money back. So, Patti used money in her IRA to repay them. She filed bankruptcy two months later.

The trustee forced Patti's parents to cough up the $20,000 for distribution to all her creditors. If Patti had filed bankruptcy *before* withdrawing the IRA, the trustee couldn't have touched the money. Then, she'd have been free, after bankruptcy, to repay her parents if she chose.

Moral of story: Parents and relatives can wait.

For example, if you paid your dentist $1,000 on an overdue bill a month before bankruptcy, the trustee can get the money back from the dentist and distribute it among all your creditors. For you, it's a lose-lose situation. The dentist won't be happy about having to give up the money, and you'll be out $1,000 that you could have used for living expenses, car payments, or house payments. Even worse, if you paid that money toward a nondischargeable debt only to have the trustee retrieve it, you wasted the dough — and the nondischargeable debt that you intended to pay is revived and continues to haunt you after bankruptcy.

You need to understand the difference between preferential and fraudulent transfers. *Fraudulent transfers* are cheating; *preferential transfers* aren't.

Whenever you pay a legitimate debt, the payment may be preferential but not fraudulent. The distinction is important because your discharge can be denied for making a fraudulent transfer but not for a preferential transfer. The former is malicious or sneaky, and the latter is essentially an accident or error in judgment. Either can affect your bankruptcy, though in different ways.

Be aware that preferential transfers can be recovered only when they're made within a relatively short time before bankruptcy, usually 90 days.

However, when a transfer is made to an insider, the trustee may be able to recover all the payments made during the entire year prior to bankruptcy. Whether an individual qualifies as an insider is determined on a case-by-case basis. *Insiders* generally include relatives and others with relationships close enough to you to strongly influence your actions. If you're still friends with your ex-spouse, he or she may be considered an insider. If you're bitter enemies, probably not. A live-in lover is deemed an insider by some courts.

Most courts say that in the case of a regular check, *payment* occurs when the check actually clears; however, with a cashier's check or money order, payment occurs when it is mailed to the creditor.

Payments on cosigned loans and joint debts

If the potential exists for a friend or relative to be left holding the bag for one of your debts if you don't pay it (for example, a joint debt or your friend cosigned for you), you may be tempted to protect her by paying that debt before bankruptcy. That's usually a bad idea (see "Poor planning brings an ugly surprise" anecdote), despite your good intentions.

For example, if your dad cosigns for your loan, he promises the lender that if you don't pay, he will. Say that before bankruptcy, you caught up on the back payments on that loan. Because every payment you make to the lender also reduces the amount of your father's potential liability, the law also treats any payment to the lender as a payment to your dad — even though he doesn't actually receive any money. So a trustee can go after your dad for the money you paid to the *lender* during the entire year prior to bankruptcy because your dad is an insider. If the cosigner wasn't an insider, the trustee can recover only the payments made during the 90 days before the bankruptcy.

Rather than making payments on joint or cosigned loans before bankruptcy, explaining things to the other person and having *her* make the payments until after you file bankruptcy is a better way to go. You can always reimburse her later. Obviously, this situation may cause some hard feelings, but your lawyer may be able to help you explain how this strategy is best for both of you.

Payments that aren't preferences

The following payments aren't considered preferences. and the trustee can't recover them:

- **Small payments:** Payments totaling less than $600 to any single creditor during the relevant time period (usually 90 days before bankruptcy, but one year for payments to insiders).

- **Payments on secured debts:** Payments for things such as your house or car aren't recoverable as preferences. You can and need to continue making these payments if you intend to keep your house or vehicle.

- **Payments for current expenses:** Regular payments on bills that aren't overdue aren't avoidable. For example, your rent payment for the current month isn't a preference. But if you paid back rent totaling more than $600, it would be a preference.

- **Payments of back alimony or child support.** The trustee can't recover payments to an ex-spouse for back alimony or child support.

Unperfected liens

The law requires lienholders to *perfect* their liens, or warn people that someone other than you claims an interest in your property. That's why mortgages must be filed as part of the public record, and security interests in motor vehicles are noted on the certificate of title.

If a lien isn't perfected by the time a bankruptcy petition is filed, it's too late for the creditor. The trustee can take over the creditor's interest in the asset.

For example, assume that you owe the bank $4,000 on a car worth $5,000, and the amount of the car that you can claim as exempt (property that is usually off-limits to creditors) is $1,500. Usually, your exemption covers any equity in the car, so the bank would have its security interest (meaning it could take the car if you don't pay), and there'd be nothing left over for the trustee. If you wanted to keep the car, you'd continue making the payments to the bank.

However, if it turns out that when the bank loaned you the money, it forgot to have its lien on your car noted on the certificate of title, the trustee can take over the bank's security interest and sell your car. The trustee then can take all the money that would have gone to the lender, and you'd be paid for the amount of your exemption only if any money was left over.

Here's another hurdle: The act of perfecting a lien also is considered a transfer of property. So, if a lien isn't perfected at the same time that the loan is made, trying to perfect it later on creates an avoidable preference if the borrower files bankruptcy within the preference period.

For example: The bank that made your car loan discovers that it failed to have its security interest noted on the certificate of title when it made the loan. If the bank tries to fix the error later by having its security interest added to the certificate of title, that attempt would be an avoidable transfer — if, that is, you file bankruptcy within 90 days of when the bank tried to fix its error.

Special problems with manufactured homes

In many states, manufactured homes begin life as personal property, subject to certificate of title laws. In other words, a security interest must be noted on the certificate of title. Whether the unit remains personal property covered by a certificate of title or becomes real property covered by a mortgage when it's installed and affixed to land isn't clear.

As you can see, manufactured housing can be very tricky, and even major lending institutions sometimes mess up their paperwork in such a way that their security interest isn't properly perfected. Trustees know to watch for these kinds of circumstances and closely examine financing documents. When they're not done right, the trustee can swoop in, and you can lose your home.

Bottom line: Whenever you have a manufactured home, show all the financing documents to your lawyer so that she can determine whether the paperwork is in order. If it isn't, she then can try to have the lender fix it before you file bankruptcy. But remember the wrinkle we point out — 90 days must pass from the time that the paperwork is corrected until bankruptcy is filed. Otherwise, the trustee can nullify the act of fixing the paperwork.

When the trustee eliminates a lien because it's unperfected, new preference issues crop up.

Remember that payments on secured loans aren't avoidable preferences (see "Payments that aren't preferences," earlier in this chapter), but payments on unsecured loans may be? Well, whenever the trustee avoids a lien, the loan is considered unsecured at the time, so all prebankruptcy payments to the creditor within the relevant time period (a year or 90 days) become avoidable preferences.

Assume, for example, that your uncle cosigned your secured car loan and during the past year you paid $1,500 on the loan. Ordinarily, these payments wouldn't be avoidable preferences because they were made to a secured creditor.

But say that the bank forgets to note its security interest on the certificate of title, which enables the trustee to avoid it. In that situation, all the loan payments become preferences, and the trustee can recover the money from your uncle. What's more, your uncle still is on the hook for the car loan because the trustee is selling the car for the benefit of other creditors.

Protecting Your Discharge

Under BARF, minor missteps may jeopardize your discharge — preventing your debts from being wiped out. Because debt elimination is probably the main reason to file bankruptcy, be sure to check out Chapter 6 to make sure that you jump through all the hoops.

Chapter 20

Living on the Edge in Chapter 13 Bankruptcy

*W*hen preparing your Chapter 13 financial reorganization plan, you have to gaze three to five years into the future, realistically calculate your income and expenses, and promise to make regular payments based on those guesstimates. Unless you have a pretty reliable crystal ball, or a resident soothsayer, that's an awfully tall order. Often, adjustments must be made because of your mistakes or because something (like an unexpected medical expense) happens to muck up your plan.

This chapter provides you with pointers for getting started on the right foot with a plan that's realistic and sensible. It addresses the importance of having a lawyer who's willing to stand by you from A to Z, describes your options when your repayment plan implodes, and offers insights into the potential successes and pitfalls that arise when things suddenly turn around and a windfall comes your way. Finally, Table 20-1 at the end of this chapter lists the various choices you can make whenever your plan isn't working, along with the implications of making those choices.

If you filed your Chapter 13 case prior to October 17, 2005, the effective date of BARF, *you don't want your case dismissed.* The old law, which was much more sympathetic to debtors, continues to apply to your present case, even if it's converted to Chapter 7. But, if your case were dismissed, any new filing would be subject to the harsh provisions of BARF.

Creating a Realistic Plan

Stuff happens — good things and bad. It's no wonder that nationally less that one-third of all Chapter 13 bankruptcies succeed. But *your* Chapter 13 needn't fail. With a reasonable plan, the odds of your success aren't all that bad. In fact, they're pretty decent.

The key is remaining *reasonable*.

Face it. If your plan is so tight that macaroni and cheese becomes an extravagant delicacy, it won't work — at least not for long. On the other hand, if your plan imposes reasonable restraint but enables you to maintain a satisfactory, albeit disciplined, lifestyle, you have a good shot.

Although statistically most plans fail, the raw stats don't tell the entire story because they fail to take into account which plans were unreasonable and therefore are virtually jinxed from the get-go, and which were reasonable and therefore had a fighting chance.

The key: Don't be discouraged by the theoretical odds. When your plan makes sense, you're probably going to come out of this situation just fine, even with those little surprises that life tends to toss in your path.

Why Chapter 13 plans fail

A Chapter 13 reorganization usually fails for one (or more) of the following reasons:

- ✔ It's poorly designed, unrealistic, and doomed from day one.
- ✔ The debtor screws up and just won't live within a budget.
- ✔ Unexpected expenses pop up.
- ✔ One of the first three listed items happens, and the debtor neglects to advise his or her lawyer, who probably could have dealt with the problem before it got out of hand and before it was too late to deal with.

Avoid these pitfalls, and you're home-free.

BARF sets up numerous booby traps to snare unsuspecting debtors. You may be required to file additional materials with the court after your case is initially filed. For example, if the trustee or creditor so requests, any federal income tax returns, including amendments that you file with the IRS while the case is open must also be filed with the bankruptcy court. Additionally, in Chapter 13, debtors must file annual reports showing all their income for the previous year. If you forget to file this paperwork, your case can be dismissed. And you don't want that to happen.

Having payments deducted from your wages

If you want to, you can have your Chapter 13 payments automatically deducted from your pay and forwarded to the trustee. Doing so is a convenient way to go that obviously makes squandering the money much harder to do because you never see it. You can do this by signing what's called a *wage deduction order.*

We have mixed thoughts about wage deductions.

Although some studies suggest that the success rate is higher, experiencing financial discipline is part and parcel of the Chapter 13 process. Working with your plan is when it's time to take control of your finances, instead of allowing others to do it for you. You certainly won't get any mileage out of burdening your boss with special payroll procedures. It's your call, of course, but we recommend making the payments yourself.

Paying the bare minimum

With a Chapter 13 plan, you can clear your slate of most debts by paying just pennies on the dollars that you owe. Still, you usually must pay a threshold minimum so that you obtain your fresh start. Typically, that minimum amount is the total of

- ✔ Back payments on your mortgage (if you want to keep your home)
- ✔ Nondischargeable priority taxes
- ✔ Prepetition support obligations
- ✔ The value of any nonexempt assets

 The total amount must be paid within 60 months, so any plan that's designed to last the full 60 months is precarious and suspect because it puts you right up against the wall from the start and offers you no wiggle room if things don't work out just the way you hoped. If the math doesn't add up under a 60-month plan, you may be tempted to propose a schedule where monthly payments start out relatively low but then increase in the latter stages of your plan. At first blush, such plans sound doable, and maybe they are. But . . .

 In our experience, we find it more often is a prescription for disaster. When the time comes for plan payments to increase, the money inevitably just isn't there. Then, the Chapter 13 case is dismissed or converted to a Chapter 7 liquidation, and any payments that you made are frequently for naught.

BARF will undoubtedly increase the percentage of Chapter 13 cases that fail — especially for those with incomes greater than the Median Income for their state. (See Chapter 5 for an explanation of Median Income.) This is because the new law requires that above-median debtors sign on for a five-year plan rather than the usual three unless creditors are paid 100 percent of their claims.

Keeping Your Lawyer in the Loop

Because the Bankruptcy Code doesn't provide clear guidance for dealing with the unexpected — job losses, unforeseen medical expenses, and so on — judges and trustees have had to improvise. They're usually pretty reasonable, but absent any formal direction, they more or less fashion their own rules and practices.

What's kosher in some areas is taboo in others, so having a guide who really knows the local practices, preferences, and eccentricities truly helps.

A Chapter 13 plan has a much better chance of succeeding when your lawyer sticks with you through the entire case — not just until your plan is confirmed.

Your lawyer needs to be willing to bargain with the Chapter 13 trustee whenever circumstances change. A lawyer who stands by you for three to five years obviously expects to be paid, but that shouldn't be a big problem. Legal fees are usually covered in regular plan payments.

Blowing It . . . Again? Not!

Sometimes, even the best Chapter 13 plan falls through because you lose your job, get sick, or you're unable to make payments as a result of other unforeseen events. All isn't necessarily lost. Depending on the type of debts and payments you're facing, your options include

- Suspending your payments
- Modifying your plan
- Requesting a hardship discharge
- Converting your case to a Chapter 7 liquidation
- Dismissing your case outright
- Dismissing your case and then filing a Chapter 7
- Dismissing your case and then filing a second Chapter 13 reorganization

Considering each of these options is enough to make your head spin. Table 20-1, at the end of this chapter, provides a thumbnail sketch (granted, a very large thumbnail sketch) of what you have to think about. You may want to glance at this table right now just to get a general overview and then refer back to it as you read through this chapter.

Whenever you miss payments to the trustee — and don't take advantage of any of the options in the previous bulleted list — the court dismisses your case, enabling creditors to resume collection efforts against you and your property. Furthermore, you may be barred from filing another bankruptcy for 180 days — regardless of how bad things get.

Something called the *180-day rule* forbids a second bankruptcy within — you guessed it — 180 days of dismissal of an earlier case. The rule kicks in if the dismissal was

✔ Requested by you after a creditor asked the court for permission to fore-close (which is called a motion for *relief from stay*)

✔ Resulted because you intentionally failed to comply with a court order

When a previous Chapter 13 case was dismissed because you couldn't make plan payments, some courts would rule that the 180-day doesn't apply. Reason: Inability to make payments is not an intentional disregard of a court order. On the other hand, some courts forbid a refiling, and 180 days is enough time for an aggressive mortgage holder to foreclose on your house.

Even if the 180-day rule doesn't apply, you may not get the benefit of the automatic stay in a second case filed within one year of dismissal.

If you had one bankruptcy dismissed less than one year before filing a new bankruptcy, the automatic stay kicks in when the new case is filed, but it expires in 30 days unless you persuade the court that the stay should remain in effect.

If more than one bankruptcy was dismissed within this one-year period, there is no automatic stay in the new case. You have to file a special request for the court to impose the stay.

The only exception is where your Chapter 7 case was dismissed for flunking the Means Test, and you're now filing Chapter 13. (See Chapter 5 for an expla-nation of the Means Test.)

You may wonder what you have to do to convince a judge to resurrect the stay if you have to refile within one year of dismissal. Good question.

With BARF, if your case was dismissed for failing to file documents, you must show a "substantial excuse" — not just negligence or inadvertence. "My dog ate my homework" probably doesn't cut it. If your earlier case was dismissed because you couldn't keep up with your plan payments, you have to prove that circumstances have changed, and now you're able to make payments. Undoubtedly, your chances of success hinge on the attitudes and prejudices of local bankruptcy judges, which can be wildly divergent.

And even if you are eligible to file, if you file within one year of dismissal, you don't get the benefit of the automatic stay (which stops all collection efforts and lawsuits —a big, big benefit of bankruptcy) unless you convince the bankruptcy court that dismissal was due to conditions beyond your control and that your financial condition has changed since the dismissal. (See Chapter 6 for more insight.)

Suspending your payments

If you miss payments because of a temporary crisis — say you get laid off or sick — the wise thing to do is to ask the trustee to allow you to suspend payments until the crisis subsides. In that situation, the suspended payments aren't forgiven; they're just paid later, and the time limit of the plan is extended.

As long as you have a good reason for suspending payments and can convince the trustee that your problem is only temporary, you'll probably be allowed some latitude.

But there's a hitch.

Because a Chapter 13 can't run any longer than 60 months, if your plan already is five years old, suspending payments and extending the life of your plan won't work. In that case, the plan must be modified, which can raise an entirely new set of problems (see the next section). This reason is just one of several why a 60-month repayment plan is inherently dicey. Quite simply, not much room is left for error.

If your income exceeds the median for your state, suspending payments probably won't work because your plan is probably already at 60 months.

Modifying your plan

When a suspension of payments won't work — because the change in your circumstances isn't temporary or because your plan already is 60 months long — it may be possible to modify your Chapter 13 plan. Doing so usually results in lower payments now and higher ones in the future.

Consider the case of Fred and Frederica. The Chapter 13 repayment plan was working just great. Fred and Frederica were diligently making up the missed mortgage payments and, finally, could see some light at the end of the tunnel. Then, their teenage son fractured his skull in a car crash, and they had to use the mortgage money to pay doctor bills. The bank asked for bankruptcy court permission to foreclose on their house.

Fred and Frederica quickly called their lawyer, who immediately filed a modified Chapter 13 plan. The plan, accepted by the court, extended the previous schedule and established payments that Fred and Frederica could make. They kept their house. And their son is doing just fine, thank you.

Modification can solve your problem the same way it did for Fred and Frederica. Of course, any proposed modification must be feasible, so the court examines your situation to see whether it's likely you'll be able to make higher payments at a later date. In other words, a judge isn't going to cut you a break now unless he's pretty sure you'll be able to make good on it later. If you can't afford higher future payments under a modified plan, consider asking the court for a hardship discharge (see the next section).

Modifying a plan after confirmation may open a Pandora's box.

Remember that any Chapter 13 plan must propose to pay the value of your nonexempt property based on the value of the property when the plan is confirmed.

If the value of your nonexempt property increases and you ask to have a modified plan confirmed, the court may insist on payments based on the increase in value. That kind of a result certainly isn't a good one, especially when you're already having problems keeping up with payments. All courts don't see things that way, but changing property values is something you need to discuss with your lawyer before requesting a plan modification.

For example, when your plan was initially confirmed, the equity in your home was within the allowable exemption. But after a couple of years, when you request a plan modification, the increase in your equity may exceed the exemption because of an appreciation in value or simply a reduction of the mortgage balance. In this situation, some courts bump up your payments to cover the increased equity.

Requesting a "hardship discharge"

A *hardship discharge* stops the Chapter 13 dead and excuses all remaining payments. To understand how it works, look at what happened to Isaac.

Isaac filed a Chapter 7 six years ago, and lo and behold, is in trouble again, with $10,000 in new credit-card bills. Because Isaac's bankruptcy was less than eight years ago, a Chapter 7 won't wipe out his debts, so he tries to make payments under a Chapter 13, but no dice. He just can't keep up. So, Isaac's attorney convinced the court to award a hardship discharge. Once again, his slate is squeaky clean.

Good deal, huh?

To qualify for such a discharge, you must

- ✔ Convince the court that your inability to make payments is for reasons beyond your control
- ✔ Show that modification of the plan isn't feasible
- ✔ Already have made payments equal to the value of any nonexempt property you had on the petition date

The major disadvantage of a hardship discharge is that you don't obtain the usual super discharge provided in Chapter 13 cases. We explain in Part IV how some debts may be wiped out in a Chapter 13 but not in a Chapter 7. That's why a Chapter 13 discharge is called a *super discharge* (although it's not all that super any more under BARF). But you obtain a super discharge only if you complete all your plan payments. In a hardship discharge, the only debts that are wiped out are the ones that are eliminated in a Chapter 7.

Nonetheless, a hardship discharge has the following advantages over converting the case to a Chapter 7:

- ✔ If you received a discharge in a bankruptcy filed within eight years (unless the prior bankruptcy was a Chapter 13 and creditors were paid at least 70 percent of their claims) of your present Chapter 13, your debts are not wiped out if you convert to Chapter 7. In contrast, you can wipe out your debts with a Chapter 13 hardship discharge if the earlier bankruptcy was a Chapter 7, 11, or 12 case filed more than four years before your present case, or a Chapter 13 case filed more than two years before your present case.
- ✔ The property you owned when your Chapter 13 was filed isn't reexamined the way it would be if you convert the case to a Chapter 7. This issue can be an especially important issue if, for example, you move out of your home (which had qualified for a homestead exemption) or the law governing exemptions was altered. On the other hand, if you convert to a Chapter 7, the court can apply the new rules, and your property may no longer be exempt. If you go the hardship discharge route, property that was exempt when you initially filed bankruptcy remains exempt despite changes of this kind.

Converting to a Chapter 7

Although a hardship discharge is frequently a better deal than converting your case to a Chapter 7, it may not be an option. Some courts interpret the "hardship" in hardship discharge strictly and literally, reserving it for debtors who have suffered some catastrophic disaster. Your lawyer should know whether your judge takes this view.

Conversion does have one advantage over a hardship discharge, however. If you convert, you gain relief from debts arising after your Chapter 13 petition was filed that wouldn't be included in a hardship discharge. For example, if you incurred some new bills after filing a Chapter 13, they ordinarily won't be wiped out in your existing bankruptcy; however, if you convert to a Chapter 7, you can add these debts to the ones you can eliminate.

With BARF, it's not clear whether a person who was not initially eligible for Chapter 7 because of the Means Test can come in through the back door by first filing Chapter 13 and then converting to Chapter 7. Our guess is that courts won't automatically allow this tactic, especially if this was your plan from the beginning. But they may go along if you did your best to make the Chapter 13 work, but just couldn't cut it.

Dismissing your Chapter 13 and filing a new Chapter 7

Instead of converting your Chapter 13 to Chapter 7, you can dismiss your Chapter 13 bankruptcy and file a brand new one under Chapter 7. Choosing between these two alternatives can be devilishly complicated.

The advantages of filing a new Chapter 7 over converting an existing case to a Chapter 7 are

✔ Beneficial changes in the law apply in a new case.

✔ You can delay filing a new case so that any debts incurred on the eve of the first case aren't presumed to be fraudulent. See Chapters 13 and 14 for an explanation of why debts incurred on the eve of bankruptcy may not be discharged.

✔ You may be able to sell assets that you'd lose in a Chapter 7 and use the money for living expenses. Chapter 10 contains more info on turning nonexempt assets into exempt assets. Chapters 7 and 19 provide more food for thought on the subject of selling assets prior to bankruptcy.

✔ You can reestablish your homestead exemption if you've changed your residence during the Chapter 13 case. We explore this option a in the section entitled "Requesting a 'hardship discharge,'" earlier in this chapter.

✔ If you dismiss your Chapter 13 and then file a new Chapter 7, you retain an option to convert the Chapter 7 into a Chapter 13 filing. When you convert to a Chapter 7, you can't convert back to a Chapter 13.

Pondering one fickle legal pickle

Nigel faithfully made all his Chapter 13 payments until the auto repair shop where he had worked for 15 years cut its workforce. To make ends meet, he got a job working nights in a convenience store and even moved into an apartment above the store so that he could rent out his house. When Nigel filed a Chapter 13, no one objected to his assertion that the home was exempt.

Nigel's convenience store boss, Garfield, filed a Chapter 13 at about the same time.

When he filed a Chapter 13, Garfield owned his personal residence, which was exempted, and a rental property, which wasn't exempt. After his income dropped, Garfield cut expenses by moving into the smaller rental property and allowing foreclosure to progress on his former residence.

Neither Nigel nor Garfield can keep up with their Chapter 13 payments, so the question becomes one of whether Nigel's and Garfield's homes are exempt if their Chapter 13 cases are converted to Chapter 7 cases.

Most courts would say that Nigel's house would be exempt after the case converts to a Chapter 7 because it was exempt on the date he initially filed under the Chapter 13. However, Garfield's house wouldn't be exempt because it wasn't his residence on the Chapter 13 petition date, even though it was when the case was converted.

But then again, other courts may rule just the opposite, saying that Nigel's home wasn't exempt because he didn't live there on the date of conversion, but Garfield's home was exempt because that's where he lived when his case was converted.

The disadvantages of filing a new Chapter 7 over converting an existing case to a Chapter 7 are

- ✔ Attorney fees and costs will probably be higher.

- ✔ Unfavorable changes in the law will apply in a new case, but wouldn't if you converted an existing case.

- ✔ If your Chapter 13 was filed on or before October 17, 2005, your case is not governed by BARF. You're not subjected to the Means Test or other burdens and indignities of the new law if you convert your case to Chapter 7. But after your pre-October 17, 2005, case is dismissed, any new filing will be.

- ✔ The automatic stay is not so "automatic" if you file within one year of having a case dismissed. To get the benefit of the stay, you have to convince the court that you had a good reason for dismissing your earlier case and that your financial circumstances have changed since then.

When a case is converted, courts disagree about whether exemptions are determined as of the date of your Chapter 13 petition or the date that the case was converted.

In other words, your property may have qualified as a homestead when your Chapter 13 was filed, but if you moved out of the property and then converted to a Chapter 7, the property may no longer qualify as a homestead and, as such, would go to the trustee.

Sounds complicated, doesn't it? Well, it is . . . and it's further complicated by the fact that to some extent the rules that apply aren't uniform or consistent and are dependent on the way your local bankruptcy court does business.

Also, your property may have increased in value since you filed Chapter 13. For example, when you filed under a Chapter 13 reorganization, say that your homestead was worth $75,000 and subject to a $50,000 mortgage. Because your state allows a homestead exemption of $25,000 at the time you filed, your property was entirely exempt — no ifs, ands, or buts about it.

But when you converted to a Chapter 7 liquidation, the value of your property had increased to $90,000, and the mortgage balance had dropped to $47,000. As a result, your equity in the house is $43,000, a considerable amount more than your state allows for an exemption. If your home is still completely off-limits, you get the benefit of this increase in value. But some courts would allow the Chapter 7 trustee to sell your home, pay you $25,000 for your exemption, and distribute the balance to creditors.

The answer's a crapshoot because it depends on where you live and how your bankruptcy court views converting to a Chapter 7 versus dismissing a Chapter 13 and filing a new Chapter 7 case.

Kind of a bummer, isn't it?

Dismissing your Chapter 13 and filing a new Chapter 13

Sometimes you're better off dismissing your Chapter 13 and starting a new Chapter 13 instead of trying to modify your existing Chapter 13 plan.

The advantages:

- ✔ You get a brand-new 60-month period to repay your debts. When you're in the fourth year of a five-year plan and problems develop, you have only one year remaining to cure any problems. This way, a new Chapter 13 gives you another five years.

- ✔ You can include debts incurred since your original Chapter 13 filing.

The disadvantages:

- When your Chapter 13 is dismissed, you lose the benefit of *cram-down* (restructuring the loan without needing the consent of the lender). Say, for example, that your car is worth $5,000, and you owe $11,000. You were keeping your car in Chapter 13 by cramming down, or paying its value — $5,000 during the life of the plan (see Chapter 11). Dismissing and filing a new Chapter 13 means having to pay for your $5,000 car all over again because you receive no credit for payments made in your earlier case.

- Whenever you file more than one Chapter 13, the court eyes all the circumstances very carefully to determine whether the second case is filed in bad faith.

- The automatic stay isn't "automatic" if the second case is filed within one year of dismissal of the first.

Tackling Car and Mortgage Payments Outside the Plan

Chapter 13 plans commonly provide that, in addition to payments to the trustee, the debtor must continue making regular house and car payments directly to the lenders for payments that come due after the date you file bankruptcy (the *petition date*). These payments are deemed *outside the plan.*

Whenever you fall behind on outside-the-plan payments, the lender asks the court for a *relief from stay* so that it can foreclose on your home or repossess and sell your car.

At this point, your options are

- Doing nothing
- Proposing a modified plan that includes missed payments
- Working out a drop-dead agreement (See the upcoming section entitled, "Working out drop-dead agreements.")
- Asking for time to sell your property

Doing nothing

If your attorney doesn't respond to a motion for relief from stay, the court will probably grant the motion by default.

You choose this option only when you're resigned to letting the property go. *Note:* You'll have to surrender your car immediately, but you can remain in your home for a while.

How long you can stay in your home depends on whether foreclosure proceedings were underway when you filed bankruptcy. If they were, you may not have much time because the mortgage company can simply resume foreclosure proceedings where they left off. On the other hand, if the foreclosure isn't already pending, you have at least three months before you have to get out.

You also need to consider whether you have any reason to remain in your Chapter 13 — especially when the only reason for filing bankruptcy was to save your home. If that's the case, you may be better off simply dismissing your case, or if you have other debts, converting to a Chapter 7. Choosing to remain in Chapter 13 after a creditor gets relief from the stay probably means that you'll have to modify your plan. Be sure to ask your lawyer about doing that.

Proposing a new plan that includes missed payments

If you still want to keep your house or car, the court may give you time to make up additional missed payments by adding them to the amount you're already paying to the trustee.

When your plan calls for monthly $500 outside-the-plan payments on your mortgage and you fall four payments behind ($2,000) with 24 months left on your plan, you can propose an increase in your plan payment to the trustee of about $90 per month to catch up on the missed postpetition payments.

This scenario is a feasible option only when the reason for missing postpetition payments was temporary, and you're able to afford increased payments to the trustee and resume regular payments to the lender.

You must also have enough time left under the plan to make up the missed payments. Remember that Chapter 13 plans can't be more than 60 months long.

If you don't have enough time left in your plan, you may consider dismissing your Chapter 13 and filing a new one. Some of the pitfalls to this tactic are that

- ✔ When a creditor moves for relief from the stay, you can't file a second case for 180 days. This rule gives the mortgage lender enough time to complete foreclosure if it acts quickly.

- ✔ The one-year no-automatic stay rule may apply.

- ✔ The bankruptcy court may enter an *in rem order,* which means that any bankruptcy filed in the foreseeable future won't interfere with foreclosure.

Working out drop-dead agreements

Sometimes, a mortgage lender agrees to withdraw its challenge to the automatic stay, provided that you agree that any further missed payments result in virtually automatic foreclosure. This sword of Damocles is known as a *drop-dead agreement* because if you blow it again, you're "dead." As chancy as it sounds — and is — it may be your only option for keeping your home.

Ordinarily, your lawyer negotiates the terms of such an agreement, but you need to pay close attention to make sure that everybody concurs on the date by which payments must be made, the amount of the payments, and whether payments are to be made directly to the creditor or to the trustee. Likewise, you need to try to get the creditor to agree to give you notice and a short time — ten days is reasonable — to make up any payment you accidentally miss.

Asking for time to sell your property

Finally, your lawyer may respond to a motion for relief from stay by asking the court to allow you a short time to sell the property and pay off the mortgage company. Doing so makes sense when you have substantial equity built up in the property. Although you don't get to keep the property, at least you won't lose your exemption.

For example, assume that your home is worth $100,000, and you owe $75,000 on the mortgage. Odds are that at a foreclosure sale, your mortgage holder will end up owning the property, and you'll get nothing. However, if you sell the property yourself, you'd sell it for $100,000 — enough to pay off the mortgage holder and leave you with $25,000, less, of course, any commission you have to pay to a real estate agent.

In some jurisdictions, Chapter 13 trustees claim that the $25,000 needs to be turned over to them for distribution to unsecured creditors and, regrettably, some judges agree. Your lawyer can fill you in on these local customs.

Addressing Debts Incurred After You File

When your budget is realistic and no unforeseen catastrophes occur after confirmation of your Chapter 13 plan, you shouldn't need any postpetition credit. In fact, you're not supposed to incur any postpetition debts without permission from the trustee. As a practical matter, incurring a new debt is occasionally necessary and sometimes even wise, but it's so potentially perilous that you never should do it without first consulting your attorney and the trustee.

The implications of postpetition debt vary, depending on whether the debt is for

- ✔ Nonemergencies
- ✔ Emergencies
- ✔ An automobile
- ✔ Support obligations
- ✔ Income taxes

Nonemergencies

Whenever you find yourself in need of credit after filing your petition, you'll probably hear big-time warning bells going off. Before you rack up any new debts, you need to figure out why your plan isn't working. If your budget was unrealistic, admit it and ask your lawyer about modifying your plan. Otherwise, things are just going to get worse. Trust us.

Postpetition debts may be dischargeable when you convert to a Chapter 7 or dismiss your Chapter 13 and file a new case, but if you incurred debts during a Chapter 13 case and you didn't tell the creditor that you were in bankruptcy, that creditor has a pretty good argument that the amount it loaned you should be excepted from discharge because of fraud.

Emergencies

True emergencies are different. If your wife got cancer and insurance covers only a fraction of the cost of her treatment, if your company downsized and you lose all your overtime hours, or if you live in Buffalo and your furnace blows in mid-January, accommodations are in order.

When something that causes your bankruptcy plan to fail truly is beyond your control, you can probably find a way to reasonably deal with it. But you need to contact your lawyer as soon as you can, preferably before incurring any expense. The Bankruptcy Code includes a procedure for obtaining trustee approval and modifications to your plan that include emergency expenses. It's in place to deal with just these sorts of things. If you need it, use it.

Automobiles

One of life's certainties is that cars die, often when you need them most. So what do you do when your car croaks while you're in the middle of a Chapter 13 bankruptcy?

If you own the late, great car outright and don't owe anything, you can probably go out and buy a new one, assuming that you have the cash, but be sure to check with your lawyer first about local rules and customs. Financing the new car isn't so easy. You need to contact your lawyer, who will have to convince the trustee and the judge that you can afford the payments and still live within your budget.

If, on the other hand, the car that died was financed, you have another problem. The creditor who financed the now deceased car was promised certain payments under your plan. Ideally, you can try modifying your plan, giving back the car, and avoiding payment of the balance of the loan. Some courts allow this kind of approach, but others will hold you to your original commitment. Again, you need to talk to your lawyer about this situation.

Support obligations

Nothing but trouble lies ahead when you start falling behind on support obligations that come due after the petition date.

The support creditor — it can be an ex-spouse, child, or governmental support collection agency — may come after you without regard to your bankruptcy. Even if a support creditor lets you slide, debts for postpetition support must be paid up by the end of your Chapter 13 case, or you won't get a discharge

When your support payments are unreasonably high, the place to look for relief is the state court, but beware. Figuring out how to pay a domestic relations lawyer is tricky because of restrictions on incurring postpetition debt. Your bankruptcy lawyer will have to forge some sort of arrangement that is acceptable to the trustee and the divorce lawyer. The specifics depend on the practices adopted in your locality.

Income taxes

Bankruptcy laws do *not* suspend your obligation to pay income taxes that accrue after filing your Chapter 13 petition. You need to pay them the same as if you hadn't filed bankruptcy.

Ideally, your employer withholds enough from your paycheck so that you won't owe additional taxes. However, consumers often are hit with unexpected tax bills on April 15, and the temptation to ignore that obligation is great because you're already on a tight budget. That's the worst thing to do. Call your lawyer instead.

Thoughtless revenuer creates problems for everyone

Joe thought he had it made in the shade.

He faithfully made all his Chapter 13 payments for four and one-half years and looked forward to his discharge in only a few months. Then disaster struck. A tax collector filed a proof of claim for postpetition income taxes that added up to far more than Joe could pay over the remaining life of the plan. The court dismissed Joe's case, which meant that all his previous efforts were for naught, sending him back to square one.

If only the tax collector had not filed that claim, Joe would have completed his Chapter 13 plan and received his well-deserved discharge. Likewise, he then would have had the ability to pay the postpetition taxes with ease.

The Bankruptcy Code arms the IRS and state income tax authorities with several options in dealing with postpetition taxes, and, to put it bluntly, you're largely subject to the whims of the tax collectors. They can ignore your bankruptcy and collect the taxes from you immediately, wait until your plan is completed and then collect, or simply file a proof of claim in your case. Any way you add it up, it's a headache for you — but there is hope.

Your lawyer needs to try to persuade the tax collector to choose an option that benefits you and the government. For example, whenever a tax problem arises early on in your case and the plan provides for relatively large payments to unsecured creditors, the best course is for the taxing authority to file a proof of claim immediately. That way, money for taxes comes out of the share designated for unsecured creditors.

If, as in Joe's case, the tax problem doesn't surface until late in the case, hopefully your lawyer can persuade the tax collector not to file a claim and to wait until your Chapter 13 is complete and your other debts wiped out before trying to collect postpetition taxes.

The lesson: Make sure that you carefully consider the possibility of postpetition income taxes *before* filing for bankruptcy. And if an unexpected tax liability pops up after you file, call your lawyer immediately.

Aside from paying the tax, you must file all income tax returns that come due after the petition date or get an extension of time from the taxing authority. And remember to file a copy of your federal return with a court. Otherwise, your case can be dismissed.

Sinking Your Ship before It Arrives

Sometimes a person's financial condition improves instead of falling apart. Funny thing, an arriving ship still may result in bad news when it isn't handled properly. Look what happened to Mary, for example.

Mary filed a Chapter 13 to save her home and relieve herself of $50,000 in credit-card debt. Her plan was confirmed, and she cured her back mortgage payments during the first year of the plan, but she still owed most of the credit-card debt.

Then Mary's long-lost Uncle Joe died, leaving her $20,000. When the Chapter 13 trustee learned of her inheritance, he tried to grab it for the benefit of credit-card lenders. Relying on a 1994 amendment to the Bankruptcy Code, Mary's lawyer responded by converting her case to a Chapter 7, figuring that doing so would enable her to keep the inheritance and wipe out the credit-card debt. The court, however, balked. Deeming Mary's conversion to a Chapter 7 bad faith, the court made her turn over the entire $20,000 to the Chapter 7 trustee.

Mary's story illustrates the fact that the Bankruptcy Code neither clearly explains what happens when a Chapter 13 debtor comes upon a valuable asset after filing bankruptcy nor adequately addresses the question of whether a Chapter 13 plan can be paid off early.

In Mary's case, assume that her plan required monthly payments of $300 per month for 36 months and that she received her inheritance in the 16th month of the plan. Can Mary simply complete her plan and discharge her credit-card debts by paying the trustee $6,000 ($300 monthly payment × 20 months remaining on plan), thereby pocketing the remainder of the inheritance for herself?

Paying off a plan ahead of time

In some areas, a Chapter 13 debtor is allowed to borrow against his homestead and pay off a Chapter 13 plan. But not all courts agree with this maneuver, and if you miscalculate, it can cost you an arm and a leg.

Consider the case of Miles.

Miles was in the middle of his Chapter 13 plan when a home-equity lender told him that he could take out a second mortgage on his home equity for $20,000, use $5,000 to pay off his Chapter 13 plan, and keep the rest for himself.

That sounded pretty good to Miles, who went ahead with the second mortgage and hoped to go happily on his way with his newfound wealth.

Well, the trustee in Miles' case was less than enamored with this maneuver and was no longer willing to accept only $5,000 to cover the Chapter 13 plan. Instead, she wanted all the money, claiming that every cent amounted to disposable income. The bankruptcy court agreed, and Mile's miscalculation cost him 20 grand. Ouch!

The answer isn't real clear. Most, but not all, courts would say "No," ruling that Mary must pay the Chapter 13 trustee all her disposable income and that the inheritance constitutes disposable income.

In these jurisdictions, it may be best for Mary's lawyer to try to negotiate a deal with the Chapter 13 trustee where the debtor can keep a large portion of the windfall to offset increased expenses (especially deferred expenses such as home maintenance, medical or dental treatment, and car repair or replacement). Fashioning a fair settlement may be better than the all-or-nothing gamble of converting to a Chapter 7 — a gamble that Mary lost.

Tying Things Together

The rules, regulations, and nuances of bankruptcy can make your head spin, and sometimes having a scorecard to keep track of what-ifs and what-fors helps. Table 20-1 makes figuring out where you stand easier when your Chapter 13 plan isn't working out.

First, find your circumstance in the left-hand column and then look at the four options in Table 20-1 (suspending payments, converting to a liquidation, dismissing your Chapter 13 and filing a new Chapter 7, and asking for a hardship discharge) to understand the implications.

Table 20-1	**Comparing Your Options**			
SITUATION	*OPTIONS*			
	Suspending Payments or Modifying Plan	*Converting to Chapter 7*	*Dismissing Chapter 13/ Filing New Chapter 7*	*Requesting a Hardship Discharge*
Debts incurred after filing Chapter 13.	Not discharged.	Discharged.	Same as converting to Chapter 7.	Not discharged.

(continued)

Table 20-1 *(continued)*

SITUATION	OPTIONS			
	Suspending Payments or Modifying Plan	**Converting to Chapter 7**	**Dismissing Chapter 13/ Filing New Chapter 7**	**Requesting a Hardship Discharge**
Discharge received in a bankruptcy filed within eight years of current Chapter 13.	Discharge available despite the earlier bankruptcy if earlier discharge was under Chapter 7, 11, or 12 and more than four years prior to present case, or if earlier discharge was in a Chapter 13 and more than two years prior to present case.	Discharge unavailable *unless* the first case was a Chapter 13 and creditors in that case received at least 70 percent of their claims.	Same as converting to Chapter 7.	Same as suspending payments or modifying plan.
Secured claim is being crammed down (value of collateral is being paid over the life of the plan). For example, if a car is worth only $2,000, and the debt is $5,000, the cramdown amount is $2,000.	No effect. If plan is completed, you'll own the car free and clear, even though you only paid $2,000.	To keep your car, you have to agree to pay the entire debt ($5,000) by reaffirming or redeem the car by paying $2,000 in a lump sum with no credit given for cramdown payments made during the Chapter 13.	Same as converting to Chapter 7.	Same as conversion to Chapter 7.

SITUATION	OPTIONS			
	Suspending Payments or Modifying Plan	*Converting to Chapter 7*	*Dismissing Chapter 13/ Filing New Chapter 7*	*Requesting a Hardship Discharge*
Property acquired after Chapter 13 petition.	Not affected *unless* trustee or a creditor gets the court to modify the plan prior to completion of payments.	Does *not* go to Chapter 7 . trustee unless conversion is deemed in bad faith.	Goes to Chapter 7 trustee if not exempt at the time the new Chapter 7 is filed.	Same as sticking with current plan.
Status of property changes during Chapter 13. Example: Debtor moves out of property that qualified as a homestead when Chapter 13 was filed, and property thereafter is un-qualified as a homestead because debtor rents it out *after* the Chapter 13 is filed.	*Probably* no effect, but check with lawyer first.	Courts dis-agree about whether prop-erty must be exempt on the date of conversion.	Exempt status deter-mined as of the date new Chapter 7 filed.	*Probably* no effect, but check with lawyer first.

(continued)

Table 20-1 *(continued)*

SITUATION	OPTIONS			
	Suspending Payments or Modifying Plan	**Converting to Chapter 7**	**Dismissing Chapter 13/ Filing New Chapter 7**	**Requesting a Hardship Discharge**
Increases in value of exempt property more than the exempt amount. Example: When filing, Chapter 13 debtor's equity was $15,000 in homestead with an allowable exemption of $17,000. After Chapter 13 is filed, debtor's equity increases to $20,000 because of an overall increase in the property value or a reduction of the mortgage balance.	Not affected *unless* trustee or a creditor gets the court to modify the plan prior to completion of payments.	Courts disagree about whether value of property must be within exemption amount at the time of conversion.	Chapter 7 trustee claims nonexempt equity.	Same as sticking with current plan.

Part VI
Enjoying Your Fresh Start

The 5th Wave   By Rich Tennant

"You'll notice in section 4 of your bankruptcy, the money owed your girlfriend has been discharged. However, she still holds a lien on your weekends."

In this part . . .

You're so close you can almost smell relief. You've survived the financial surgery of bankruptcy. That malignant debt is a thing of the past. Now, you can build your strength back and get on with your life. In this part, we go over some strategies for restoring your credit and avoiding the traps that can undermine all your good efforts and hard work.

Chapter 21

Repairing Your Credit

. . . .

In This Chapter

▶ Realizing that you're already on the path to credit repair

▶ Ordering credit reports after bankruptcy

▶ Finding mistakes on your credit report

▶ Disputing items on your credit report

▶ Reestablishing credit

▶ Building credit in your own name if you're married

. . . .

*L*ike life insurance or aspirin, credit is something that's better to have than use. Knowing it's there if you really, really, really need it is nice. However, you don't want to use credit just because it's there any more than you want to die so that you can finally make the insurance company fork over all those premiums you paid though the years or conk yourself on the head so that you can use up that aspirin before the expiration date.

Granted, you'll probably have to borrow money if you intend to buy a home, but that isn't a big deal when you have a halfway decent job and don't set your sights on the snazziest house in town. Under current guidelines, if you have steady employment, you can qualify for a conventional mortgage (with the same interest rate and fees as everyone else) within four years of filing bankruptcy. If you're willing to pay a little more in interest and fees, you can get a mortgage sooner.

You *may* even need to borrow to buy a car, but it's usually better for you to save and pay cash for a reliable used car than to borrow heavily to finance a flashy new vehicle that drains your bank account for years to come. And you'll probably want a credit card so that you can rent a video or reserve a hotel room.

Despite misgivings about credit in general, in this chapter, we explain how to get your credit back, point out how you've already taken the first step by filing bankruptcy, describe how to access and (if necessary) clean up your credit reports, and show you how to continue building a reputation for creditworthiness.

Realizing that You've Already Taken the First Step by Filing Bankruptcy

Counterintuitive as it may sound, bankruptcy is frequently the first step on the road to credit repair.

A decade ago, lenders avoided customers with bankruptcies on their records like the plague, but now, they're making so much from their unconscionably high interest rates that they've become less discriminating. In fact, several companies specifically target folks who've recently obtained bankruptcy discharges. To these lenders, you're a financial virgin — squeaky clean, unable to file bankruptcy again in the near future, and ripe for picking.

Nevertheless, that doesn't mean you won't ever encounter some short-sighted, mean-spirited, vindictive type, dead set against giving you the benefit of the doubt and resentful of your fresh start. So, getting all your ducks in order makes sense. And one way of doing that is to make sure that your credit reports are accurate. After you know that your credit reports show that your debts were eliminated through bankruptcy and that your slate is clean, you can start writing a new chapter.

Recovering from bankruptcy

Today, so many people are on the rebound from bankruptcy that "prosperity advisor" Paula Langguth Ryan has devoted her life to helping recovering bankrupts "heal" their relationship with money. Ryan, who endured bankruptcy herself, authored *Bounce Back From Bankruptcy: A Step-By-Step Guide to Getting Back on Your Financial Feet* (Pellingham Casper Communications, 1998). Her book covers post-bankruptcy from soup to nuts and provides lots of comforting advice on putting your financial life back together. You can order the book by calling 1-800-507-9244. Also, you can check out her Web site at www.artofabundance.com.

Using the Fair Credit Reporting Act to Your Advantage

The federal Fair Credit Reporting Act (FCRA) together with the Fair and Accurate Credit Transactions Act (FACTA), which came into effect December 1, 2004, offer you some measure of protection against inaccurate credit reports by guaranteeing your rights to

- ✔ Know what's in your credit file
- ✔ Find out the name and address of any credit bureau that produces a report that results in a denial of credit or employment and obtain a copy of that report
- ✔ Dispute inaccurate information with both the credit bureau and directly with the entity ("the furnisher") that provided the information to the bureau — usually the creditor
- ✔ Force the credit bureau to verify any information that you claim is wrong and to delete incorrect information when it can't be verified within 45 days
- ✔ Insist that corrected reports be sent to anyone who received an incorrect version within the past six months (within the past two years when the incorrect report was ordered for employment-related reasons)
- ✔ Receive a free updated copy of your credit report within 45 days when an error has been corrected
- ✔ Expunge adverse information after seven years (ten years after a bankruptcy)
- ✔ Include a written statement in your credit file explaining any issues that you dispute

Hopefully, you can use this information to make sure that your credit reports are reasonably accurate.

Getting Your Credit Reports after Bankruptcy

Your ability to secure credit is determined largely by credit reports issued by Equifax, TransUnion, and Experian. The reports of these three companies show who has extended credit to you, the amounts, your payment records, and other information that can be obtained from creditors or gleaned from public records (such as public filings of judgments and liens). Most major lenders and many smaller local ones subscribe to one or more of the credit bureaus. In return for receiving credit reports from the big three, subscribers agree to furnish current information about your account.

Credit reports do *not* contain subjective judgments or comments. The reports are supposed to include only the facts — your Social Security number, birth date, addresses, employers, the status of your accounts, and information from public records like bankruptcy, judgments, or tax liens.

A few weeks after your bankruptcy discharge is granted, you need to order credit reports from

- Equifax, P O Box 74024, Atlanta, GA 30374-0241; phone 800-685-1111; Web site www.equifax.com.
- Experian, P O Box 2002, Allen, TX 75013; phone 888-567-8688, Web site www.experian.com.
- TransUnion, P O Box 1000, Chester, PA 19022, phone 800-888-4213, Web site www.experian.com.

Getting credit reports for free

You're entitled to a free copy of your credit report whenever you

- Have been denied credit during the past 60 days because of that report
- Are unemployed and intend to apply for work within the next 60 days
- Receive welfare assistance
- Believe that the report contains inaccurate information as a result of fraud

Although some companies offer reports that combine the information from all three credit bureaus (see Chapter 2), you may find that correcting mistakes is easier when you deal directly with each individual credit bureau.

Under a new law, the three nationwide consumer reporting agencies — Equifax, Experian, and TransUnion — must provide consumers, upon request, with a free copy of their credit report once every 12 months. Call (877) 322-8228 for more information or write to: Annual Credit Report Request Service, P.O. Box 105281, Atlanta, GA 30348-5281. Requests by phone or mail will be processed within 15 days of receipt.

Knowing the score

Many lenders find it more efficient and cheaper to forego individual credit reports in lieu of statistical credit scores prepared by the three national credit bureaus. Each company produces its own score, but they're all based on the same computer-credit model developed by a California company, Fair, Isaac & Company, Inc. Your Fair, Isaac Credit Bureau Score — sometimes called *FICO Score* — is the result of an intricate analysis of your credit history.

You can get your FICO Scores for all three credit bureaus from www.myfico.com for about $45. For general information about credit scoring, check out www.creditscoring.com.

You need to look for two things on the reports:

✔ Mistakes unrelated to your bankruptcy

✔ How your bankruptcy is reported

Correcting mistakes on your credit reports

Unfortunately, about half of all credit reports contain errors — such as adverse information about someone with a similar name, duplicate accounts, and obsolete data.

When you receive your report, check to make sure that it doesn't

✔ Misstate your name, Social Security number, birth date, or marital status

✔ Include information about someone with a name similar to yours

✔ Contain obsolete information. Most items must be removed after seven years. Bankruptcies may remain for ten years. Judgments remain until the statute of limitations (which can be as long as 20 years) lapses.

✔ Report the same account more than once

✔ Inaccurately indicate that you were party to a lawsuit

✔ Include credit inquiries older than two years

Mistakes usually are easy to address, but *you* must take the initiative. Completing the investigation request form that usually comes with a copy of your credit report is the first thing to do. You also may want to write a letter identifying each mistake and requesting an investigation. You should also dispute errors with the *furnisher* — the entity providing the information — by sending a "return receipt requested" letter stating the account number, the basis for the dispute, and any supporting documentation. Credit bureaus and furnishers should respond to you within 45 days.

Deleted items have a nasty habit of reappearing on credit reports, usually because of some computer glitch. You need to order new reports a few months after adverse information has been deleted. If the same stuff pops up again, write another letter to the credit bureau, and, with a little luck, this time, they'll fix it for good.

Whenever a mistake isn't so obvious or involves something that isn't verifiable as a matter of public record, the credit bureau checks with the creditor, and it tends to take the creditor's word. Subscribing creditors are the backbone of a credit bureau's business, so any time an issue comes down to your word versus the creditor's, guess who the bureau is going to believe?

When a creditor insists that the information is correct, the credit bureau won't remove it. In a situation like that, you must contact the creditor directly and in writing so that there's a paper trail. Under the FCRA, creditors who use credit bureaus are prohibited from intentionally reporting false information.

Among the other duties of furnishers are

- ✔ Notifying the credit bureau whenever they discover that information they already provided is wrong

- ✔ Providing credit bureaus with corrected information

- ✔ Including notices of the dispute — if you're disputing that you owe the money — when reporting the debt to credit bureaus

If the furnisher sends you a letter agreeing that information is incorrect, you need to send a copy of that letter to the credit bureau, requesting a correction just to make doubly sure.

When the furnisher insists that the information is correct, call the credit bureau to ask whether it can provide any suggestions. You can at least prepare a written statement that explains your side of the story. In all likelihood, however, such a statement probably won't do any immediate good because most creditors are linked to credit bureaus by computer, and your statement isn't transmitted with the credit report. Nevertheless, submitting a written statement establishes a record. **Note:** The credit bureau may limit your statement to 100 words, but only if it helps you write it.

Submit your statement using certified mail, with a return receipt requested, in all communications with credit bureaus or creditors concerning disputed issues. Doing so tends to focus their attention much more than regular mail and establishes a written record that proves useful if you eventually end up in court.

Oops! Many credit reports are inaccurate

A study of credit bureaus by the U.S. Public Interest Research Group, entitled "Mistakes Do Happen," concludes

✔ Nearly one-third of all consumer credit reports contain errors that are serious enough to cause a denial of credit, or even a job.

✔ Seventy percent contained errors of some kind.

✔ Twenty percent were missing information that could demonstrate that a consumer was in fact creditworthy.

✔ Twenty-six percent of the accounts listed as active in reports actually had already been closed by the consumer.

You can order a copy of "Mistakes Do Happen" from U.S. PIRG Reports, 218 D. Street 8E, Washington, DC 20008.

Although the FCRA gives you the right to sue in court or complain to the Federal Trade Commission (FTC), as a practical matter, polite persistence is probably your best tactic. And although credit bureaus naturally are biased toward their subscribing creditors, they really don't want any legal trouble or fights, particularly when it looks like you're going to win. A well-drafted letter from your attorney should get their attention.

Making sure that your credit reports properly reflect your bankruptcy

After receiving a bankruptcy discharge, all your prepetition accounts are supposed to show zero balances. If they don't, or if other mistakes are evident, follow the instructions for disputing issues that accompany your credit report. Send in the dispute form (always using certified mail, with a return receipt requested), copies of your bankruptcy schedules D, E, and F (which show all the debts you listed), the court's notice of your 341 meeting with creditors (which shows the date that you filed bankruptcy), and the court's order of discharge (which proves that your debts were wiped out). See Chapter 6 for an explanation of your bankruptcy schedules, the 341 meeting, and the order of discharge.

Be sure to specifically request a copy of the corrected report for you and insist on distribution of corrected copies to all creditors who potentially received the inaccurate version within the past six months (or within the past two years for reports requested for employment-related purposes).

Obtaining New Credit

You know how some recent college graduates complain that they can't get a job because they don't have experience, and they can't get experience because they can't get a job? Sometimes, obtaining new credit works the same way. You can't build a record of creditworthiness until you have credit, and some lenders won't give you credit until you've established a good record.

When your postbankruptcy credit reports show a clean slate, you're halfway home — but *only* halfway. Now, you must establish a good payment record and ensure that your efforts are reflected on the credit reports. Creditors want to know that you're now good for your debts, and if you continue making payments on a prepetition debt, such as a house or car loan, you're off to a good start. Check out the following sections for other things you can do to start building a solid credit record.

Applying for an unsecured credit card

At the moment, obtaining an unsecured credit card (one not secured by the items you purchase or anything else) with a modest limit is pretty easy. Many lenders target people who have recently obtained bankruptcy discharges.

If you obtain an unsecured credit card, keep the purpose for your card firmly in mind, remembering that the objective is to show that you can responsibly handle debt. Use the card only for small items and make sure that you keep up with all the payments (actually, you'd be wiser using the card only when cash won't do, like when renting a car or making hotel reservations). And if you find yourself only making minimum payments, watch out! You may be drifting into financial trouble all over again. See Chapter 22.

Beware of *catalog cards* that enable you to charge items from particular merchants. For one thing, the company probably doesn't sell anything that you should even consider buying at this point. For another, you can't be sure that the company actually reports your payment history to credit bureaus. So, whenever you use one of these cards, you may end up buying stuff you don't need without doing diddly squat to improve your credit rating.

Settling for secured credit

If you can't get an unsecured credit card, you may be able to obtain some form of secured credit.

Local banks or credit unions may give you a small loan if you agree to maintain a specific balance in an account, which they, of course, promptly seize if you don't pay. If you go this route, however, make sure that the lender reports your good payment history to the credit bureaus.

You may also be able to get a secured credit card. Some credit-card issuers guarantee you a credit card as long as you keep enough money on deposit to pay off the account. If, for example, you have a $300 line of credit, you need to keep $300 on deposit.

Again, be certain that the issuing bank reports your diligence to the credit bureaus. Otherwise, what's the point?

Likewise, don't confuse secured credit cards with debit cards that allow only immediate deductions from your bank account. Because you don't borrow money with a debit card, nothing about your creditworthiness can be reported to credit bureaus.

When shopping around for secured card, ask whether the lender flags the card as secured when reporting to credit bureaus. If so, try to find a lender who doesn't. Similarly, you may want to look for a lender that's willing to convert the secured card to an unsecured card after a record of timely payments is established.

Several online outfits provide comparisons between secured cards and instructions for obtaining one. Keep in mind that because these companies are heavily dependent on cooperation from the credit-card industry, they provide a wealth of useful information about credit. Check out

> ✔ **CreditComm Services LLC:** www.creditcom.com.
>
> ✔ **Ram Research Group:** www.ramresearch.com
>
> ✔ **BankRate Monitor:** www.bankrate.com

You may also want to consider buying a used car from one of those we-don't-turn-anyone-down-for-financing outfits. But be real careful. Don't let them sell you a car that you can't afford because you certainly won't accomplish your purpose that way. And, be prepared to pay sky-high interest rates on the loan.

Informing credit bureaus of your good work when the creditor doesn't

If you're making payments to a creditor that doesn't report to the credit bureaus, you still can write the agencies yourself, asking them to include that information on your report. They're not obliged to comply, and chances are good they won't, but nevertheless, asking is worthwhile. When you do, be sure to include the creditor's phone number and your account number so that the credit bureaus can verify the information. After you've established a good payment history, you also have the option of using the creditor as a credit reference. Just make sure beforehand that the creditor is willing to back you up.

Taking it easy when building new credit

Although building a credit history is important, you need to begin slowly. If you go wild, applying for credit all over the place, your report probably is going to show that you tried to get credit and failed. That kind of report makes lenders nervous, and they begin thinking that you're headed toward trouble again or that they're missing some egregious problem.

After you reestablish credit and (despite our warnings about the evils of plastic) want to start regularly using credit cards, shop around for the best deal. Many lenders entice you with ads for low interest rates but, after they've got your attention, come up with some cockamamie reason why you don't qualify and try to sell you on a higher one. Others offer low teaser rates, but then hike the interest after a short period of time or when you miss a payment. Some impose outrageous fees for late payments, sticking you with a $25 fine when you're a day late on a $5 payment. Late fees represent as much as one-third of the income of some credit-card issuers.

The smartest move — other than avoiding credit cards altogether (Have we convinced you yet? We didn't think so . . .) — is paying off the entire balance every month. That way, you never have to pay interest. Of course, credit-card companies aren't particularly fond of folks who pay their bills in full because they lose out on collecting a ton of interest, and some even have the nerve to cancel your account.

Watching Our for Credit-Repair Scams

Credit-repair companies can't do anything legitimate that you can't do for yourself. Some are shady, some are not, and you have to be on the lookout for scams. Run for cover whenever the company

- ✔ Tries to loan you money
- ✔ Plans to sell your name to other lenders
- ✔ Boasts that it can remove truthful information from your credit reports

One common ploy that credit-repair hustlers use is repeatedly disputing negative but truthful information on your credit report, hoping that the credit bureau drops the ball, doesn't investigate the dispute, and, as a result, has to delete the item. Credit bureaus are onto this game, and they don't like it. Even when your credit repairer succeeds in getting a legitimate item off your report, the chances are good that the credit bureau will look a little harder in the future and put it right back in.

Creating a new credit identity by applying for and then using a new Social Security number to obtain a new credit file is another *dumb trick.* That obtaining a Social Security number for fraudulent purposes is illegal is a no-brainer. And yet, some credit-repair advisors advise you to go that route. If you do, you'll pay the consequences. The judge just isn't going to care that you took the advice of some bonehead credit-repair advisor.

Sometimes, advisors suggest that you apply for credit using a Social Security number similar to but slightly different than your real number, hoping that the credit bureau won't match this fake number with an existing file but that it will create a new one. Taking this step is illegal and stupid.

Establishing Good Credit When You're Married

Each partner in a marriage needs to take responsibility for building his or her own credit history. Married people are considered an economic unit only in Arizona, California, Idaho, Louisiana, Nevada, New Mexico, Texas, Washington, and Wisconsin, the nine community-property states. In the other states, married folks are entitled to establish separate credit identities and can structure their finances so that they're not legally responsible for the financial blunders of the other.

Still, if your husband or wife can't get credit in his or her own name, a joint card may be a good idea. If you're both legally responsible on an account and regular payments are made, that helps *both* of you establish a good credit record. Of course, the opposite is just as true — delinquencies also reflect badly on the credit of *both* spouses.

Bear in mind that this joint credit applies only when both spouses are legally responsible on the account and doesn't apply to cases when one spouse is merely an authorized user on the account. The *authorized user* isn't legally responsible on the account, and payments help only the credit history of the spouse who is liable on the account.

The federal Equal Credit Opportunity Act (ECOA), and laws in many states, indicate that a creditor can't refuse to extend credit because of gender, marital status, race, religion, or because you're older than 62. In noncommunity property states, if you apply for credit in your own name, the lender isn't supposed to request information about your spouse — unless, of course, you're relying on your mate's income to qualify for a loan.

If you're about to get married, don't merge your credit-card accounts. Keep your spouse's separate from yours, and, for good measure, each partner needs to maintain one checking account in his or her own name. Similarly, whenever you take your spouse's name, inform your creditors and the credit bureaus of the name change in writing. Creditors aren't supposed to cancel your credit simply because you got married.

The great number of people who end up in bankruptcy because of the misdeeds of someone who turned out to be Mr. or Ms. Wrong is a shame. Time and time again, we see folks with a lifetime of perfect credit financially ruined because of a spouse's spending or problems with drugs, alcohol, or gambling. After you discover these kinds of problems, you need to write to your creditors and cancel any joint accounts and, if you've given your spouse authority to charge on your accounts, terminate it right away. Doing so won't eliminate your responsibility for charges that already were made, but it should protect you from future charges.

The same applies when you consider splitting up with your spouse. Be sure to send the letter by certified mail, with a return receipt requested, and then save copies of the letter and receipt. That way, you'll have proof if a creditor claims that it was never notified.

If you and your spouse are bent on maintaining a joint account and are building a good payment record, at least make sure that each person's credit reports reflect this good record. If not, write a letter to your creditors requesting that they report this favorable information to the credit bureaus — under your name *and* your spouse's name.

Chapter 22

Staying Out of Financial Trouble

*Y*ou know how doctors and pharmacists always tell you to take *all* your antibiotics even after you're feeling better, lest the infection recurs and knocks the stuffing out of you? Well, the same is true with the debt bug. When you stop taking the medicine, even though you think you're cured, your problems almost certainly return with a vengeance. A painful financial relapse is probably as close as a single missed paycheck or one ill-advised spending binge.

But now that you're ahead of the pack, you need to maintain your lead. This chapter shows you how by explaining the importance of building a support network and creating a realistic budget. It offers suggestions for changing your lifestyle and reveals some telltale signs that the barbarians are again at the gate.

Addressing Compulsive Spending

Compulsive spending is very much like an addiction and often is as difficult to overcome. It has serious and often devastating consequences — emotional, financial, professional, social, and so on. Mental health professionals estimate that perhaps 25 percent of the American public has a buying problem, and as many as one in six are compulsive spenders. It kind of gives the "Shop 'til you drop!" slogan a literal meaning, doesn't it?

Experts on compulsive disorders say you can't really make progress without understanding the nature of the beast and directly confronting the host of personality traits and emotional needs that feed your compulsion. And that may require some uncomfortable soul-searching. Ask yourself

- ✔ Why do I buy things I don't need and don't even particularly want?
- ✔ Why do I buy little, or big, gifts for people when it isn't their birthdays or Christmas?
- ✔ Am I afflicted with *affluenza,* the curse of consumption and materialism?

Admitting that you have a problem

If you've become guarded and secretive about your buying, if you routinely spend more than you intended to, if you buy to take your mind off other things (the same way an obese person may stuff him or herself after a marital spat), you may have a problem. If you're unable to pass up a "good deal," tend to live from paycheck to paycheck and suspect you'd live that way no matter how much money you made, or you continually obsess over how you can juggle this debt or that bill to keep the collectors at bay, you already know that you have a problem. Know, however, that you have loads of company.

Enrolling in Debtors Anonymous

Admitting your problem is an important first step. So, getting help is a close second. Many compulsive spenders find aid through Debtors Anonymous (see Chapter 2). With its 12-step process and support groups, Debtors Anonymous helps you understand that your problem is common and that many people have found ways to cope quite nicely with it. Contact them by writing to Debtors Anonymous, General Service Office, P.O. Box 920888, Needham, MA 02492-0009; phone 781-453-2743; Web site www.Debtors Anonymous.org.

If joining support groups just isn't your thing, you may want to look for a private counselor who works with compulsive disorders. In any case, this chapter identifies some ways to get your spending urges in check, regardless of whether you get outside professional help.

Building a Consensus with Loved Ones

You needed the support of your friends and relatives when you first thought about filing bankruptcy, and you need it just as much now. The people closest to you need to understand that the same way a person recovering from open-heart surgery isn't the best candidate to play center in a bruising pickup hockey game, you're not the one to grab the tab or the one to hit up for a donation every time little Buster sells candy bars for Little League. In short, the expectations that loved ones have for you need to conform with the new reality.

And you know what? They will. When you stay on the financial wagon, your pals and kin adjust accordingly. And so will you.

Establishing common ground with your mate on money matters

Regardless of whether your significant other filed bankruptcy with you, you are, to a large extent, in this together, for better or worse. Obviously, the household budget will implode if one of you is acting responsibly and the other isn't. It's kind of like riding a bicycle built for two — the stoker has to go where the pilot goes, or everyone's gonna get some boo-boos. So, remember that the project is a joint one, and you need to tackle it in tandem.

Creating realistic expectations from your offspring

When you're deep in financial do-do, chances are that your kids need to get real as much as you. Maybe that costly excursion to the amusement park needs to be a once-a-year treat rather than an every-weekend entitlement. Yeah, the kids may get cranky, but they'll get over it. And dollars to donuts, you'll all find something to do that's much less expensive but just as satisfying — like going to the public park or the library or . . .

Using a Budget

In Chapter 2, we recommend keeping a record of every penny you spend. That's good advice there, and it's good advice here. But you're more likely to succeed in budgeting when you view your spending plan not as something that restrains you, but rather as something that empowers you. In other words, look at a budget as your way of taking control, not as something that controls you.

Developing a system for tracking what you spend

Many computer programs can help you track expenses and create a budget. Although computer programs can make budgeting a game, they can also be a pain in the rear when the novelty wears off. In our experience, you're better off with a little notebook, and one big rule: Everything — and we mean *everything* — gets recorded. After you know exactly where your money goes, you'll almost certainly stop, or at least slow, the bleeding.

The worksheets in Chapter 2 help you create a budget. We're not going to suggest what you should spend on specific items. By now, you know enough to be sure that you aren't spending more than you have coming in every month and that you're saving for that inevitable rainy day.

Sticking to the plan

Sticking with any personal development schedule — whether it's an exercise plan, a diet, whatever — is difficult, and staying on a budget is particularly stressful. One good way to save money is to enroll in a payroll deduction program, like the kind offered through credit unions. That way, a certain amount of your paycheck goes directly into savings. It's right there if you really need it, and safely stashed until that need arises. Again, however, think *need,* not *want.*

Avoiding Temptation

Although offering credit to folks with obvious spending problems is the moral equivalent of providing booze to a recovering alcoholic, credit-card companies do it all the time. Everywhere you turn, you face temptation. Although resisting the lure of credit isn't easy, you *can* do it, but it nevertheless helps when you can eliminate at least some sources of enticement.

Reducing credit-card solicitations

Those credit-card offers that clutter your mailbox certainly are a pain, but you can try sending a note to the solicitor asking to be removed from its mailing list. That may work, but in all honesty, you'll probably be ignored. One of our favorite jokes is stuffing all the crap that they send you into their prepaid envelope and mailing it back. Turning the tables on credit-card companies, making them not only open junk mail, but also receive nothing in return, *and* pay the postage to boot is incredibly satisfying. Ah, revenge is sweet — particularly when it's justice personified! And solicitors listen much more carefully when something actually costs them money.

Removing your name from direct-marketing lists

As unlikely as it seems, those mosquitolike companies using the direct marketing tactic really don't want to get under your skin. The Direct Marketing Association even provides a service called the Mail Preference Service (MPS). When you sign up, your name is placed in a do-not-mail file. (Although signing up online at www.the-dma.org costs $5, you can register for free via snail mail by printing the online form at www.dmaconsumers.org/cgi/off mailinglist and mailing it to Mail Preference Service, Attn: Dept: 7377757, Direct Marketing Association, P.O. Box 282, Carmel, NY 10512.)

Members of the Direct Marketing Association are required to check the list before sending solicitations. Doing so is a smart move on their part because they don't want to waste their time and money on people like you who aren't going to take the bait, and they realize no mileage can be gained from ticking you off.

Also, the Federal Trade Commission has set up a toll-free number that allows people to stop *all* credit-card solicitations: 888-567-8688 (888-5-OPTOUT).

Reigning in telemarketers

The Federal government created the national registry to make it easier and more efficient for you to stop telemarketing calls. You can register online at www.donotcall.gov or call toll-free, 1-888-382-1222 (TTY 1-866-290-4236), from the number you wish to register. Registration is free.

Placing your number on the registry will stop most, but not all, telemarketing calls.

Some states also offer do-not-call registries that may block telemarketers who are presently exempt from the federal regulations, such as political pollsters and charities. Check with your state's consumer protection bureau (it may be part of the attorney general's office) to see whether your state offers this service.

Making a Few Lifestyle Changes

When you keep track of what you're spending, you'll probably discover that many of your expenditures are simply a matter of habit — the $2 latte you get on the way to work, the $1 you plop in the soda pop machine, the $2.50 you spend for an afternoon snack. It all adds up, big time. But you can save a bundle by bringing your own coffee, soda, and snack — bought at supermarket prices. By simply tracking your expenses, you're sure to cut out many of these impulse buys.

Figuring out your priorities

Studies show that Americans spend 6 hours per week shopping, but only 40 minutes actively playing with their kids. Something is seriously askew about that ratio.

But more and more people are getting their priorities in order and opting out of the consumption rat race by *downshifting* — working less, spending less, making more meaningful use of their time, and devoting more energy to raising their children. The seminal downshifting organization is probably the Seattle-based New Road Map Foundation (www.scn.org/earth/lightly /vsacpbak.htm). You may also want to check out the Center for a New American Dream at www.newdream.org. Both of these Web sites provide links to tons of information on living a simpler and more rational life.

Thinking about ways to save moneys

Simple awareness of what you have and where it goes helps you save money. Can you save a couple bucks by parking a block farther away? Do you really want dessert with your meal? Can you get a better rate on a plane ticket through Priceline.com? When you train yourself to be more conscious of what things cost, you naturally cut your expenditures.

Discovering how to live without credit

Life without credit is as basic as forcing yourself to use cash. Give yourself a monthly cash allowance and make your credit cards off-limits, or better yet, cut them up and throw them away. If you don't have the dough in your pocket to make a purchase, you know right away that you can't afford whatever you're thinking about buying. Granted, some expenditures require more than you have in your wallet, but you're still almost always better off using your savings than going into hock.

If you absolutely must borrow money to buy a car, focus on the *total* amount you're borrowing, not the monthly payment. When dickering with a car sales-man, don't even go down the monthly payment path. The issue isn't how much it will cost you every month but rather how much you'll end up paying in the end.

Discovering cheap ways to have fun

After growing up poor during the Great Depression, our parents were experts at finding inexpensive ways of having fun and discovering myriad imaginative uses for cardboard boxes. We can all garner some lessons from our beloved parents, Big Jim and Fitz: Take a hike, literally. Rent a video rather than going to see a movie. Borrow a book from the library instead of buying it (except for this one, of course). Watch an amateur baseball game at the park rather than a pro game at the stadium. The possibilities are limited only by your imagination.

Recognizing Danger Signs

In the same way that a scratchy throat signals an oncoming cold, plenty of telltale signs warn you that the debt demons are back on your track. You must keep your eyes open, but these gremlins are fairly easy to detect and stare down when you know what you're looking for.

Watching for telltale signals

At this point, you know when you're headed for trouble. If you're using one credit card to pay off another, buying junk you don't need, or ignoring your budget, cut it out! Remember, you're in control and the responsibility is yours. As soon as you adopt a victim's mind-set, you've ceded power to the creditors. Never forget that control of your finances is in your own hands — and the moment you feel like you're losing control, you probably already have.

If you get to this point, immediately stop buying on credit and borrowing money. Then, turn to Chapter 2 for pointers on stopping the financial hemorrhaging.

Living without savings

If you have nothing squirreled away for a rainy day, you're living on the edge. The best thing you can do with your extra cash is put it in a savings account used only for emergencies. Financial planners usually advise that you have at least six months' worth of income set aside.

When developing a budget (see our earlier discussion in this chapter in the section "Using a Budget" and also Chapter 2), be sure to include an item for savings.

Using debt-to-income and equity ratios

Financial advisors frequently suggest that you watch your debt-to-equity ratios to see whether you're drifting too far into debt. In our view, that's great when you're a CPA or figurehead. But using such formulas is pretty useless for most folks because they don't have realistic ideas about how much their assets are really worth. In any case, here are a couple formulas if you're the numbers-crunching type:

- ✔ **Debt-to-income ratio formula No. 1:** Many so-called experts say that you're okay as long as your debts are between 10 to 20 percent of your income. However, these same experts disagree about whether to include mortgages as a part of your total debts and whether using gross income or net income is appropriate. If you're taking this approach, we recommend including all mortgage debts, except the first mortgage on your home. We also suggest using net income rather than gross income.

- ✔ **Debt-to-equity ratio formula No. 2:** Taking the value of your assets into account is important in this method of determining how much debt you should carry. Divide the total amount of your debts, including all mortgages, by the value of all your assets. As a general rule, 30 percent is deemed acceptable.

Part VII
The Part of Tens

The 5th Wave   By Rich Tennant

"No, Mrs. Moskowitz. There's just no way we can list the unpaid debt of gratitude your son owes you on his credit history."

In this part . . .

*T*his part includes some nifty lists of ten things you can do right now — regardless of whether you end up filing for bankruptcy — to ease your financial burdens, ten mistakes you want to avoid, and ten of the most common questions we hear from folks pondering bankruptcy in the aftermath of the Bankruptcy Abuse Reform Fiasco (BARF) of 2005.

Chapter 23

Ten Common Bankruptcy Mistakes

. . . .

In This Chapter

▶ Borrowing to beat bankruptcy

▶ Dealing with assets and debts

. . . .

*O*ne mantra that we definitely preach: Play it straight and simple. Some debtors get into trouble because they try to manipulate the system, or they outright lie and cheat. For them, we have no sympathy whatsoever. May a thousand red ants invade their armpits!

Many more people turn their lawyers' hair gray with well-intentioned but ill-conceived efforts at making the most of a bad situation. That's unfortunate and unnecessary. You can easily avoid most pitfalls when you know where they are. This chapter lists the most common errors so that you can sidestep them now and avoid the hassles of dealing with them later.

Borrowing Money from Relatives

Asking your parents, children, or rich uncle for a loan is awfully tempting — but if you do, you'll probably live to regret it. For one thing, asking for a loan inevitably stresses relationships, and you're going to need the support and encouragement of your family as you undertake the bankruptcy process. For another, you simply can't borrow your way out of debt. Unless your benefactor has more money than she knows what to do with, filing bankruptcy and wiping out debts that you can't afford to pay just makes more sense to us than hitting up your loved ones.

Repaying Money Owed to Relatives

If you ignore our advice and end up accepting a loan from a relative, about the worst thing you can do is pay it back if you're planning to file bankruptcy within the next year. Strange as it may seem, a bankruptcy trustee can sue any relative who received $600 or more from you during the year prior to bankruptcy — even if the payment was on a perfectly legitimate debt. The rationale is that your relatives shouldn't be paid when other creditors are left holding the bag.

Chipping Away at Debts with a Home-Equity Loan

We can't say it often enough: You can't borrow your way out of debt. It's pretty obvious that banks and other lenders are really pushing home-equity loans, and it's pretty obvious why. If they can get you to sign over the most valuable and most important asset in your life, they have you right where they want you — scared out of your wits and willing to eat regurgitated dog food if necessary to keep up with your payments. Don't yield that kind of power to lenders. Odds are that if you file bankruptcy instead of obtaining a home-equity loan, you'll not only wipe out those pesky debts, but you'll also be able to keep your home.

Draining Retirement Accounts to Pay Debts

Read that heading again! That's a bad, bad idea — albeit one that some credit counselors advocate. If there's even a remote chance that you'll end up in bankruptcy court, there's no point in squandering your retirement account. Oftentimes, pensions are protected in bankruptcy — meaning that you get to keep your retirement benefit and creditors can't touch it. However, if you voluntarily sign over your pension or drain it to pay the credit-card company, that money's lost; it's gone forever.

Neglecting to Accurately List All Creditors

A bankruptcy petition is no place to wing it. Don't guess. Instead, get it right. Make sure that *all* your creditors are listed. If you screw up, you can amend your petition later . . . maybe. But that's a bunch of trouble, and if the judge thinks you tried to hide something or mislead the court, she may well become very grumpy. Although some exceptions are in place, you nevertheless need to assume that if you fail to list a creditor with an accurate mailing address, that debt may not get wiped out.

Concealing Your Assets

People who monitor bankruptcies aren't stupid, and they generally don't have much of a sense of humor. When you go out of your way looking for trouble, you'll surely find it. Don't play games. Don't assume that things will go unnoticed. Don't "forget" to mention the vintage Mercedes sitting in your garage. Just play it straight.

Transferring Assets to Keep Them Away from Creditors

Many people transfer their assets with the best of intentions, often shifting property to their children or other loved ones to keep it away from the groping paws of creditors. You can't do that. And, if you try, you'll almost certainly cause trouble for yourself and quite possibly for the relative or friend to whom you transferred property.

Making Payments that You Can't Afford to Make

Making payments to a bill collector that you can't afford to make is money down the drain, simple as that. Coming up with a few bucks here and a few there to temporarily pacify bill collectors puts a great deal of pressure on you. But the finger-in-the-dike approach quickly becomes overwhelming. You simply don't have enough digits, or dollars, to plug all those holes, and you'll probably stretch yourself to the breaking point if you try.

Thinking that Bankruptcy Is Your Last Resort

Much can be said for preventive medicine — in matters of health as well as in matters of finance. So, we urge you to look at bankruptcy as a financial-planning decision rather than as your fiscal funeral. You don't have to wait until your home equity is blown, your relationships are shot, and your pension is kaput before exerting your right to a fresh start. As a rule: If you can't fully pay off all your debts (except mortgages) within three years while living a reasonably restrained lifestyle, you definitely need to consider bankruptcy.

Filing Bankruptcy Too Soon

Although filing for bankruptcy sooner rather than later usually is better for most folks, in some circumstances, delaying a bit is to your advantage. For example, if you're contemplating divorce, expecting a sizeable income tax refund, in the process of repaying debts to family members (or have been in the recent past), or owing taxes that may be dischargeable in the near future, it can be better to wait. However, it's never too early to discuss your situation and your options with a good bankruptcy lawyer.

Chapter 24

Ten Things You Can Do Right Now to Ease Your Financial Woes

In This Chapter

▶ Getting your financial affairs in order

▶ Establishing what your assets are worth

*F*olks swimming against the high tide of debt frequently feel powerless. Some are even inclined to just let go and allow the current to take them wherever it may — even if it's smack into the jagged rocks. Don't do that.

No matter how bleak things may seem, you're still in control, and the list of what you can do to relieve the burdens on your bank account (if you still have one) and your psyche (we assume that you have one) is a long one. Maybe you can't quite manage to swim upstream, but plenty of branches are jutting out from the banks for you to grasp so you at least won't go over the falls. You only need to grab hold, hang on tight, and keep your head up, even if — especially if — you're up to your neck in debt doo-doo.

Think of this chapter as your temporary lifeline. It shows you how to survive until you get your bearings and how to take those first tentative steps toward dry land.

Stop Feeling Guilty

Okay, so maybe you screwed up. Get over it. Although in our experience, the far more likely scenario is that something unexpected pushed you over the edge. No matter how you ended up in your present predicament, you won't gain any mileage by beating yourself up. What has happened, has happened. The past is past, but tomorrow is money in the bank — literally and figuratively.

Cut Up Your Credit Cards

Start with this premise: You can't borrow your way out of debt (are we getting redundant on that? Good!). Using Card B to pay off Card A isn't going to solve the problem. It'll only make matters worse.

In all but a few situations, you don't really *need* a credit card. Sure, a credit card makes shopping easier, especially from mail-order catalogs and online merchants, but the last thing you need right now is more temptation.

Pick *one* credit card to save — preferably one with a zero balance — and put it in a drawer, not your purse or wallet. Reserve that card for those few situations where only plastic will do, such as auto rentals and possibly hotel reservations. Now take a deep breath and cut up all the rest of your cards and put the pieces in an envelope so that you can remind yourself of the commitment that you've made. Join the ranks of smart and happy campers who pay cash or do without. You'll be surprised how liberating escaping the yoke of credit cards can be. It just feels good, kind of like the way it feels to take a shower when you're all sweaty.

Again, take control.

Order Your Credit Reports

The first step toward taking control is knowing the score and understanding just where you stand. Of course, you can pluck the petals off a daisy, playing "she loves me/she loves me not," but you'll probably get a more realistic answer from your credit reports. Obtaining them shouldn't cost any more than ten bucks. You can order your reports from the big three reporting agencies:

- ✔ Equifax, P.O. Box 740241, Atlanta, GA 30374-0241; phone 800-685-1111; Web site www.equifax.com
- ✔ Experian, P.O. Box 2002, Allen, TX 75013; phone 800-682-7654; Web site www.experian.com
- ✔ TransUnion, P.O. Box 1000, Chester, PA 19022; phone 800-851-2674; Web site www.transunion.com

See Chapter 6 for more tips on tracking down your creditors.

Keep Track of Everything You Buy

Keep a list of everything you buy. Write it down, write it all down — everything from donuts to dentists. Yeah, doing so is a definite pain in the rear, but that's actually the point. If you have to do some work every time that you buy a gumball, you may figure that impulse to buy is more trouble than it's worth. Besides, identifying the holes in your pockets so that you can realistically consider what's needed, what's not, and what's in between is the smart thing to do.

Get Your Name off Any Joint Accounts

Joint accounts are often convenient, especially for married couples. But they can create plenty of headaches in times of financial distress. Keeping your credit accounts separate is better because when you have a joint account, you're legally responsible for the debts of your mate (and vice versa).

Stop Making Partial Payments on Credit-Card Bills

Whenever you're making only partial payments on your credit cards, bankruptcy may be on the horizon and, quite frankly, is more likely probable, although most people put off the inevitable as long as possible. In short, making partial payments on your credit-card debt is money down the flusher. Besides, you have no incentive for making payments now, for a couple of reasons. One main reason is that if you file bankruptcy, you stand a good chance of not having to pay those debts (or at least not all of them). The second reason: At this point, you'd do better using that money for bare necessities, so you're better equipped to resist temptation to pull out your credit card for groceries.

Call a Lawyer Now If You're Being Sued or Foreclosure Is Underway

If you don't respond to a lawsuit, the other side automatically wins and obtains a judgment, which may limit your options if you end up filing bankruptcy. Have a lawyer look at the lawsuit papers while you still have time to respond.

If a foreclosure already has started and you want to keep the property, find out the date of the foreclosure sale and call a bankruptcy lawyer right away. If bankruptcy isn't filed before the foreclosure sale date, it may be too late to save the property.

Find Out How Much Your Home and Car Are Worth

Odds are your house and vehicles are among the most valuable assets you have. But you need to know just how valuable they are. For your home, you can check with the local assessor to obtain a ballpark figure of what it's worth. However, those figures are notoriously inaccurate, and you'd do better finding out what similar homes in your neighborhood are selling for. For your car, check out the *Kelley Blue Book* at www.kbb.com.

Empty Accounts in Banks Where You Owe Money

If you owe a bank money, and the bank is sitting on your cash, you can pretty well figure out what happens next. Before it dawns on the banker to seize whatever stash you have, pull it out of his reach. You need to decide where your assets will do the most good at this point (hint: not the mall), and you don't need the bank making that decision for you. Oh, your money may, of course, go back to the bank at some point, but, for now, you need to marshal your forces until you figure out how they'd be most effectively deployed.

Sharpen Your Pencil and Start Filling Out the Worksheets in Chapter 2

You have some homework to do, and we bet you'll feel much better when it's done. Filling out the worksheets in Chapter 2 gives you a firmer grasp of your situation. An enemy is much easier to overcome when you know the nature of the beast. Regardless of whether you eventually file bankruptcy, taking an inventory is crucial. We've tried to make that chore as painless as possible with our worksheets in Chapter 2.

Chapter 25

Ten Common Questions about Bankruptcy

In This Chapter

▶ Putting bankruptcy hobgoblins to rest

▶ Glimpsing the pros and cons of bankruptcy

*B*ankruptcy — the B-word — conjures up images of horror, torment, and eternal financial damnation. In this chapter, we lay many of these bugaboos to rest, and place others in proper perspective.

Will Bankruptcy Damage My Credit Rating?

Yes.

Credit bureaus are allowed to report your bankruptcy for up to ten years from the date bankruptcy is filed, and generally do just that in Chapter 7 cases. With Chapter 13 cases, major reporting agencies usually delete mention of your bankruptcy after seven years, assuming, that is, you successfully complete the court-approved repayment plan. In either case, for seven to ten years, any time you seek credit — for a house, a car, for anything — your bankruptcy will factor in.

Under the federal Fair Credit Reporting Act, only certain people and entities are allowed access to your credit information, including credit-card companies, insurance firms, and prospective employers who sometimes review credit reports to determine whether a job applicant is financially stable. No one else is entitled to look at your credit report.

On the other hand, bankruptcy filings are public court records, available for-ever to anyone who wants to scour the files. The record is there in the court-house or in federal archives whenever anyone cares to see it, and as more and more records are stored on computers, searching that kind of data will become easier and easier.

Nevertheless, even with a bankruptcy, the odds of your obtaining credit are very good. With a little work and perseverance, you can reestablish credit almost immediately. (Some credit-card companies actually *target* folks right after bankruptcy because they know their slates are clean.) So, don't lose any sleep worrying about your credit. Instead, see Chapter 21 and get to work restoring your good credentials. You may have to pay a higher interest rate for a few years until your credit is fully restored, but you may not if you shop around.

Will Bankruptcy Affect My Job?

It shouldn't.

Employers are barred by federal law from firing or in any way discriminating against you because of a bankruptcy petition. And unless you volunteer infor-mation about your bankruptcy, your employer probably won't even know.

You may not want to tell your employer *before* your bankruptcy is actually filed because it is unclear whether someone who reveals plans to file bank-ruptcy in the future (but has not filed) is protected from firing or discrimina-tion. In addition, remember that *prospective* employers are among the entities legally entitled to check out your credit reports. A poor credit rating or a bankruptcy may lead a potential employer to reject you.

Will I Lose My Home?

Probably not.

Few people ever lose their homes solely because of bankruptcy, but it can happen. It all boils down to how much your house is worth, your mortgage balance, how far you're behind in your payments, and which state you live in. See Chapter 12 for more information.

Will I Lose My Personal Belongings?

Probably not.

Debtors are allowed to keep all their stuff in about 94 percent of personal bankruptcies. The reason debtors keep their stuff is that most personal belongings are off-limits to creditors or simply aren't worth enough to bother with.

Will I Ever Be Able to Buy a House?

Probably.

As a general rule, you stand a pretty good chance of getting a conventional mortgage about four years after your debts have been wiped out in bankruptcy, assuming, of course, that your income is high enough for you to qualify. You may qualify even sooner when you're willing to go through a finance company and pay more fees and higher interest rates.

Does My Spouse Have to File Bankruptcy, Too?

Not necessarily.

You're usually not responsible for your spouse's debts, unless, of course, you cosigned and promised the creditor that you'd cover for your wife or husband. A divorce decree sometimes also makes you liable for your ex's spending.

However, when you live in one of the nine community property states (Arizona, California, Idaho, Louisiana, Nevada, New Mexico, Texas, Washington, and Wisconsin), the story is different. In those states, so-called community property belonging to both spouses is subject to debts incurred by either spouse. *Community property* includes the earnings of you and your spouse, and any property acquired by either of you (except for gifts and inheritances) during the marriage.

Can I Keep Some Debts Off My Bankruptcy and Deal with Them Separately?

No.

Your bankruptcy petition must list every one of your creditors.

If you mistakenly forget to list a creditor, you can amend your bankruptcy papers. But doing so is a hassle, and life's much simpler when you get it right from the get-go. Additionally, if the court somehow thinks you intentionally excluded a creditor, you can find yourself in a heap of trouble.

You can voluntarily repay any creditor *after* you file. And you can always continue regular house or car payments so that those creditors aren't affected by your bankruptcy.

Can I Cancel My Bankruptcy If I Change My Mind?

That depends.

You can't dismiss a Chapter 7 — or a Chapter 13 that was converted from a Chapter 7 — unless you convince the court that dismissal is in the best interest of creditors. But, absent fraud or other misconduct, you can dismiss a Chapter 13 that was never in Chapter 7 without court permission. However, remember that even if your case is dismissed, the bankruptcy may still show up on your credit reports.

Is Filing Bankruptcy a Long, Protracted Process?

Not at all.

Your petition can be filed within a matter of days, and, after that happens, the automatic stay kicks in, collection activities cease, and you're on your way.

About 40 days later, you and your lawyer meet with creditors (the 341 meeting) — see Chapter 6. At that hearing, you take an oath and answer some questions about your financial affairs.

Most Chapter 7 cases are closed within four months of the petition date. Chapter 13 repayment cases remain open for the length of your plan (basically three to five years). But, as a practical matter, after the judge approves your repayment plan, the procedural stuff is dispensed with as long as you continue making your payments.

Does It Cost a Bundle to File?

It shouldn't.

You have to pay a court filing fee of $274 for a Chapter 7 or $189 for a Chapter 13. You also have to pay your lawyer, and BARF creates more work for attorneys. It's too early to tell how much lawyers will have to increase their fees to cover the additional hours they spend on even run-of-the-mill bankruptcies. If the cost seems high, yell at the politicians who voted for this consumer-hostile measure.

Will BARF Make it More Painful to File Bankruptcy?

Yes, it will. Congress — or, more accurately, the credit lobby — wanted to make filing bankruptcy more cumbersome. It succeeded. Lots of new hurdles are in your way, such as the Means Test (see Chapter 5), but for the most part, they amount to little more than a distraction and annoyance. In the final analysis, if you can't pay your bills, you're entitled to a fresh start.

Appendix

Homestead Exemption Laws

Although bankruptcy law is generally the province of the federal government, a number of states have their own provisions with regard to exemptions, giving people the chance to choose between exemptions offered under the Bankruptcy Code (federal exemptions) and those provided by their own state legislature.

Debtors can choose local or Bankruptcy Code exemptions in the following places: Arkansas, Connecticut, District of Columbia, Hawaii, Kentucky, Massachusetts, Michigan, Minnesota, New Hampshire, New Jersey, New Mexico, Pennsylvania, Puerto Rico, Rhode Island, Texas, Vermont, the Virgin Islands, Washington, and Wisconsin. Bankruptcy Code exemptions may be available in other states in certain circumstances where you changed states in the past two years (see Chapter 10).

Choosing between Federal and State Exemptions

You generally apply the law of the state of your permanent home for the two years before bankruptcy. If, for example, you lived in the same state two years ago as you do now, the laws of your present state apply.

But if your permanent home has not been in a single state for this two-year period, the law that applies is that of the state where you lived for 180 days immediately prior to that two-year period, or for the longer portion of this 180-day period than any other state.

Generally, you have to stick with one set of exemptions; the law usually doesn't allow debtors to shop for the best deal. Also, joint debtors must both agree to choose local or federal exemptions. In other words, one spouse can't pluck the state exemptions if the other elects to go the federal route.

Identifying the Federal Homestead Exemption

Keep in mind that at each three-year interval ending on April 1, the exemption allowed under the Bankruptcy Code is adjusted to reflect changes in the Consumer Price Index. The Judicial Conference of the United States publishes the dollar amount in the Federal Register 30 days before the change takes effect. The amounts next change on April 1, 2007. So far, every adjustment has increased the amount of the homestead exemption, so if the federal exemption applies to you and you're near or over the limit, you may be better off waiting until the next adjustment.

Married debtors may each claim the full amount for separate property and double these amounts for jointly owned property. The present exemption amount is $18,450 and isn't limited to real property (land and buildings), so mobile homes, and possibly even travel trailers, qualify. But the property must be your actual home or the home of your dependent.

Surveying State Homestead Exemptions

To find out more about exemptions for your particular state, log on to www. bankruptcyaction.com or americanbankruptcy.com/pdfexemption tables/states.htm or www.bankruptcyinformation.com/services. html. But be careful because state exemption laws are always changing, and these Web sites aren't always up to date. The only way to know for sure whether your property is exempt is to ask your lawyer.

Note: If you acquired your present home within 1,215 days of bankruptcy, your homestead exemption may not exceed $125,000, even if state law allows more. But this restriction is limited to the extent that you used the proceeds of a prior homestead in the same state to purchase your present home — unless, of course, the first residence was also acquired within 1,215 days of bankruptcy. For example, assume that you moved to Florida in 1995 and bought a home for $500,000 cash. Then, in 2005, you sold this home and used the money to buy a new home in Florida for $500,000. The $125,000 limitation doesn't apply even if you filed bankruptcy within 1,215 days of acquiring your new home.

There is also an absolute $125,000 cap on homesteads if the debtor has been convicted of specified federal securities law or has committed criminal acts or other intentional or reckless acts that caused serious injury or death within five years of bankruptcy.

Although BARF isn't clear on the subject, we believe that if a husband and wife own their homestead together and file a joint bankruptcy, the $125,000 limit could be doubled to $250,000.

Alabama: Up to $5,000, and land can't exceed 160 acres. Husband and wife may double.

Alaska: $64,800. Although joint debtors may each claim exemption, combined amount may not exceed $64,800.

Arizona: $150,000 real property or mobile home. Joint debtors may not double.

Arkansas: Unlimited.

California: $50,000 if single and not disabled; $75,000 family residences; $150,000 if debtor is 65 or older; disabled; or if 55 or older and, if single, earns $15,000 or less or, if married, joint income of less than $20,000.

Note: Debtors may choose a homestead exemption under a different set of California exemptions that are similar to the exemptions under the U.S. Code.

Colorado: Real property, certain manufactured home, or mobile homes — $45,000. Husband and wife may not double. House trailer used as residence — $3,500. Mobile home used as residence — $6,000.

Connecticut: $75,000. Husband and wife may double.

Delaware: $50,000.

District of Columbia: Unlimited.

Florida: Unlimited value, up to 2 acres in municipality or 160 contiguous acres elsewhere.

Georgia: $10,000. Husband and wife may double.

Hawaii: $30,000 for head of family or individual 65 or older, all others $20,000. Husband and wife may double.

Idaho: $50,000.

Illinois: $15,000. Husband and wife may double.

Indiana: $15,000. Husband and wife may double.

Iowa: Unlimited value, up to 40 rural acres or one-half acre in city.

Kansas: Unlimited in amount, up to 160 rural acres or one acre in town or city.

Kentucky: $5,000. Husband and wife may double.

Louisiana: $25,000 may not exceed 5 acres in city or town, 200 acres elsewhere. Husband and wife may not double.

Maine: $35,000; if minor dependents live with debtor, $70,000; if debtor is 60 or older or disabled, $70,000. Husband and wife may double.

Maryland: No specific exemption, but some general exemptions totaling $12,000 may be applied to homestead. Husband and wife may double.

Massachusetts: $500,000. Husband and wife may not double.

Michigan: $30,000, $60,000 if debtor has dependents. $45,000, $90,000 if debtor over 65 and has dependents.

Minnesota: $200,000 up to 160 rural acres or one-half acre in city. Husband and wife may not double.

Mississippi: $75,000 up to 160 acres. Husband and wife may double.

Missouri: $15,000. Husband and wife may not double.

Montana: $100,000. Husband and wife may double.

Nebraska: $12,500 if debtor is married or head of a household. Husband and wife may not double.

Nevada: $350,000. Husband and wife may not double.

New Hampshire: $100,000. Husband and wife may double.

New Jersey: None.

New Mexico: $30,000. Husband and wife may double.

New York: $50,000. Husband and wife may double.

North Carolina: $18,500. Husband and wife may double.

North Dakota: $80,000. Husband and wife may double.

Ohio: $5,000. Husband and wife may double.

Oklahoma: Unlimited for property outside city limits up to 160 acres, up to one acre within city limits.

Oregon: Real property — $30,000, $39,600 if owned by joint debtors. Mobile home with land — $23,000, $30,000 if owned by joint debtors. Mobile home without land — $20,000, $27,000 if owned by joint debtors.

Pennsylvania: None.

Puerto Rico: $1,500. Husband and wife may double.

Rhode Island: $200,000. Husband and wife may double.

South Carolina: $5,000. Husband and wife may double.

South Dakota: $30,000. Husband and wife may double.

Tennessee: $5,000, joint owners are entitled to $7,500.

Texas: Unlimited value, limited in area to one acre of urban property or 100 acres (200 for families) of rural land.

Utah: $20,000. Husband and wife may double.

Vermont: $75,000. Husband and wife may not double.

Virgin Islands: $30,000.

Virginia: $5,000, plus $500 for each dependent. Husband and wife may double.

Washington: $40,000. Husband and wife may not double.

West Virginia: $25,000. Husband and wife may double.

Wisconsin: $40,000. Husband and wife may not double.

Wyoming: $10,000. Husband and wife may double.

Index

• D •

• J •

• K •

• L •

• *M* •